Cambridge Studies in Oral and Literate Culture 12

THE SOCIAL HISTORY OF LANGUAGE

Cambridge Studies in Oral and Literate Culture

Edited by PETER BURKE and RUTH FINNEGAN

This series is designed to address the question of the significance of literacy in human societies: it assesses its importance for political, economic, social and cultural development, and examines how what we take to be the common functions of writing are carried out in oral cultures.

The series is interdisciplinary, but with particular emphasis on social anthropology and social history, and encourages cross-fertilisation between these disciplines: it is also of interest to readers in allied fields, such as sociology, folklore and literature. Although it includes some monographs, the focus of the series is on theoretical and comparative aspects rather than detailed description, and the books are presented in a form accessible to non-specialist readers interested in the general subject of literacy and orality.

Books in the series

THE SOCIAL HISTORY
OF LANGUAGE

Edited by
PETER BURKE
Fellow of Emmanuel College, Cambridge

ROY PORTER
Senior Lecturer in the Social History of Medicine,
Wellcome Institute for the History of Medicine, London

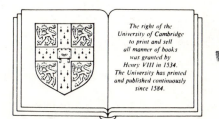

The right of the
University of Cambridge
to print and sell
all manner of books
was granted by
Henry VIII in 1534.
The University has printed
and published continuously
since 1584.

CAMBRIDGE UNIVERSITY PRESS

CAMBRIDGE
NEW YORK   NEW ROCHELLE   MELBOURNE   SYDNEY

Published by the Press Syndicate of the University of Cambridge
The Pitt Building, Trumpington Street, Cambridge CB2 1RP
32 East 57th Street, New York, NY 10022, USA
10 Stamford Road, Oakleigh, Melbourne 3166, Australia

First published 1987
Reprinted 1988

Printed in Great Britain by
Billings and Sons Ltd., Worcester

British Library cataloguing in publication data

The Social history of language.–
Cambridge studies in oral and literate culture; 12).
1. Sociolinguistics–History
I. Burke, Peter II. Porter, Roy, 1946–
401'.9   P40

Library of Congress cataloguing in publication data

The Social history of language.
(Cambridge studies in oral and literate culture; 12)
Bibliography.
Includes index.
1. Sociolinguistics. 2. Social history.
I. Burke, Peter II. Porter, Roy, 1946–
III. Series.
P40.S544 1987   401'.9   87-6560

ISBN 0 521 30158 0 hard covers
ISBN 0 521 31763 0 paperback

CONTENTS

ILLUSTRATIONS

NOTES ON CONTRIBUTORS

Peter Burke was educated at Oxford and taught at the University of Sussex from 1962 before moving to Emmanuel College, Cambridge in 1978. His books include *Culture and Society in Renaissance Italy* (1972), *Popular Culture in Early Modern Europe* (1978), and *The Historical Anthropology of Early Modern Italy* (1987).

James Obelkevich is Lecturer in Social History at the Centre for the Study of Social History, University of Warwick. After receiving degrees from Columbia University and the University of Cambridge, he was Assistant Professor in the Department of History at Princeton University. He is the author of *Religion and Rural Society: South Lindsey 1825–1875* (1976) and editor of *Religion and the People, 800–1700* (1979), and co-editor (with Lyndal Roper and Raphael Samuel) of *Disciplines of Faith: Studies in Religion, Politics and Patriarchy* (1987).

Roy Porter read history at Christ's College, Cambridge. His publications include *The Making of Geology*, *Images of the Earth* (edited with L. J. Jordanova), *The Ferment of Knowledge: Studies in the Historiography of Eighteenth-Century Science* (edited with G. S. Rousseau), *A Dictionary of the History of Science* (edited with W. F. Bynum and E. J. Browne), and *The Enlightenment in National Context* (edited with M. Teich). He is now working on a history of psychiatry in Britain, and is also researching the history of quack doctors, and the history of medicine from the point of view of the patient. He is Lecturer in the Social History of Medicine at the Wellcome Institute for the History of Medicine, London.

David Garrioch studied French and history at the University of Melbourne, and subsequently completed a D.Phil at Balliol College, Oxford. He has held Junior Research Fellowships at Wolfson College and St Anne's College, Oxford, and now lectures in European history at Monash University, Melbourne. He is the author of *Neighbourhood and Community in Paris, 1740–1790* (1986).

Dorinda Outram gained her Ph.D from the University of Cambridge in 1974, and has published extensively on French and Italian history of the revolutionary period. Her most recent book was *Georges Cuvier: Vocation, Authority and Science in Post-Revolutionary France* (1984). She is now engaged in a full-length study of the political culture of the French Revolution, and is the co-editor of *Women, Families, Careers: Women in Science 1789–1968* (forthcoming). She currently teaches at University College, Cork.

Janis Langins is a former chemical engineer, now historian of science and technology, who is currently a research associate at the Institute for the History of Science and Technology at the University of Toronto. He is the author of *La République avait besoin des savants* (1987). His present research is on the history of French engineering at the end of the eighteenth century.

D. F. Mckenzie, a New Zealander, is Reader in Textual Criticism, and Fellow of Pembroke College, Oxford. He is currently editing the complete works of William Congreve for Oxford University Press.

Jonathan Steinberg has been University Lecturer in History, and Fellow and Tutor at Trinity Hall, Cambridge since 1966. He is the author of *Yesterday's Deterrent: Tirpitz and the Birth of the German Battle Fleet* (1965) and *Why Switzerland?* (1976). He recently translated Pino Arlacchi: *Mafia, Peasants and Great Estates: Society in Traditional Calabria* (1983), and is also a regular contributor to *New Society*.

1

INTRODUCTION

Peter Burke

It is high time for a social history of language, a social history of speech, a social history of communication. In the last generation or so, as the rise of feminist and regionalist movements shows, dominated groups have become more sharply aware of the power of language as well as the involvement of language with other forms of power. Whatever their other differences, the philosophers, critics and others associated with structuralism and deconstruction do at least share a strong concern with language and its place in culture. Whether they are involved with one or more of these movements, or with oral history (another relatively recent development), a number of historians have recently come to recognise the need to study language as a social institution, as a part of culture, as well as to develop a sensitivity to linguistic conventions so as to avoid misinterpreting the sources for more traditional kinds of history.[1] All the same, there remains a gap between linguistics, sociology (including social anthropology) and history, a gap which can and should be filled by the social history of language.

It is hardly news that language has a history. Ancient Romans and Renaissance humanists were interested in the history of Latin, while treatises on the origin of Italian, Spanish and other languages were published in the seventeenth century.[2] The dominant school of nineteenth-century linguists, the so-called 'Neogrammarians', was much concerned with the reconstruction of early forms of language, such as 'protoromance' and 'protogermanic', and with the formulation of laws of linguistic evolution.[3] This was the approach against which the linguist Ferdinand de Saussure, now seen as the father of structuralism, reacted, because he considered that the historical school of linguists was too little concerned with the relation between the different parts of the language system.[4] In Saussure's day, however, the historical approach remained dominant. The *Oxford English Dictionary*, planned, as its title-page declares, on 'historical principles', began publication in 1884, while its French equivalent, edited by Emile Littré, goes back to 1863. Classics such as Jespersen's *Growth and Structure of the English Language* and Brunot's massive *History of the French Language* date from the early years of this century.[5]

1

However, this approach to the history of language lacked a full social dimension. Children of their time, the nineteenth-century scholars thought of language as an organism which 'grows' or 'evolves' through various stages and which expresses the values or 'spirit' of the nation which speaks it. Their concerns were national, or even nationalist, rather than social. They showed little interest in the varieties of the 'same' language spoken by different social groups, an interest which is central to contemporary sociolinguists, which crystallised into a discipline some thirty years ago.

Of course, awareness that different groups in a given society speak differently is far from new. Shakespeare expressed it in a number of passages in his plays, such as the famous scene in *Henry IV* in which Hotspur criticises his Kate for saying 'in good sooth' because this turn of phrase was not aristocratic: 'you swear like a comfit-maker's wife'. What Hotspur wanted to hear was 'a good mouth-filling oath'.

A similar consciousness of the social meaning of speech differences is to be found in many nineteenth-century novels. Think, for example, of Rosamond Vincy, in *Middlemarch*, objecting to her mother's phrase 'the pick of them' as 'rather a vulgar expression', while her carefree brother Fred counters with the assertion – which has its parallel among linguists today – that so-called 'correct' English is nothing but 'the slang of prigs'. When the old lawyer Standish, in the same novel, swears 'By God!', the author intervenes to explain that he was using that oath as 'a sort of armorial bearings, stamping the speech of a man who held a good position'. He used it, as we might say, as a status symbol. There would not in fact be any need for a social history of language if ordinary speakers were not aware, often acutely, of the social meaning of speech styles, while anyone wishing to rise socially has had to be hyperconscious of such matters.

Again, it is no new idea that language may be an instrument in the hands of the powerful, employed to mystify and control as well as to communicate, and that in Europe, for example, Latin was long used as a device to maintain the power of the clergy and other professional men such as doctors, lawyers and of course academics. In a dialogue published in 1546, the Florentine writer Gianbattista Gelli, who was not a member of the ruling class but a shoemaker, made one of his characters denounce the Latin liturgy as a trick of the clergy to keep the faith secret so as to 'sell it to us retail', while in 1584 another autodidact, the miller Menocchio Scandella, recently rescued from oblivion by the Italian historian Carlo Ginzburg, told the inquisitors who were interrogating him that 'speaking Latin is a betrayal of the poor' because ordinary people cannot understand what is going on in court 'and if they want to say four words they have to have a lawyer'.[6] A similar point about the use of 'law French' in English courts was made by Archbishop Cranmer, by James I, and by radicals such as John Lilburne and John Warr during the English Revolution.[7]

All the same, as the philosopher Whitehead once remarked, 'Everything of importance has been said before by somebody who did not discover it': in other words, there is a considerable difference between a vague awareness of a particular problem and systematic research into it.[8] Pioneering explorations of the relation between language, thought and society were made in the 1920s by Ogden, Richards and Malinowski, and in the 1930s by the Russian psychologist Lev Vygotsky, who was concerned with the acquisition of speech and writing (separate 'linguistic functions' in his view), and by the American linguist Benjamin Whorf, whose controversial but influential essays argued that the thought of a particular people, such as the Hopi – their conceptions of time, space and so on – was shaped by the structure of their language, its genders, tenses, etc.[9]

As for the stage of systematic research, it was reached a generation later, in the late 1950s and early 1960s, with the development of what is variously called 'sociolinguistics', 'ethnolinguistics', 'the sociology of language', 'the ethnography of speaking' or 'the ethnography of communication', labels which stand for substantial differences in approach, but should not be allowed to obscure what the different schools have in common. If, in the 1980s, social historians wish to pay more attention to language, they would be well advised to turn for orientation to the work of such linguists as Dell Hymes, Joshua Fishman, John Gumperz and their pupils.[10]

What do these ethnographers and sociologists have to offer? An acute awareness of 'who speaks what language to whom and when', and an analytical framework, which includes a rich vocabulary. Just as the Bedouin have many words for 'camel', and Eskimos for 'snow', because they draw finer distinctions in these areas than the rest of us need to do, so the sociolinguists have many words for 'language'.

In this vocabulary, a central concept is that of 'variety', 'style' or 'code', defined as a way of speaking employed by a particular group or 'speech community'.[11] Simplifying brutally – as brief introductions must – it may be suggested that sociolinguists have used this idea of 'variety' to make four main points about the relationships between languages and the societies in which they are spoken (or written). These points may well seem rather obvious when they are stated in a bare and simple form, but they have not as yet been fully integrated into the practice of social historians. They are as follows:

1. Different social groups use different varieties of language.
2. The same people employ different varieties of language in different situations.

3. Language reflects the society (or culture) in which it is spoken.
4. Language shapes the society in which it is spoken.

The next few pages will comment on these points one by one and offer a few historical illustrations.

1 Different social groups use different varieties of language. Regional dialects are perhaps the most obvious example, but they are far from being the only one. The language of women, for instance, was and is different from that of men in the same society in a number of ways, which often include a predilection for euphemism and for emotionally charged adjectives, and a closer adherence to standard forms. Even their intonation is distinctive, a point which was not lost on Shakespeare: 'Her voice was ever soft/ Gentle and low, an excellent thing in woman' (*King Lear*, Act 5, scene 3). As the last example suggests, women do not simply happen to speak differently from men but have been trained to do so in male-dominated societies, expressing their subordination in their speech. Even Mrs Thatcher has bowed to this convention and taken lessons in elocution in order to lower her pitch.[12]

Again, distinctive varieties of language have often been the mark of minority religious groups. In the sixteenth and seventeenth centuries, for example, English puritans were supposed to be recognisable by their nasal twang and also by their vocabulary, in which terms such as 'abomination', 'backsliding', 'discipline', 'edify', 'godly' and so on made a frequent appearance.[13] Quakers stood out from the rest not only because they insisted on using the familiar 'thee' and 'thou' to everyone, but also by their refusal to use certain common words, such as 'church' (which George Fox replaced by 'steeple-house'), and also by their special use of silence.[14] On the Continent, too, religious minorities were betrayed by their speech. In seventeenth-century France, for example, the speech of the Huguenots was so frequently larded with phrases from the Bible that it was known irreverently as 'the patois of Canaan'. The German Pietists were supposed to speak in a 'whimpering', 'whining' or 'sighing' manner, and also to employ distinctive turns of phrase such as 'the fullness of the heart' (*Fülle des Herzens*).[15]

Another cluster of speech varieties is associated with professional beggars and thieves, whose secret language (known in English as 'cant', in French as *jargon* and in German as *Rotwelsch*), appeared in print a number of times in the course of the sixteenth and seventeenth centuries.[16] Varieties of language have also been associated with social classes, as two lively discussions which took place in Britain in the 1950s and 1960s may remind us.

It was the linguist Alan Ross who coined the term 'U' to describe the language of the British upper class, and 'non-U' for that of everyone else.

He explained, or more exactly asserted, that 'looking-glass' was U, but 'mirror' non-U; 'writing-paper' U, 'notepaper' non-U, and so on.[17] Considerable anxiety seems to have been aroused by this essay, and it is likely that usage changed in some circles as a result. However, there was nothing new about this type of distinction, and although it is widely believed to reflect a peculiarly English obsession with class, it does in fact have many parallels in other parts of the world.

In Philadelphia in the 1940s, for instance, it was U to refer to one's 'house' and 'furniture', but non-U to call them 'home' and 'furnishings'; U to 'feel sick', but non-U to 'feel ill'.[18] In Victorian England there were parallel distinctions, as the remark by Rosamond Vincy about 'the pick of them' would suggest.[19] In eighteenth-century Denmark, the playwright Ludvig Holberg put a character on stage to comment on the way in which language was changing to reflect some people's higher social aspirations. Such people, no longer content with such traditional, homely terms as 'boy', 'fiddler' and 'clerk', preferred to speak of a 'lackey', an 'instrumentalist' and a 'secretary'.[20] In seventeenth-century France, François de Callières, later private secretary to Louis XIV, pointed out differences between 'bourgeois ways of speaking' (*façons de parler bourgeoises*) and those of the aristocracy in his *Mots à la mode*.[21] In sixteenth-century Italy the controversial man of letters, Pietro Aretino, wrote a dialogue in which one of the characters claimed that a window should be called a *balcone*, and not (as was more common), a *finestra*; that it was proper to say *viso* for 'face', but improper to say *faccia* and so on. Aretino's tongue was well into his cheek (as, doubtless, were those of Holberg and Ross), but the joke would have had little point if other people had not been taking the matter rather more seriously.[22]

It is not only in the west that varieties of speech function as symbols of status. In Java, for example, the traditional elite have their own dialect (or 'sociolect'), distinctive in grammar as well as in vocabulary, while among the Wolof of West Africa, accent, or more exactly pitch, is a social indicator. The nobles speak in low-pitched quiet voices, as if they do not have to make an effort to gain their listeners' attention, while commoners speak in high-pitched loud voices.[23]

Whether the associations between a particular variety of language and a specific social group are necessary or arbitrary it is hard to say. From a historian's point of view, the important thing is to note that linguistic status symbols are subject to change over time, so that words which are U in one generation may not be so in the next. Regional accents have not always been non-U. Sir Walter Raleigh is said to have spoken broad Devonshire, and that arbiter of correct English, Dr Johnson, broad Staffordshire.[24]

However, it does not follow from this propensity to change that the social symbolism of varieties of language is completely arbitrary. At the end of the last century, the Norwegian–American sociologist Thorstein Veblen produced the fascinating suggestion that the ways of speaking of an upper class (or 'leisure class', as he called it), were necessarily 'cumbrous and out of date' because such usages imply 'waste of time' and hence 'exemption from the use and the need of direct and forcible speech'.[25] The Wolof example quoted above would seem to illustrate this point, for which it would not be difficult to amass many supporting examples. Some sixty years after Veblen, his idea of necessary links between varieties of language and the social groups employing them was reinforced by another sociologist, Basil Bernstein, whose arguments have generated considerable controversy.

Studying the language of the pupils in some London schools, Bernstein distinguished two main varieties, or as he called them, 'codes', the 'elaborated' and the 'restricted'. The restricted code employs expressions which are usually concrete and it leaves meanings implicit, to be inferred from the context. The elaborated code, on the other hand, is abstract, explicit and 'context-independent'. Bernstein has explained the contrast in terms of two very different styles of bringing up children, associated with two types of family, associated in turn with two social classes. Roughly speaking, the elaborated code is middle-class while the restricted code is working-class.[26]

Originally designed to explain the relative failure of working-class children to achieve good results at school, the theory has far wider implications. Like Vygotsky and Whorf, Bernstein has been exploring the relationship between language and thought. From the point of view of the historian of mentalities, there are intriguing similarities between the idea of the two codes and the contrasts which have so often been drawn between two styles of thought, whether they are labelled 'primitive' and 'civilised', 'traditional' and 'modern', 'prelogical' and 'logical' or, most usefully, 'oral' and 'literate'.[27] Bernstein's substantive points about British children at the time he was writing aroused a storm of criticism on the grounds that he failed to take account of the influence of the media or to examine the class system closely enough, that he suggested that people are prisoners of the code they use, and that he emphasised the weaknesses of the restricted code at the expense of its special strengths, while stressing the positive features of his own code, the elaborated one.[28] However, at a more general level, Bernstein's hypotheses about the way in which styles of speech and thought are acquired remain extremely suggestive.

2 The second of our four points is that in different situations, the same individual will employ different varieties of language, or, as sociolinguists say in this context, different 'registers'.[29] This point too had been picked up by some nineteenth-century novelists. Hardy's Tess, for example, 'who had passed the 6th Standard in the National School under a London-trained mistress, spoke two languages; the dialect at home, more or less; and English abroad and to persons of quality'. What the sociolinguists offer to supplement this observation is an analysis of the 'strategies', conscious or unconscious, involved in switching from one register to another.[30] Studies of bilingual individuals and communities show how they switch from one language to another not at random but according to the situation, including under this heading not only the other participants but also the topic under discussion, the 'speech domain', as it is called. As the polyglot emperor Charles V is said to have remarked, French was the language to use to ambassadors, Italian to ladies, German to stable boys and Spanish to God. Alternatively, the switching may operate, as in Tess's case, between two varieties of the same language, 'high' or 'low', standard or dialect. Religion, for example, often seems to demand a relatively high or formal register, such as classical Arabic in the Middle East.[31]

Historians will have no difficulty in finding examples from many periods of the use of different registers. Latin, for instance, was a second language, spoken as well as written in medieval and early modern Europe by anyone with pretensions to learning, and associated with particular settings such as universities and schools. Lectures, disputations, orations were all in Latin, and not these alone. As late as 1677, at Queens' College, Cambridge, the President and Fellows gave instructions that the undergraduates should speak Latin in Hall at both dinner and supper. Schoolboys were often expected to speak Latin in the playground as well as in class, and a 'spy' (literally 'wolf', *lupus*) might be appointed by the master to ensure that lapses into the vernacular were reported and punished. In Luther's *Table-Talk*, the written record of the master's conversations at meals, kept by various disciples, we find him regularly switching from the vernacular into Latin, either because German in his time still lacked an adequate vocabulary for discussing certain topics, or because the dignity of a particular speech domain required a shift of this kind.[32] Even in the nineteenth century, Latin might be required on formal occasions in European universities, and scandal was caused in Leiden when a new professor insisted on giving his inaugural lecture in Dutch. The Latin speeches given at degree days in Oxford and Cambridge today are the vestiges of a long academic tradition.[33]

Again, in medieval and early modern Europe, French was a second language for a number of elites. In England and in southern Italy in the fourteenth century (as a result of the Norman conquests), in the Dutch Republic in the seventeenth century, in Prussia in the eighteenth century, and in Russia – as *War and Peace* reminds us – in the nineteenth century, speaking French was U, and people with aspirations to rise socially might make the effort to master it for that reason. As one fourteenth-century Englishman cynically observed, 'oplondysch men wol lykne hamsylff to gentil men, and fondeth with gret bysynes for to speke Freynch for to be more ytold of'.[34] It would be good to know more about the kinds of situation in which all this French was spoken outside France.

Of course, elites were not the only groups to speak more than language. On the borders between languages bilingualism was and is common, while people living near major trade routes have often learned a pidgin or lingua franca, such as the language of trade in the Mediterranean world (from which the term 'lingua franca' is itself derived), a language relatively well documented for North Africa in the nineteenth century, but one which has left documentary traces at least as far back as the fourteenth century, if not further.[35] In seventeenth-century Languedoc, where occitan was still spoken by most people most of the time, the Huguenots preferred French for talking to God, in other words as the language of the liturgy. When the French Protestants were persecuted in the late seventeenth century and a movement of resistance was organised in the Cévennes, some of its leaders, more especially the women, would not infrequently fall into convulsions and prophesy – but when they did so it was not in their everyday language but in French. French was for them a linguistic symbol of the sacred, as glossolalia has been from New Testament times to our own.[36]

Switching between dialect and a literary language is also well documented, at least for some regions and periods. In early modern Italy, for example, educated men were able to speak as well as to write Tuscan (the dialect which was in the process of becoming standard Italian), but they continued to employ their local dialect (Venetian, say) on occasion, although there has so far been little attempt to study what these occasions were in any systematic way. Venetian patricians might, for example, write erotic poetry in dialect, perhaps because they considered the subject deserved a 'low' style. Conversely, in nineteenth-century France, peasants who normally spoke patois might sometimes switch register into French. One of the few historians to have taken this subject seriously so far, Eugen Weber, tells us that a boy might employ French as a sign of formality when inviting a girl to dance, and also that peasants who discussed local politics in patois would switch to French to talk about national issues.[37]

Unfortunately, our knowledge of such matters remains fragmentary. It is interesting to learn that Venetian was spoken in courts of law in the Republic in the eighteenth century, or that Tennyson used to tell bawdy stories in a Lincolnshire accent (although, unlike Sir Walter Raleigh and Dr Johnson, he did not speak with a regional accent the rest of the time), but these pieces of information are not fully intelligible without a knowledge of their contexts, including a knowledge of the relevant language system, the rules for speaking in a particular culture. Ethnographers of speaking have been investigating these rules – how to be polite (or insulting), how to joke, how to ask for a drink and so on – but they have so far been rather neglected by social historians.[38]

Even silence deserves study from this point of view. 'We have no history of silence', as the literary critic George Steiner has observed. He was thinking of its place in modern literature and music, but a social history of silence would also have its interest. It would have to deal with changes in the rules – who should be silent (monks, women, children, servants and so on); when; where; and on what topics speech was taboo. It would have to be considered in relation to secrecy (who keeps what secret from whom, and what indirect methods are available, in a given culture, for 'mentioning the unmentionable').[39] It would also have to be considered in conjunction with noise, a subject which has engaged the interest of Raphael Samuel.

Without this kind of knowledge of linguistic rules, explicit or implicit, historians run a serious risk of misinterpreting many of their documents. To see through the glass clearly, rather than darkly, we need to become aware of the properties of that glass, for language is not unproblematically transparent. As the Canadian critic Marshall McLuhan used to say, 'the medium is the message'.[40] More exactly, the medium, code, variety or register employed is a crucial part of the message, which the listener or reader or historian–eavesdropper cannot afford to miss.

The most obvious example to take here is that of the written language. This is only in rare instances a transcription of the spoken language, despite Jane Austen's famous advice to 'write as you would speak', and needs to be treated as a separate variety with its own rules, varying with time, place, writer, intended reader, topic and, not least, literary genre, including in this category such everyday forms as letters of various types – the love-letter, begging letter, threatening letter, or whatever is appropriate to the particular culture.[41] In eleventh-century Japan, for example, a 'next morning' letter from a courtly lover to the mistress from whom he had just parted was not only *de rigueur*, but had to be composed according to strict rules which governed not only the poem which formed the focus of the message but also the calligraphy, the choice of paper, and even the spray of blossom to which the letter (properly folded) was attached. In traditional China, as in other societies, official documents had their own distinctive forms, which extended to calligraphy as well as phraseology, and these forms were taken as models for communication with the world of spirits, which was imagined to be organised into a 'heavenly bureaucracy'.[42]

Although a social historian of Britain working on family papers of the
seventeenth century (say) in a local record office office may be unlikely to
find anything so elaborately formal as the 'next morning' letter or the
official request to the gods, there remains a general need for awareness of
the rules of communication – written and unwritten – and of the rhetoric
of everyday life. One of the most immediate tasks for social historians of
language is to work out who, in a given place at a given time, used the
medium of writing to communicate with whom about what: for much that
has interested members of cultures of restricted literacy, or even cultures
of near-universal literacy, was not written down. Sixteenth-century
Venetians, for example, seem to have preferred not to discuss politics in
writing, for obvious reasons of prudence (see below, p. 34). Much of
popular culture long went unrecorded in writing, not only because most
ordinary people were illiterate, but because the literate were either
uninterested in popular culture, or ashamed of their interest, or simply
unable to transcribe or transpose an oral culture in dialect into a written
variety of the language. When it was eventually written down, much of
this oral culture was bowdlerised. Whether this was to accommodate it to
middle-class readers, or to the medium of writing, or both, is not
altogether clear.

Since there are so many lacunae, readers may well be wondering
whether a social history of speech is a viable enterprise at all, before the
coming of the wire and later of the tape-recorder. However, in Western
Europe from the later Middle Ages onwards, there are some extremely
voluminous and relatively reliable sources for speech, notably the records
of the courts. As David Garrioch remarks in his chapter on insults (see
below, p. 107), courts were careful to have witnesses testify to the exact
words spoken on particular occasions. The Inquisition took even more
care. The instructions to the Roman inquisitors, for example, told them
to ensure that the notary who had to be present at interrogations
transcribed 'not only all the responses of the accused but also all the other
remarks and comments he made and every word he uttered under
torture, including every sigh, scream, groan and sob'.[43] A chilling
directive, but its results, 400 years later, turn out to be invaluable for the
social historian of language.

The students recording Luther's table-talk were presumably rather less
accurate (how could they write and eat at the same time?). However,
their text does have a colloquial flavour, and so do some transcriptions of
sermons (those of S. Bernardino of Siena in the fifteenth century, for
example), and some reports of speeches in assemblies such as the House
of Commons, even before the professionalism of Hansard.

To these sources may be added the evidence of plays and novels,
already utilised more than once in this introduction. They have to be used

with care because novelists and dramatists stylise the speech they represent, but to anyone aware of these conventions they have a good deal to reveal. In short, studies of the uses and conventions of literacy form a necessary complement to the many quantitative studies of literacy carried out over the last few years. Without awareness of these constantly changing conventions it is impossible to tell whether a given text is serious or ironic, servile or mocking: whether it follows the rules or subverts them.

The first two sociolinguistic theses are essentially descriptive. The remaining two are more analytical and also more controversial.

3 Language reflects (or better, perhaps, 'echoes') society. The point is not simply that the accent, vocabulary and general speech style of an individual reveals, to anyone with a trained ear, a good deal about that individual's social position. Linguistic forms, their variations and changes, also tell us something about the quality of social relationships in a given culture, or cluster of cultures. It has, for example, often been pointed out that the greater hesitancy of women's language indicates their subordinate position. 'Statistical measurements show that men speak more loudly and more often than women; are more apt to interrupt, impose their views, and take over the conversation; and are more inclined to shout others down. Women tend to smile obligingly, excuse themselves and stutter, or in fits of insecurity attempt to imitate and outdo men.'[44] Alternatively, they employ strategies of indirectness, like the wives who practise the art of asking their husbands 'tiny and discreet questions', a point recently made about a village in Spain but one which may be assumed to have a much wider relevance, the limits of which will have to be charted by social historians.[45]

The use of *tu* and *vous* in French and of equivalent terms in other languages makes a particularly useful social litmus paper, which reveals patterns of familiarity and deference. The two terms (T and V, as they are called in cross-language comparisons), may be used either reciprocally or non-reciprocally. Usage has varied not only with the relative status or mutual intimacy of the speakers, but also (in Russian, at least), with the topic of conversation. As might have been expected, the rules for the use of T and V in European languages have changed over time, notably in the last generation or two, with a general shift towards reciprocity, symbolising the spread of egalitarian values.[46] In this context, the early abandonment of T in English in the eighteenth century would appear to be significant, although what it signifies is not easy to say.

Again, it is for social historians to chart the chronology, geography and sociology of this shift, as well as to interpret the specific overtones or undertones of usage in particular contexts, distinguishing the deferential from the patronising or ironic usages. Meanwhile, we have learned something about social relationships in fourteenth-century Languedoc when told that a priest would use T to his flock, but receive V in return.[47] We have been helped to assess the significance of the German Peasants' War of 1525 and of some rural revolts in nineteenth-century India by authors who describe the use of T by peasants to their lords and masters, in place of the expected V.[48] We have discovered something about social change in nineteenth-century Russia on reading, in Turgenev's *Smoke*, that Litvinov's mother (a member of the provincial nobility) addressed the servants with V, instead of the traditional T, because she believed that this was the progressive and the Western thing to do, just as we have a sudden insight into relationships between the sexes when we read that Tolstoy's wife Sonia was afraid to say T to her husband on their wedding night.[49]

That these pronouns were heavily charged with social meaning became obvious whenever the system, social and linguistic, was challenged, as it was by the Quakers when they used T to everyone regardless of their worldly status. A similar point was made by the French revolutionaries' use of T and of *citoyen*, and also by the Saminists in Java at the end of the last century, who rejected both the social hierarchy and the traditional linguistic etiquette and replaced the conventional modes of address by the term *sedular* ('brother').[50] The parallel with attempts by contemporary feminists to reform our male-dominated language ('mankind', 'chairman', etc.), will be obvious enough, another reminder of the symbolic importance of the apparently trivial.

Modes of address are the most obvious but not the only linguistic clue to social relationships. The choice of a particular variety of language conveys information about the speaker's loyalties, expressing solidarity with those who speak in the same way and social distance from those who speak differently. So when the upper classes of western Europe gave up using the local dialect, as they seem to have done in the seventeenth and eighteenth centuries, they were distancing themselves from a popular culture in which their ancestors had participated.[51]

Again, the development of certain occupational languages, notably the languages of the law, the army and the civil service, needs to be interpreted not only in a utilitarian way, as the creation of technical terms for practical purposes, but also in a symbolic way, as the expression of a growing professional self-consciousness and of a growing distance from outsiders, such as the inhabitants of 'Civvy Street'. A similar point might be made about the languages of some religious sub-cultures such as the Puritans. The 'cant' of professional beggars and thieves is an extreme case of this expression of social distance. It has been interpreted as an 'anti-language' which 'brings into sharp relief the role of language as a realisation of the power structure of society', and at the same time reflects the organisation and the values of a 'counter-culture'.[52]

More generally, the structuralists, such as the late Roland Barthes, would argue that the language system of a given culture, like its culinary system, its vestimentary system, its architectural system, and other systems of signs, reflects the whole culture; in other words, that food, clothes, buildings and so on are so many 'languages' making statements about that culture to anyone who, like the semiologist, knows how to 'read' them.

Whether 'reflection' is an altogether appropriate metaphor for the relationship between languages and societies is, however, open to question. 'Refraction', with its implication of a more indirect relationship, seems a better image. After all, linguistic conventions sometimes persist although social structures have changed. In People's Poland, for example, forms of politeness once associated with the nobility have passed into general currency, and it is normal to address strangers as *Pan* and *Pani* ('Sir' and 'Madam'). The Communists attempted to sweep this usage away, along with much else, and to introduce *Wy* (modelled on the Russian form of V), in its place. However, this innovation has not been generally accepted, for reasons which it would be politically naïf to reduce to the power of 'tradition'. As a result, unintended by all concerned, the use of *Wy* has become a badge of Party membership.[53]

4 In any case, both 'reflection' and 'refraction' carry the misleading implication that the role of language in society is a purely passive one. This brings us to the last sociolinguistic thesis, which is that language is an active force in society, used by individuals and groups to control others or to defend themselves against being controlled, to change society or to prevent others from changing it. This is not just a point about the content of one specialised form of language which historians have been taking relatively seriously – propaganda – but one with much wider implications. Like other forms of social history, the social history of language cannot be divorced from questions of power.[54]

For example, as the late Michel Foucault and others have emphasised, labelling certain groups 'insane', 'criminals', 'witches' and so on is a way of controlling them.[55] Again, the sociologist Pierre Bourdieu has suggested that the standard variety of a language is a form of 'symbolic domination' (meaning domination by means of symbols, not symbolic as opposed to 'real' domination).[56] It legitimates the rule of the U over the non-U, Prospero over Caliban ('the red plague rid you,/ For learning me your language!', *The Tempest*, Act 1, scene 2).

Some sociolinguists would also argue that language is a part of ideology, defining this slippery term in the words of the philosopher Louis Althusser as a representation of the imaginary relationship of individuals to their real conditions of existence.[57] Others, unhappy with this sharp distinction between the 'real' and the 'imaginary', might prefer to say that language is constitutive of society (or culture) as well as being created by society; that it plays a central part in the social construction of reality. To expose the power of language is one of the principal aims of the supporters of 'deconstruction'. The philosopher–critic Jacques Derrida, the 'architect' of deconstruction, goes further than most in this direction by suggesting that language uses its speakers rather than the other way round, and that we are the servants rather than the masters of our metaphors (including this one).[58] His point has its parallels in Foucault's emphasis on discourse at the expense of individual speakers; in Lévi-Strauss's aphorism that we do not think with myths but myths think themselves in us; and, earlier in the century, in Whorf's argument, already discussed, that the structure of a particular language produces the fundamental categories with which its users interpret the world: 'If Aristotle had spoken Chinese or Dakotan he would have had to adopt an entirely different logic.'[59]

These arguments certainly have their force, and they expose the weaknesses of any simplistic view of language as a mere tool in the hands (or mouths!) of its users. But like most attempts to turn common-sense views upside-down, the counter-arguments themselves have their weaknesses. They too are simplistic, and fail to make important distinctions. Some of us are more in control of language than others, and more skilled in controlling others through language. One thinks of the many groups of professional 'communicators' in contemporary society – copy-writers, speech-writers, script-writers, newsmen, publicity men, whose job is to sell anything from soap-powders to presidents to their viewers, listeners and readers.[60] Their style is unmistakably that of the late twentieth century, the age of the commercial. All the same, social historians should have no difficulty in placing them in a tradition which includes such specialists in the art of persuasion as the Greek sophists (who were attacked by Socrates for making the worse case appear the better), the humanists of the Renaissance (rhetoricians by profession, and often prepared to flatter rulers and justify their actions) and the eighteenth-century quacks (whose techniques are dissected by Roy Porter in Chapter 4 below).

We should not assume either that these professional persuaders believed all their own propaganda, for ideas, people or commodites, or that they were all cynically detached from it. There is a real need for a special term to apply to the situation in between, in which individuals are both masters and servants of their language. 'Ideology' is a possible candidate, a term with the rather dubious advantage that it is already used both in the narrow manipulative sense and in the wider sense (Althusser's, for example) in which it is an inescapable part of daily life.

Alternatively, there is the term 'cultural hegemony', popularised if not coined by the Italian Marxist Antonio Gramsci, to refer to one of the ways in which a ruling class dominates the subordinate classes, a mode of domination which would not be effective if the ruling class were not seen to believe in these ruling ideas which happen to serve their turn.[61] This term would be more useful if it were not currently employed so widely, to refer to almost every society where there is a ruling class, whether or not they exercise coercion, and whether or not they are involved in systematic attempts to persuade the subordinate classes (by means of schools, newspapers and other media), of the legitimacy of their rule, as has been the case increasingly over the last two centuries. Cheap print, followed by photography, cinema, radio and television, has made it possible to expose more people more of the time to highly professional performances carrying all sorts of moral, political and economic messages. The languages of persuasion (including images) seem to be growing ever more insistent and more invasive.

These developments have a particular moral (or message) for the social historian. They are a reminder that although languages are partially autonomous they cannot be understood without reference to the society in which they are spoken, and that 'society' includes not only the different social groups and their ways of life but the basic political, economic and technological structures as well. It might also be argued that social historians have a role to play in making people conscious of these 'hidden persuaders', thus bringing them into the open.

Whether or not they regard themselves as 'consciousness raisers', it is clear that social historians need to think seriously about the role of language in creating and changing the social reality they study. Some of the examples already discussed lend themselves to reinterpretation in active terms. Feminist linguists, for instance, have pointed out that ordinary language, male-dominated as it is, not only expresses the subordinate position of women but keeps women in that subordinate place.[62] Even in the French Revolution, as Dorinda Outram argues (see below, Chapter 6), women were excluded from what a contemporary called *le langage mâle de la vertu*. Again, the master using the familiar T to a servant who replies with the respectful V is not simply expressing or symbolising the social hierarchy, he is re-enacting or confirming it; and so is the servant, unless he or she manages to inject a measure of irony or what the military authorities used to call 'dumb insolence' into the respectful verbal forms.

Similarly, the technical languages of particular professions and crafts need to be understood not only as reflections of a sense of distance from outsiders, but also as a means of ensuring that outsiders remain outside and preventing them from penetrating the mysteries of the clergy, masons, lawyers, quacks and so on. The inhabitants of Polish prisons, according to a recent study, show their awareness of the power of language by compelling the new inmates to learn the prison jargon (*grypserka*), just as the newcomers to Winchester and other public schools are compelled by the older boys to learn and use the school slang. The private language is employed to socialise recruits into the community.[63]

Again, as Jonathan Steinberg is concerned to show (in Chapter 9, below), governments have become increasingly aware of the power of language – the standard language, as opposed to the local dialects – in the course of the nineteenth and twentieth centuries. From the French Revolution onwards, as recent studies have been made abundantly clear, the government of France was unusually aware of the 'politics of language' and concerned to ensure that all the inhabitants of the hexagon knew French.[64] More generally, the erosion of Breton, Irish, Catalan and other 'dominated languages' was an essential part of the process by which these regions were subjected to the rule of Paris, London and Madrid (in Franco's day, newspapers were not allowed to be printed in Catalan). The use of Spanish in America and of English in India, Wales, Africa and elsewhere – at least in certain speech domains – deserves more historical analysis from this point of view than it has so far received.[65]

Conversely, there is a need for the study of revivals of dominated languages as part of movements of resistance to central governments perceived as alien powers; and also of the alternative strategy, the appropriation of dominant languages to resist dominant nations and classes. In East Africa, for instance, Swahili, a traditional lingua franca encouraged by the British because it facilitated local administration, was given a new function during the independence movement, since it was a means of uniting people from different tribes in a common political enterprise, of giving them a common consciousness. And so, ironically enough, was English: the language of the rulers could become the language of resistance.[66]

The active role of language can also be illustrated from recent studies of the 'rhetoric' or 'discourse' of revolution and protest, studies which take words more seriously than historians of these movements used to do. Thus Gareth Stedman Jones has criticised earlier social interpretations of English Chartism as reductionist because they neglected the language of the Chartists. 'Consciousness', he argues, 'cannot be related to experience except through the interposition of a particular language which organizes the understanding of experience.'[67] Historians of the French Revolution have also expressed dissatisfaction with a reductionist view of language (as a mask for class interests, for example), and have suggested that its role in the Revolution be understood as a means of national integration, or as a substitute for power, or as a part of a new political culture in which words like *patrie* had a 'magical quality'.[68]

Historical examples of all these uses of language could easily be multiplied, and some of them are worked out in detail in the chapters which follow. In such a small collection, many important topics have had to be omitted. Insults are discussed but not politeness, the language of medicine but not the language of the law, while the case-studies are confined to England, France and Italy, from the end of the Middle Ages to the present century. As for the present introduction, its purpose has essentially been to whet the appetite of the reader, and to make two suggestions: in the first place, that language is too important historically to leave to the linguists – so intimately involved with the processes of social interaction and social change that social historians need to give it much more attention than they have done so far; in the second place, that social historians of language have much to learn from the ethnographers of communication, sociologists of language and others who entered the field before we did. We would do well to begin by learning *their* language. We will doubtless discover the need to make alterations in order to adapt it to our own purposes: whether the adaptation should be treated as a case of 'pidginisation' or 'creolisation' is not for us to say. In the meantime, this collection is offered as a few stepping-stones into the unknown.

NOTES

[1] Indicators of this growing awareness include History Workshop 14, 'Language and History', held in Brighton in 1980, and the discussion on the social history of language held at King's College, Cambridge, the same year.

[2] C. Cittadini, *Le origini della volgar toscana favella* (Siena, 1604); B. Aldrete, *Del origen y principio de la lengua castellana* (Rome, 1606).

[3] T. Bynon, *Historical Linguistics* (Cambridge, 1977), Chapter 1.

[4] J. Culler, *Saussure* (London, 1976), especially Chapter 3.

[5] O. Jespersen, *Growth and Structure of the English Language* (Leipzig, 1905); F. Brunot, *Histoire de la langue française* (14 vols, Paris, 1905–).

[6] G. B. Gelli, *Capricci del bottaio* (Florence, 1546), the fifth dialogue; C. Ginzburg, *The Cheese and the Worms* (1975; English translation, London, 1980), p. 9.

[7] *Year Books of Edward I*, vol. 1, ed. F. W. Maitland (London, 1903), p. xxxv; D. Veall, *The Popular Movement for Law Reform* (London, 1970).

[8] Quoted by R. K. Merton, *Social Theory and Social Structure* (revised edition, London, 1957), p. 3.

[9] C. K. Ogden and I. A. Richards, *The Meaning of Meaning* (London, 1923), with an appendix by B. Malinowski on 'The Problem of Meaning in Primitive Language'; L. Vygotsky, *Thought and Language* (1934; English translation, Cambridge, Mass., 1962); B. Whorf, *Language, Thought and Reality* (New York, 1956).

[10] Introductory statements include D. Hymes, 'Toward Ethnographies of Communication' (1964), reprinted in *Language and Social Context*, ed. P. P. Giglioli (Harmondsworth, 1971), Chapter 1; J. Fishman, 'Who speaks What Language to Whom and When' (1965), reprinted in *Sociolinguistics*, ed. J. B. Pride and J. Holmes (Harmondsworth, 1972), Chapter 1 and 'The Sociology of Language' (1969), reprinted in Giglioli, Chapter 2. Other useful anthologies include *Directions in Sociolinguistics*, ed. J. Gumperz and D. Hymes (New York, 1972), and *Explorations in the Ethnography of Speaking*, ed. R. Bauman and J. Sherzer (Cambridge, 1974).

[11] The term 'code', used in opposition to 'message', is coming to be abandoned because of its ambiguity. *Cf.* Hymes, 'Ways of Speaking', in Bauman and Sherzer, Chapter 21, and M. A. K. Halliday, *Language as Social Semiotic* (London, 1978), p. 111. On the speech community, J. Gumperz, 'The Speech Community' (1968), reprinted in Giglioli, Chapter 10.

[12] R. Lakoff, *Language and Women's Place* (New York, 1975); S. McConnell-Ginet, 'Intonation in a Man's World', *Signs* 3 (1978), 541–59; on Mrs Thatcher, M. Atkinson, *Our Masters' Voices* (London, 1984), p. 113.

[13] M. van Beek, *An Enquiry into Puritan Vocabulary* (Groningen, 1969).

[14] R. Bauman, *Let Your Words be Few: Symbolism of Speech and Silence among the Quakers* (Cambridge, 1983).

[15] A. Langer, *Der Wortschatz des deutschen Pietismus* (Tübingen, 1954). *Cf.* M. Fulbrook, *Piety and Politics* (Cambridge, 1983), p. 149.

[16] *Coney-Catchers and Bawdy Baskets*, ed. G. Salgado (Harmondsworth, 1972), makes a useful introduction to the English variety of this international counter-culture.

[17] A. S. C. Ross, 'Linguistic Class-Indicators in Present-Day English', *Neuphilologische Mitteilungen* 55 (1954), 20–56. A simplified version appears in *Noblesse Oblige*, ed. N. Mitford (London, 1956). *Cf. U and Non-U Revisited*, ed. R. Buckle (London, 1978) and A. Barr and P. York, *The Official Sloane Ranger Handbook* (London, 1982), pp. 14f.

[18] D. Baltzell, *Philadelphia Gentlemen* (New York, 1958), p. 51.

[19] *Cf.* K. C. Phillipps, *Language and Class in Victorian England* (London, 1984).

[20] L. Holberg, *Erasmus Montanus*, Act 1, scene 2: 'I mi Ungdom talede man ikke saa her paa Bierget som nu; det som man nu kalder Lakei, kaldte man da Dreng; det som man nu kalder Matresse kaldte man da Bislaaperske; en Frøken hedte da Statsmo, en Musikant Spillemand, og en Sikketerer Skriver.'

[21] F. de Callières, *Mots à la Mode* (Paris, 1693), pp. 58f.

[22] P. Aretino, *Sei Giornate*, ed. G. Aquilecchia (Bari, 1975), p. 82.

[23] C. Geertz, 'Linguistic Etiquette' (1960), reprinted Pride and Holmes, Chapter 11; J. Irvine, 'Strategies of Status Manipulation in the Wolof Greeting', in Bauman and Sherzer, Chapter 8.

[24] K. V. Thomas will discuss the history of the English regional accent in an essay to be published in his forthcoming collection.

[25] T. Veblen, *The Theory of the Leisure Class* (New York, 1899). *Cf.* R. A. Hall, 'T. Veblen and Linguistic Theory', in *American Speech* 35 (1960), 124–30.

[26] Bernstein's papers on this subject are collected in his *Class, Codes and Control* (London, 1971). For an assessment, see Halliday, *Language*, Chapter 5.

[27] Recent contributions to this long debate include J. Goody, *The Domestication of the Savage Mind* (Cambridge, 1977); C. R. Hallpike, *Foundations of Primitive Thought* (Oxford, 1979); and W. J. Ong, *Orality and Literacy* (London, 1982), who refers to Bernstein (p. 106).

[28] H. Rosen, *Language and Class* (Bristol, 1972). *Cf.* W. Labov, 'The Logic of Non-standard English' (1969), reprinted Giglioli, Chapter 9.

[29] Hymes, 'Ways of Speaking', pp. 440f; Halliday, pp. 31f.

[30] J. Gumperz, *Discourse Strategies* (Cambridge, 1982); R. Tyler, *The Emperor Charles V* (London, 1956), p. 20.

[31] C. Ferguson, 'Diglossia' (1959), reprinted in Giglioli, Chapter 11.

[32] B. Stolt, *Die Sprachmischung in Luthers Tischreden* (Stockholm, 1964).

[33] Printed in the Oxford University *Gazette* and the Cambridge University *Reporter*.

[34] Trevisa's translation of Higden, quoted in B. Cottle, *The Triumph of English 1350–1400* (London, 1969), p. 19.

[35] K. Whinnom, 'Lingua Franca: Historical Problems', in *Pidgin and Creole Linguistics*, ed. A. Valdman (Bloomington and London, 1977), pp. 295–310.

[36] E. Le Roy Ladurie, *Les paysans de Languedoc* (1966; English translation, *The Peasants of Languedoc*, Urbana, 1974), p. 272. On glossolalia, see W. Samarin, *Tongues of Men and Angels* (New York, 1972).

[37] E. Weber, *Peasants into Frenchmen* (London, 1979), Chapter 6.

[38] Two classic studies are W. Labov, 'Rules for Ritual Insults', in *Studies in Social*

Interaction, ed. D. Sudnow (New York, 1972), pp. 120–68; and C. O. Frake, 'How to Ask for a Drink in Subanun' (1964), reprinted in Giglioli, Chapter 5.

[39] For an ethnographic approach, K. Basso, 'Silence in Western Apache Culture' (1970), reprinted Giglioli, Chapter 4; for the silence of medieval monks, C. W. Bynum, *Jesus as Mother* (Berkeley, 1982), pp. 43f; for that of medieval children, S. Nagel and S. Vecchio, 'Il bambino, la parola, il silenzio', *Quaderni Storici* 19 (1984), 719–63; for that of Quakers, Bauman (note 14 above). On secrecy as a 'communicative event', B. L. Bellman, *The Language of Secrecy* (New Brunswick, 1984).

[40] M. McLuhan, *Understanding Media* (New York, 1964), Chapter 1.

[41] K. Basso, 'The Ethnography of Writing', in Bauman and Sherzer, especially pp. 428f; on the rhetoric of the threatening letter, E. P. Thompson, 'The Crime of Anonymity', in *Albion's Fatal Tree*, ed. D. Hay *et al.* (London, 1975), Chapter 6.

[42] I. Morris, *The World of the Shining Prince* (London, 1964), pp. 187f; E. A. Ahern, *Chinese Ritual and Politics* (Cambridge, 1981), Chapter 2.

[43] Translated from E. Masini, *Sacro Arsenale* (Bologna, 1665 edition), p. 157.

[44] I. Illich, *Gender* (London, 1983), p. 135.

[45] S. Harding, 'Women and Words in a Spanish Village', in *Toward an Anthropology of Women*, ed. R. R. Reiter (New York and London, 1975), pp. 283–308.

[46] R. Brown and A. Gilman, 'The Pronouns of Power and Solidarity' (1960), reprinted in Giglioli, Chapter 12.

[47] E. Le Roy Ladurie, *Montaillou village occitan* (Paris, 1975), pp. 515–16. Since his source translates the occitan into Latin, it is fortunate that both languages make the distinction between T and V.

[48] R. Guha, *Elementary Aspects of Peasant Insurgency in Colonial India* (New Delhi, 1983), pp. 49f.

[49] I. Turgenev, *Smoke* (Moscow, 1867), Chapter 2. Cf. P. Friedrich, 'The Russian Pronominal Usage' (1966), reprinted in Gumperz and Hymes, pp. 272–300; J. Lyons, 'Pronouns of Address in *Anna Karenina*', in *Studies in English Linguistics for R. Quirk* (London, 1980), pp. 235–49.

[50] On the Quakers, see Bauman; on the Saminists, J. Scott, *The Moral Economy of the Peasant* (New Haven, 1976), p. 237.

[51] P. Burke, *Popular Culture in Early Modern Europe* (London, 1978), pp. 270f.

[52] Anti-languages are discussed from this point of view in Halliday, Chapter 9. On the militarisation and bureaucratisation of German in the nineteenth century, see G. Craig, *The Germans* (New York, 1982), appendix.

[53] N. Davies, *Heart of Europe* (Oxford, 1984), p. 9.

[54] A point made somewhat dramatically by T. Judt, 'A Clown in Regal Purple', *History Workshop Journal* 7 (1979), 66–89.

[55] P. Burke, *Sociology and History* (London, 1980), p. 58.

[56] P. Bourdieu, *Ce que parler veut dire* (Paris, 1982), pp. 34f.

[57] L. Althusser, 'Ideology and Ideological State Apparatuses' (1970), translated in his *Lenin and Philosophy* (London, 1971).

[58] For a famous example of his approach, J. Derrida, 'Plato's Pharmacy', in his *Dissemination* (1972; English translation, Chicago, 1982), Chapter 1. On the movement, cf. J. Culler, *On Deconstruction* (London, 1983), and C. Norris, *Deconstruction: Theory and Practice* (London, 1982).

[59] F. Mauthner, *Beiträge zu einer Kritik der Sprache* (3 vols., Stuttgart, 1902–3), quoted in Ogden and Richards, p. 35n. Cf. G. Weiler, *Mauthner's Critique of Language* (Cambridge, 1970), especially p. 143.

[60] Among the many studies of such groups are J. McGinniss, *The Selling of the President* (London, 1970), and A. Schwartzenberg, *L'Etat–Spectacle* (Paris, 1977).

[61] For selections from Gramsci on hegemony, with comments, see *Culture, Ideology and Social Process*, ed. T. Bennett *et al.* (London, 1981), pp. 191–218.

[62] R. Lakoff, *Language and Woman's Place* (New York, 1975).

[63] On Polish prisons, see J. Kurczewski, 'Bluzg, Grypserka, "Drugie Zycie" '; there is a brief discussion in Halliday, pp. 164f.

[64] M. de Certeau, D. Julia and J. Revel, *Une Politique de la langue* (Paris, 1975); cf. J. Y.

Lartichaux, 'Linguistic Politics during the French Revolution', *Diogenes* 97 (1977), 65–84, and P. Higonnet, 'The Politics of Linguistic Terrorism', *Social History* 5 (1980), 41–69.

[65] A beginning has been made by S. B. Heath and R. Laprade, 'Castilian Colonization and Indigenous Languages', in *Language Spread*, ed. R. L. Cooper (New York, 1982), pp. 118–43; A. Mazrui, *The Political Sociology of the English Language* (London, 1978), on Africa, and V. E. Durkacz, *The Decline of the Celtic Languages* (Edinburgh, 1983).

[66] W. Whiteley, *Swahili: the Rise of a National Language* (Cambridge, 1969). *Cf.* O. Macdonagh, *States of Mind: a Study of Anglo–Irish Conflict 1780–1980* (London, 1983), Chapter 7, 'The Politics of Gaelic'.

[67] G. Stedman Jones, *Languages of Class* (Cambridge, 1983), p. 101.

[68] L. Hunt, *Politics, Culture and Class in the French Revolution* (Berkeley, 1984), Chapter 1.

2

THE USES OF LITERACY IN EARLY MODERN ITALY

Peter Burke

In the middle of the twentieth century, when many new nations were embarking on massive literacy campaigns, scholars in several disciplines began to take the subject of reading and writing more seriously than before. Sociologists argued, for instance, that 'Literacy is the basic personal skill which underlies the whole modernising sequence' because it 'gives people access to the world of vicarious experience'.[1] Anthropologists suggested that the traditional distinction between 'logical' and 'prelogical' thought should rather have been framed in terms of 'literate' and 'preliterate', because what made abstract thinking possible was literacy.[2] Historians too began to concern themselves with this topic, to measure the extent of the diffusion of literacy in different periods and to discuss the economic, social and political consequences of these techniques.[3]

Less than a generation later, a reaction against this approach has set in, marked by a critique of its assumptions. Scholars who have written about the literacy revolution are accused of exaggerating the distance between oral and literate cultures; of underestimating the achievements and resources of societies without literacy; and, most serious of all, of treating literacy as a uniform neutral technology which can be studied in detachment from its social context, as if the meaning, uses and conventions of literacy did not vary from one society to another.[4]

This reaction against an older approach is itself part of the context of what is now called the 'ethnography of writing', an approach which has grown out of the ethnography of communication (see above, p. 3) and emphasises the settings in which literacy is learned and the purposes for which it is used, whether in the United States or in Liberia.[5] The dust has not yet settled on this debate, and it is doubtless too early to say whether or not there are common features underlying the different literacies, their settings and conventions. What has become clear is the need to occupy the middle ground between the grand theories of literacy and its consequences on the one hand, and the empirical but limited research on literacy 'rates' and 'levels' on the other. This essay will therefore focus, like some other recent historical studies, on what Richard Hoggart called 'the uses of literacy.[6] To work on Italian literacy in the early modern period is in some ways frustrating. The preliminary work of more or less approximate measurement is much more difficult to carry out than it has been in the case of Britain, let alone Sweden. Despite the growing interest of the bishops in the attitudes of the laity, there was nothing in Italy like the Swedish church-inspired house-to-house investigations ('husverhör'). Nor was there anything like the British Protestation Oath of 1642, the signatures to which have been used as an indicator of male literacy.[7] There was not even a tradition of signing marriage registers, and there was, of course, no unified Italy till 1860. Until the coming of national surveys, like the one carried out in 1911, there is little to be done but collect fragmentary information from fragmentary sources.[8]

One famous fragment which is often used as a baseline is the testimony of the Florentine merchant chronicler Giovanni Villani, to the effect that in 1338, between 10,000 and 12,000 Florentine children were going to school. This figure, if accurate (as many historians believe it to be), is quite extraordinary for a fourteenth-century city with a population of under 100,000. It is likely that most if not all the schoolchildren were male, and on this assumption it would follow that from 45% to 60% of Florentine boys of school age were actually attending a school of some kind.[9] This figure makes a remarkable contrast with the statistics from the 1911 survey, which found the national average literacy rate to be only 38% of the population over the age of six, even if we allow for the fact that the 38% is an aggregate which is pulled down by the figures for women, for the countryside, and for the south.

For Venice too in the late Middle Ages – or early Renaissance – there are figures which suggest a population which was relatively highly schooled. In the early fifteenth century, when the city contained about 85,000 people, there were fifty or sixty teachers, in other words one to every 350 males under twenty. By the late sixteenth century the ratio had improved to one to 135, for more than 250 practising schoolmasters are recorded in a population which had risen to about 135,000.[10] In Milan at the end of the sixteenth century, there were said to be 120 schools of Christian doctrine, combining religious instruction with elementary literacy.[11] Rome seems to have lagged behind till the end of the seventeenth century, but in 1703, 126 schoolmasters are recorded in a population of about 150,000.[12] Although systematic comparisons have not been made, it seems likely that literacy in northern Italy, at least, was high relative to other parts of Europe (with the possible exception of the Netherlands) from the year 1000, if not before, till about 1600, and that the Italian lead was only challenged in the seventeenth century, with the rise of the Dutch Republic and of the great literacy campaign in Sweden. Yet this conclusion, however plausible, cannot be established; that is what is so frustrating. Prospects improve if we turn from the literacy rate to the true subject of this chapter, the question of the ways in which this hard-won and highly prized skill was used. This is, of course, not so much one question as a whole cluster. The ethnographers of writing have emphasised the need for studying a whole range of problems: who, in a given culture, writes to whom, in what social settings, and also on what subjects – for not all information is necessarily considered to be appropriate for transmission by written channels. It is on these problems that I shall concentrate.

A similar set of questions could be asked about reading, which should ideally be discussed separately from writing because of the likelihood that many people who could not write were able to read. Villani describes children in elementary schools who 'stick to reading' (*stanno a leggere*), while writing was taught to fewer pupils elsewhere. We need to ask who read what, indeed who read what to whom (since there was much reading aloud), and in what settings. To learn, for example, that in the early fifteenth century Pope Eugenius IV used to read in bed is to have acquired more than a piece of picturesque trivia, for the example helps to document the slow but significant shift from public to private reading.[13] To discover that the legend of Santa Margherita was read aloud to women in childbirth in sixteenth-century Italy tells one something about contemporary attitudes to the power of the word. However it is with the manifold uses of writing, or active literacy, that this chapter is principally concerned, whether the writing was in Latin, or in what was becoming standard Italian, or in dialect; whether the handwriting was gothic, or the elegant italic script which was spreading in humanist circles, whether the message was written on parchment or paper, or carved in stone, or indeed scribbled on walls.[14]

So far as these questions are concerned, there is certainly no shortage of evidence. On the contrary, it is copious; so copious as to create serious problems for historians who want to use it. From the eleventh century, if not before, Italy – or at least, the many towns of the north and centre – was becoming what might reasonably be called a 'notarial culture', with a high proportion of notaries in the population (eight per 1,000 in Florence in 1427), thanks to the high demand for the registration of wills, contracts of marriage, apprenticeship and partnership, and other legal 'acts' and 'instruments'.[15] Italy was not alone in this respect. The notarial culture seems to have extended over much of the Mediterranean Christian world in the later Middle Ages. Yet a contrast with England, which might be extended to other parts of northern Europe, is suggested by the remark of an Italian notary who visited this country in the thirteenth century. 'Italians,' he wrote, 'like cautious men, want to have a public instrument for practically every contract they enter into; but the English are just the opposite, and an instrument is very rarely asked for unless it is essential.'[16] The remains of this notarial activity are massive. The idea of writing on this subject came to me while waiting for documents in an Italian archive (a process which not infrequently affords leisure for contemplation), together with the realisation, at once intoxicating and sobering, that every document in that vast repository would be of relevance to the research. One would in a sense be interrogating the documents about themselves, rather than, as usual, about something else; asking for what purposes they were originally made, and dividing them into genres – notarial acts, bills, certificates, licences, passes, denunciations, petitions and so on.

The uses of literacy obviously include what we call 'literature' and what the humanists knew as *bonae litterae* (categories which overlap to a considerable extent but do not coincide). This function will not be discussed here, not because it is unimportant (the period under consideration runs, after all, from Petrarch to Goldoni), but because it has attracted so much scholarly attention, while practical or 'pragmatic' literacy, as it is now called, has not. Sociolinguists distinguish what they call 'domains of language behaviour', different styles of speech which are to be found in different settings.[17] In a similar way I should like to distinguish four principal domains of practical literacy and discuss them in turn: business, the family, the Church and the State. Although it is impossible to distinguish four styles of writing, one to each domain, there is evidence of variation in style as one moves from one 'use' to another. In three of the domains, distinct types of handwriting were customarily employed. Merchants used 'business hand' (*lettera mercantescha*) in its regional varieties (*mercantile fiorentina*, *venetiana*, etc.). Administrative documents were generally produced in 'chancery hand' (*lettera cancellarescha*), while clerks in the service of the Church used 'ecclesiastical hand' (*lettera ecclesiastica*), together with special styles for papal bulls and briefs.[18] Latin was the language not only of the Church but of the law and of much public administration. The alternative to it was not Italian but dialect. Although Tuscan was gaining ground in the early modern period in the domain of literature, it had not yet invaded the public domains of business, politics and the Church, let alone the privacy of the family.

Literacy and business

The uses of literacy in business are relatively well known. In the fourteenth and fifteenth centuries, writers of advice to merchants – a genre which itself illustrates one of the practical uses of literacy – counselled them not to spare their pens and told them that the good merchant had inky fingers.[19] In the early seventeenth century, the Genoese patrician Andrea Spinola was still giving similar advice to anyone who wanted to succeed in business. Even nobles ought to know how to write a good hand and to keep accounts; it was 'really shameful' that some of them relied on other people to do this for them.[20]

The numbers of surviving bills, receipts, contracts and so on suggests that the advice was often taken. The business papers of one fourteenth-century merchant, Francesco Datini of Prato, near Florence, are so vast as to daunt historians who wish to study them and make them wonder how Datini and his agents found the time to do anything besides produce this mass of documentation, which includes some 500 account-books and ledgers, piously inscribed 'in the name of God and of profit'.[21] In Datini's time it was in fact normal for nine different ledgers to be kept in a single firm, dealing respectively with income, expenditure, wages, petty cash and so on, not forgetting the master ledger or 'secret book' (*libro segreto*). The ledgers employed the method of double entry which the Italian businessmen pioneered.[22]

Keeping accounts in this way was a skill which had, of course, to be learned, and numeracy was taught to a relatively high level in what were known as 'abacus schools' (such as the six in Florence mentioned by Villani). The abacus was a board with counters on the ancient Roman model, not the system of beads on wires used in the Far East. The curriculum of these abacus schools seems to have been a practical, business-oriented one.[23] The evidence comes from surviving school-books, which include questions about buying and selling wool and converting different weights, measures and currencies. The existence of schoolbooks such as these from the fourteenth century – in other words, well before the invention of printing – deserves emphasis, even if the books were intended for the teachers rather than the students. So does the abacus. It is mind-boggling to imagine Italian merchants adding up long columns of Roman numerals, but in fact there was no need to do so, thanks to the abacus, which also allowed the otherwise illiterate to calculate at speed.[24]

It is the numeracy of the Florentines in the fourteenth and fifteenth centuries which has attracted most attention from historians, but the same skills can be documented for a later period and other cities. The *Summa of Arithmetic*, published in 1521, discusses rates of interest and exchange. The *Universal Treasure*, published in Venice about 1530, claimed to teach book-keeping and 'all business methods' (*ogni ragione di mercantia*), and it gave examples with a distinctly Venetian flavour, such as the buying and selling of sugarloaves and spices and the journey time of a galley going to Crete.[25] In 1587, again in Venice, there were 143 pupils at one school who were learning arithmetic and double-entry

book-keeping.[26] One begins to wonder whether there were enough
businesses to employ all these pupils after they had finished the course,
and to understand why the *Universal Treasure* was directed to 'friars,
priests, students, doctors, gentlemen, craftsmen and especially to the
sons of every father who desires his son's welfare'.

Business affairs depended on other kinds of document besides account,
on letters, for example. Over 125,000 letters survive in the Datini archive
in Prato. Letters brought news and news was a matter of life and death –
economic life and death at least – for the business community. Priority
was crucial. 'If you are in business,' goes one famous piece of advice, 'and
your letters come in the same packet as other letters, you must always
think of reading your own letters before passing the others on.'[27]

Letters did not merely give news of supply, demand and prices elsewhere. Payments could be made by particular forms of letter. The Medici
bank in Bruges, for example, sold what were called 'letters of credit' to
travellers to Italy, the letters being addressed to its Milan branch; the
travellers bought the letters in one local currency and redeemed them for
the other on arrival. Also in general use in the fifteenth century were bills
of exchange, again in the form of a letter, which allowed the advance of
funds in one place and repayment in another.[22]

With all these letters to write and accounts to keep, not to mention the
bills and receipts which had to be made out, it is no wonder that the
fingers of the good merchant were so inky. And not his fingers alone; for
running a family, as well as running a business, could generate a good deal
of paper.

Literacy and the family

The second domain of practical literacy to be discussed here is that of the
family, more especially the urban patrician family (although its
dominance of the written record may be in part the result of a higher
documentary survival rate). For what purposes, in early modern Italy,
were family papers written and preserved? At this point we need to
distinguish three kinds of family document. In the first place, *carte di
notaio*, as they were called, in other words notarial papers such as wills,
marriage contracts, inventories *post mortem* and so on, documents which
were supposed to be preserved with care in chests in case disputes about
the inheritance should arise, as they often did.

In the second place, family letters. What the Paston letters are to
the historian of fifteenth-century England, the letters of Alessandra
Macinghi Strozzi are to the historian of Florence in the same period. The
Strozzi letters were printed in the nineteenth century, but the letters of a
number of families of the period remain unpublished: those of the Donà,

for example. The Donà were a Venetian patrician family whose letters survive in considerable numbers from the middle of the sixteenth century onwards. As in the case of the Strozzi, the letters were written because of the absence of the adult males of the family. Alessandra's sons Filippo and Lorenzo were in exile, living in Bruges and in Naples. 'If I were with you,' she wrote in her vivid, colloquial way, 'I shouldn't be writing these old letters' (*queste letteracce*).[29]

She wrote about the possible marriages of the daughters of her household, as well as letting off steam about her servant problems, more exactly slave problems (since Florentines bought Circassian and other slaves at this period). Similarly, when the head of the Donà household, Gianbattista, was away in Cyprus on busines, his wife Paola wrote to him with news of the children (one of them, as it happens, a future Doge): 'Lunardo is learning very well and I believe that we can expect well of him ... Antonio ... is beginning to speak and is my solace.'[30] It should be clear that the 'sense of childhood' as the late Philippe Ariès called it, was not a discovery of the seventeenth and eighteenth centuries, at least not in Italy,[31] for Paola Donà's interest in her children has a number of parallels in the family papers of the time. In 1501, for example, Isabella Gonzaga, Marchioness of Mantua, wrote to her husband (another absentee from home) about their little son: 'Our little boy began to walk today, and went four steps, to his great pleasure and ours, with no one holding him (though he was watched carefully) ... he staggered a little, so that it seemed as if he was imitating a drunkard. Asking him if he wanted to send his regards to Your Lordship, he replied Ti Pa.' The next year, she again reported her son's progress to her absent husband: 'Yesterday I was saying my prayers when he came in and said he wanted to look for Daddy [*il Pa*], and he went through the prayer-book himself and found a bearded face, which delighted him, and kissing it more than six times he said "fine Daddy" [*papà bello*], with the greatest joy in the world.'[32] The Medici papers tell a similar story of the sense of childhood and the uses of letters. In the late fifteenth century Clarice, wife of Lorenzo the Magnificent, wrote to him about their three-year-old son Giovanni (better known as Pope Leo X), telling him that 'he keeps saying, when will Loencio come?' Giovanni's younger brother Giuliano, at the age of six, was described in a letter by a gentleman in Medici service as 'as fresh as a rose', and as saying 'with a long O: O, O, O, O, where is Lorenzo?' (it is interesting to find that these children called their father by his first name).[33]

With the exception of the last example, all these domestic details come from letters from wives to husbands. On the other hand, there is no surviving letter from G. B. Donà to his wife asking for news of the children; he wrote to his grown-up son about the arrival of ships and other business, adding various messages to be passed on to different individuals. The letters were clearly family rather than individual affairs, which helps explain their preservation. Politics, however, was a taboo subject, at least for Gianbattista Donà, who once reprimanded his son for having referred to it in a letter. 'Never write about the concerns of the authorities [*cose di signori*, a remarkable phrase from the pen of a patrician], neither to approve nor to disapprove, because it can get you into trouble.'[34] The problem was that one could never be certain who would see one's letters, since they circulated in bundles, as was implied by the advice to merchants quoted above. A Florentine apothecary of the late fifteenth century records receiving a letter from his godfather 'though it was addressed to other citizens'.[35]

A third use of literacy within the family was to compile what the Florentines called *ricordanze*, a term which might perhaps be translated as 'memoranda'. From Florence alone, about a hundred such memoranda survive from the fourteenth, fifteenth and sixteenth centuries, generally from patrician families such as the Guicciardini, Medici, Pitti and Rucellai, but also from craftsmen and shopkeepers such as Landucci the apothecary and Arditi the tailor.[36] They are rarer elsewhere, but patricians in Venice and Genoa also kept memoranda, and so did a few ordinary citizens, including a builder from Bologna and a carpenter from Milan.[37]

Memoranda of this kind overlap with urban chronicles, but their emphasis is on private rather than public life. They are sometimes called 'diaries' by their editors and others, but this term is rather misleading, for they were not, for the most part, records of the individual deeds and thoughts of the writer. Like the letters we have just discussed, and like many portraits of the Renaissance, these memoranda are concerned not so much with the individual as with the family, as is shown by the fact that in some cases, such as Landucci's and that of the Vellutis, they were continued by another member of the family after the first 'remembrancer' had died.[38] The prologues to particular texts tell the same story, explaining that the purpose of the record – which was presumably read out on occasion – was to remind the family (the *nazione*, as it is sometimes called) of its past. They deal, therefore, with the origin of the family or branch, with the births, marriages and deaths of its members, and with the acquisition of property.[39]

Beyond that, the memoranda have a somewhat miscellaneous character. They are a 'mixed salad' (*una insalata di più erbe*), as one remembrancer rather charmingly put it.[40] Some of them, like the journal kept by the Genoese patrician Pallavicino, lean towards local history. Others concentrate on the family finances, so that it would not be too unfair to describe them as glorified account-books. Even the memoranda of the great sixteenth-century historian Francesco Guicciardini, which constitute one of the most self-consciously literary examples of the genre, bear the marks of their origins. Like some diaries in early modern England, Guicciardini's manuscript was bound up with his book of debtors and creditors.

The assumptions behind these records are made explicit in a fourteenth-century text, itself on the margins of the genre, the collection of proverbs and other pieces of advice compiled by the Tuscan merchant Paolo da Castaldo for his son, brothers and others. 'Foresight is an excellent thing,' he wrote, 'so you should always plan all your affairs ahead.' Among other things he recommended keeping a record of all the occasions when a notary has drawn a document up, together with the date and the names of the witnesses, and also carrying in one's purse a paper listing everything that has to be done, so as to catch the eye whenever the purse is opened.[41]

These documents bear witness not only to the habit of active literacy but also to a particular mentality, prudent and calculating (it is tempting to add 'bourgeois'). The statistics of school attendance in the Villani chronicle, with which this chapter began, are of interest not only for what they tell us about education but as evidence of the mentality of the chronicler, a 'numerate mentality' for which there is considerable supporting evidence from late medieval Italy.[42] Whether the memoranda also bear witness to what Burckhardt called 'the development of the individual' is more doubtful, not least because of the concern with the family which they reveal – not only the nuclear family but also, on occasion, a wider group of kin. Burckhardt's view must be described as anachronistic, or at the very least as somewhat premature, in the sense that what a later age would call 'autobiography' does seem to have developed out of this habit of keeping memoranda, which were made for the whole family but were necessarily made by one individual at a time, encouraging him (for the individual is male in the vast majority of these cases), to express his own opinions.[43]

Studies of literacy in our own century often suggest that it encourages self-consciousness. At all events it was Italy, and more especially Tuscany, the heartland of memoranda, which produced the best-known and the most numerous personal documents in early modern Europe (at least in the period 1350–1600), from Petrarch's 'Private Book' (*Secretum*) to the autobiography of Benvenuto Cellini. Cellini's self-celebration is linked to the tradition of the memoranda by his concern for his family. Of course the autobiography had religious roots as well. The tradition of Augustine's *Confessions* was well known to Petrarch. All the same, even the spiritual autobiography was perceived in this culture as a kind of accounting. Petrarch's disciple Giovanni da Ravenna called his the 'Account-Book of his Life' (*Rationarium Vitae*).[44] Looking back, we can see how the spiritual autobiography gradually became secularised, and the family record individualised in the sense not only of dealing with a single individual but of being intended for that individual's eyes alone. A striking Florentine example, all the more striking because the individual concerned is not particularly interesting in other ways, is the journal (described by its author as *Ephemerides seu Diarii*) kept in the first years of the seventeenth century by the young patrician Girolamo da Sommaia when he was studying at the university of Salamanca.[45] He protected himself against other readers, as Samuel Pepys was to do later in the century, by recording his frequent sexual encounters in a simple private code, the Greek alphabet. Transliterated, the entries take the form of *dolcetudine con Francisca, Isabella* and so on.

Literacy and the Church

In the two domains described so far, business and the family, there has been little to say about change. The arithmetic books of the sixteenth century are difficult to distinguish from those of the fourteenth century, while a guide to the notary's art written in the thirteenth century was considered relevant enough over 300 years later to be worth reprinting.[46] Family memoranda seem to have become more numerous (especially outside Florence) and more personal as time went by, but the shift was neither sudden nor sharp. The situation in the remaining two domains, religion and politics, makes a dramatic contrast. Here change positively forces itself on the historian's attention. It will also be necessary, in these cases, to say rather more about reading.

The clergy had, of course, long needed to be literate in order to 'say' Mass, since this oral performance was in fact a public reading from a service-book, the 'Missal'. Priests were also obliged to recite other prayers or 'Offices' in private every day, reading them from a smaller book, the 'Breviary'. It was, of course, useful for them to read other works too, whether they were theological, devotional or practical; an obvious example of the third class is the *Mirror of Conscience*, a manual for confessors compiled in the mid-fifteenth century by Archbishop Antonino of Florence.

All the same, there is evidence from the records of episcopal visitations in rural Tuscany and Lombardy in the fifteenth and sixteenth centuries that occasional parish priests were 'illiterate' (*ignarus litterarum*), while others were reported as 'knowing nothing', whatever these phrases meant (unable to read? unable to write? ignorant of Latin?). Others lacked breviaries, and were given a month to acquire them, while one illiterate priest was told to learn these basic skills by Easter and was suspended from his functions until he had done so.[47]

Given the relatively high literacy of the laity in Florence and elsewhere, even a few cases of clerical illiteracy, if this is what it was, are striking, and one can see why the bishops were shocked. On the other hand, only a few cases are recorded. From the perspective of the uses of literacy, the existence of the sources from which this information is derived is what deserves emphasis; the existence of written records of official inspections of every parish in a given diocese. Records of this kind have survived in small numbers from the fifteenth century, but they become increasingly common in the sixteenth, especially after 1560 or thereabouts, as the movement which historians now call the 'Catholic Reformation' or 'Counter-Reformation' grew in strength. The systematic, separate, professional education of the clergy in seminaries was another part of this movement. Seminaries were founded in Italy from the 1560s onwards in Milan, Verona, Rome, Bologna, Padua and so on. As a result, priests became better-educated, and also more remote from ordinary people.[48]

What about the literacy of the laity? From the Church's point of view, both the literate and the illiterate laity presented a problem. The illiterate were a problem because they were what the clergy called 'superstitious', which meant, in the sixteenth century at least, that they were addicted to magic. At this time what might be called the magical uses of literacy were extremely important: the use of writing to communicate with supernatural forces unofficially, without going through proper ecclesiastical channels. These were what might be described as the uses of literacy for the illiterate, signs of the respect for the written word common in societies where literacy is restricted.[49]

Inquisition records and other sources of the sixteenth and seventeenth centuries reveal the importance of the written word in the equipment of Italian cunning men and wise women in town and country alike, and the belief in its power to cure the sick. A common amulet, which was supposed to cure fevers if worn round the neck of the sufferer, took the form of a triangle lettered abracadabra, thus:

A
AB
ABR
ABRA
ABRAC
ABRACA
ABRACAD
ABRACADA
ABRACADAB
ABRACADABR
ABRACADABRA

Again, words would be inscribed on 'papers of goodwill' (*carte del benevolere*), which by touching someone would prevent them bearing ill will towards the person carrying the paper. Diocesan synods not infrequently denounced the 'superstitious words' inscribed on sheets of paper ('*bollettini*', '*brevi*', '*polizze*', etc.). To give them more power, words would be inscribed in the form of a cross, or a triangle (as above); or they would be written by a virgin on virgin paper; or on the leaf of a herb; on almonds; on bread; or on a host.[50]

Not only spells but whole books had their magic. At least one devotional book, the legend of Santa Margherita, was popularly believed to possess healing powers. According to some sixteenth-century editions of this text, it should be recited to a woman who was having a difficult childbirth, or alternatively, placed on her stomach. Whether it was taken internally or externally, the book was medicine.[51] There were also books which gave instruction in magic, and which could be found in the possession of villagers as well as in the libraries of the learned. A man from Friuli, for example, who claimed, in 1630, to recognise the bewitched and to tell who had bewitched them, possessed 'a book in which he had learned all this'.[52] Oral and literate cultures not only co-existed but interacted. If some ordinary people had not been able to read, the life of Santa Margherita would not have been recited from the book. If, on the other hand, literacy had not been restricted, books and papers would hardly have possessed such glamour. From the Church's point of view, illiteracy encouraged superstition.

On the other hand, the literate laity were also a problem in the eyes of the Church. There was a good deal of orthodox devotional literature in circulation in Italy from the introduction of printing onwards: at least 735 editions of 248 titles between 1465 and 1494.[53] All the same, there was anxiety lest the laity fall into heresy as a result of reading the wrong books, a fear which became more acute from the 1520s onwards as Protestant literature began to be available in Italy. Around the year 1530, one preacher went so far as to declare that 'all literate people [or intellectuals?] are heretics' (*tutti i literati siano heretici*).[54] Reading the Bible in the vernacular was thought by the clergy to lead the laity into unorthodox paths; they may well have been right. Thanks to Carlo Ginzburg, we all know what Menocchio Scandella, the miller of Friuli, made of his reading – the Bible, the Golden Legend, Mandeville's travels and so on.[55] To take a less extraordinary case, one among many, from the records of the Venetian inquisition, we find a tailor from Burano accused of heresy in 1585. He was described as having 'no grammar' (as we would say, no secondary education), but all the same he owned a Bible in the vernacular and talked about it.[56]

The Church was thus caught in a classic double bind, with a problem if it encouraged the spread of literacy and another problem if it did not. Its leaders seem on the whole to have opted for spreading literacy, but in a controlled way. Carlo Borromeo, Archbishop of Milan in the later sixteenth century, was exemplary in this area as in other forms of pastoral activity. He recommended fathers of families to read aloud after dinner from a devotional book or the life of a saint ('if you can read').[57] He also promoted the 'schools of Christian doctrine' which have been mentioned already (see p. 22), requiring each parish to have such a school, which functioned on Sundays and feast days. In other words, a Catholic Sunday-school movement was under way in northern Italy before the end of the sixteenth century. It is a pity that little is known about the working of these schools – whether, for example, they taught writing, reading or only the elements of the faith. However, we do know that broadsheets printed with the Pater Noster, Ave Maria and Credo – in Latin and Italian – were distributed, and also that one layman who was associated with these schools in Milan taught writing *gratis* 'for the honour of God, the salvation of souls, and the common good'. He was the carpenter already mentioned who kept a journal, thus illustrating the link, familiar to English historians, between piety and diary-keeping.

Having opted for the encouragement of literacy, the Church was aware of the need to control these dangerous media, notably by investigating schoolmasters and asking them to sign professions of religious orthodoxy, as at Venice in 1587 and, of course, by the censorship of publications.[58] It was also aware of the ways in which the media could help them in their campaign to supervise and control the beliefs and behaviour of the laity. Visitation records have already been mentioned. There were also 'communion tickets' (*biglietti di communione*), used by the famous reforming bishop Matteo Giberti in his diocese of Verona, an example which was imitated elsewhere. Annual confession and communion was a duty for the laity. At confession an individual would be given a ticket with his or her name on it, which had to be returned at communion. The names could be checked against a register of the inhabitants of the parish so as to identify the negligent and the heretical. Even travellers might find themselves in the net. Some Englishmen left Rome hurriedly at Easter 1593 because 'the priests came to take our names in our lodging' to check on the annual communions.[59] Another use of literacy for the purposes of control is revealed by the letters of denunciation of heretics, blasphemers and other sinners, still preserved in the files of the Inquisition in Venice and elsewhere. Literacy was not necessarily on the side of the unorthodox.

Literacy and the State

The obvious uses of literacy for 'social control', or more exactly, the control of the subordinate classes by the ruling class, were perceived not only by the Church but also by the State. The connexion between literacy and bureaucracy (or, less precisely but more accurately, officialdom), goes back at least as far as the administrative lists of ancient Mesopotamia. The administrative uses of writing for storing and sorting information have been obvious for a very long time.[60] However, there is evidence to suggest that the connexion between writing and administration became a closer one in Italy from the fourteenth century onwards, especially in the case of the larger states such as Milan, Venice, Florence, Rome and Naples.

Some kinds of official documents were common enough all over Europe, most obviously the various kinds of letter going upwards with information or requests and going downwards with orders; each state had its own categories. In Rome and in Venice (until 1501 in the latter case), the man who sealed important documents was required to be illiterate, to ensure that the documents were not tampered with; illiteracy, like literacy, had its political uses.[61] Literacy was a threat to secrecy. As a defence against the breaches of security which the spread of literacy made more likely, cipher was invented. A historian of diplomacy has pointed out that 'The first extant ciphered document in the archives of Venice dates from 1411, at Florence from 1414, at Milan from 1454 and at Genoa from 1481.'[62] In the sixteenth century, the post of cipher secretary came into existence. Giovanni Sora, for instance, exercised this function in the service of the Venetian state from 1502 onwards. Books were written explaining how different kinds of cipher worked, and the publicity made it necessary for yet more complex ciphers to be invented.[63]

Cipher was a field in which the Italians were pioneers. The same goes for a special kind of official report, the *relazione*. It was normal European practice for ambassadors to present written reports on their return from missions, but in Venice the custom went back earlier than elsewhere – to the thirteenth century – and by about 1500, if not before, this report was required to be particularly thorough and to follow a fixed form, dealing with the geography, history and political structure of the state visited, the personality of the ruler, his foreign policy and so on. These reports were filed in the chancery and they could be consulted by newly appointed ambassadors before they set out.[64]

Another important type of document developed by Italian states in this period is what (despite the variety of local names such as '*anagrafo*', '*catasto*' and so on) it is convenient to call the 'census'. The precocity of the Italian censuses of the fourteenth and fifteenth centuries deserves particular emphasis. It was obviously easier to make a census of a small state like Florence than of a large one like France; but only a state with a high literacy rate – and a high numeracy rate – could have carried out a project of this kind. A census was no small enterprise. In the case of the famous *catasto* of 1427, which listed every household in Tuscany under Florentine rule – some 60,000 of them – the services of at least twenty-three clerks were required, not counting the specialists who estimated the value of each household's property. The declarations (*portate*), had to be copied into registers (*campioni*), and summaries had to be made to facilitate reference to this huge document (the history of information retrieval is still to be written, but it is likely that the Italians of this period will have quite an important place in it). This was an expensive business: the bill for paper alone came to more than 250 florins, enough to keep twenty-five students at university for a year.[65] It is easy to see why a census was regarded in this period not as an ordinary part of the business of administration, but as an extraordinary or even an emergency measure. The 1427 *catasto*, for example, was part of the war effort. Famine lay behind the Neapolitan censuses of the 1590s, and plague behind those of Florence and Venice in the 1630s.

In these cases, the government was concerned with organising the distribution of bread. Recipients might have to present tickets or cards (*cartelli* or *polizze*) to ensure that they did not claim twice. The procedure is not unlike that of communion tickets; did the Church imitate the State, or the other way round? Yet another type of official document which the Italians seem to have pioneered, and of which they made increasing use in the period, was the pass (*bolletta, bollettino*). Passes or licences were issued allowing certain people to carry arms in a certain city, or to be out in the streets after curfew. There were also 'health passes' (*bollette di sanità*), required from the late fifteenth century onwards for people and goods on the move in time of plague.[66] They spread widely in Italy but they seem to have been an Italian speciality, to judge by the comments of foreign travellers. Montaigne at Ferrara noted the inscription 'remember your pass' on all the doors of his inn (*ricordati della bolleta*), while Philip Skippon was so fascinated by these documents that he copied several of them into his journal, as well as recording the occasions on which they were issued and inspected.[67]

Reports, censuses and passes far from exhaust the administrative uses of literacy in early modern Italy. There were public notices, for example, more especially the proclamations or edicts of various sorts (called '*bandi*' in Rome, '*parti*' in Venice, '*gride*' in Milan and so on). Armies were already producing a mass of paper including billeting regulations, paysheets, and muster rolls, which described the horses more carefully than the men because it was particularly important to ensure that they were not counted twice.[68] In the navy, too, literacy and numeracy had its uses. Clerks sailed with Venetian galleys, and a writer on naval matters in the early seventeenth century argued that gunners needed to be numerate (*il bombardiero dovrebbe essere abachista*).[69] In republics, the selection of officials required many lists. In Florence, for example, the names of individuals qualified for office had to be written in registers, and also on slips (*polizze*) which were placed in bags and – in theory at least – drawn out at random.[70] In Venice, the patricians, who were the only people eligible for most offices, had to be registered soon after birth in the so-called *Golden Book*, and a record was also kept of the numbers of votes cast for candidates for particular offices.[71]

Another political use of literacy, and not the least important, was secret delation. Visitors to Venice in particular often remarked on the stone letter-boxes, the slots in the shape of lions' mouths, which were used for denunciations of deviants. The inquisitive and precise Skippon noted fourteen of these mouths in the Doge's palace alone.[72] That the mouths were in regular use is clear from the denunciations – of blasphemers, for instance – still preserved in the Venetian Archives.

How efficiently all this material was organised after it had been collected is hard to say. In Venice there were officials in the Doge's Chancery employed to make indexes by name and subject. In other parts of the Venetian administration, however, officials seem to have been overwhelmed by the task of organising the documents.[73] Elsewhere, in the sixteenth century in particular, we find archive-conscious rulers such as Grand Duke Cosimo of Tuscany and Pope Gregory XIII; but the distinction between private and public was not drawn as sharply then as later, and it was quite normal for officials to treat official documents as their private property and pass them on to their heirs.

In many ways, literacy facilitated the State's control of its subjects, as it facilitated the Church's control of its flock. However, the effects of technological change are rarely simple. Literacy could also serve the cause of heresy and political protest. The authorities were well aware of the danger and operated a political as well as a religious censorship of printed books. Much was published in Venice that could not be printed elsewhere, but in the early seventeenth century several important books were unable to appear in print for political reasons. One was a history of Venice by the late Doge Nicolò Contarini; another was Paolo Sarpi's history of the Council of Trent; a third was the commentary on Tacitus by Traiano Boccalini. However, the number of surviving manuscript copies suggests that these works had considerable circulation in private in the seventeenth-century equivalent of *samizdat*.

More spectacular, however, and addressing a far wider audience, was the use of graffiti and placards (*cartelli*) for the purpose of protest, or at least for candid unofficial commentary on politics. In Florence this tradition goes back at least as far as the fourteenth century, and by the sixteenth it can be found in Venice, Padua, Brescia and Naples. It was an institution in Rome, birthplace of the *pasquinade* in the fifteenth century. By the eighteenth century, the practice had spread to rural communes such as Altopascio in Tuscany.[74] It is a pity that, *pasquinades* apart, no anthologies have been made of these graffiti, which give a vivid view of politics from below, and were taken seriously, and with good reason, by the authorities. Placards inciting the population to rebel appeared in the streets of Naples in 1585 and 1647; in both cases the advice was taken. The comments were usually pithy and pungent. 'Nine fools are out' (*è usciti nove pazzi*), said a placard on the Palazzo della Signoria of Florence in 1466, referring to the outgoing administration.[75] 'House to let' (*Caxa d'afitar*), was the laconic message on the empty State granary in Venice in 1529.[76]

The demand for documents in these four domains was great enough to call into existence all sorts of specialist producers of the written word, the number and variety of whom will be obvious to anyone who cares to read through early modern censuses, those of Florence and Venice in particular. The best-known and most numerous of these groups was that of the notaries. There were eight notaries to every thousand people in Verona in 1605 as there had been in Florence in 1427.[77] Then there were the schoolmasters, more particularly the writing-masters. Such was the prestige of calligraphy in early modern Italy, as in traditional China and Japan, that some of these writing-masters became famous, especially in the sixteenth century, notably Leonardo Arrighi, Gianantonio Tagliente, Gianbattista Palatino and Gianfrancesco Cresci. There were the printers, of course, to be found in many Italian towns, even small ones, but especially numerous in Venice, where Aldo Manuzio among others settled. There were the book-sellers and stationers, down to the *leggendaio*, the humble itinerant hawker of the lives of saints, one of those who 'sell the stories of saints, and prayers to saints, and sing them and also ask for alms'.[78] There were private secretaries, an occupation which included a number of distinguished writers on their way to fame, a famous sixteenth-century example being Annibale Caro. There were clerks (*scrivani*), and freelance copyists (*copiascritture*). The numbers of clerks in the law courts of Naples in 1728 made a deep impression on one visitor, Montesquieu: 'les seuls scribes font une petite armée, rangée en bataille, le canif à la main'.[79] There were official couriers and more humble messengers (*portalettere*). There were also the specialists in numeracy, such as accountants, book-keepers, cashiers and valuers (terms which recur in the censuses are 'carriere', 'computista', 'calcolatore' and 'stimatore'), as well as the teachers in abacus-schools.

The evidence is so abundant that the historian has to be careful not to exaggerate the importance of all these activities, which have left traces in the archives while oral transactions have not. We need to remind ourselves that the majority of Italians, throughout this period, must have been illiterate – some professional men, most peasants and almost all women.[80] Let us look at the relationship of women to literacy in a little more detail.

In the fourteenth and fifteenth centuries, some men argued that girls should have nothing to do with reading and writing, and suggested that they should stay at home and wait for a husband rather than go to school. Reading was dangerous because girls might read love-letters.[81] In fact illiteracy was not enough to stop girls receiving and sending love-letters through intermediaries, as a case which came before the Tribunal of the Governor of Rome in 1602 vividly illustrates. Margherita, the sixteen-year-old daughter of a notary, could not read or write, but she corresponded with the boy next door *via* another friend, throwing the notes from the kitchen window into the courtyard. By the time her parents had discovered the correspondence, Margherita was no longer a virgin.[82]

It is easy enough to find exceptions to the rule of female illiteracy, but very hard to say how common these exceptions were. The wife of Francesco Datini, the superlatively inky-fingered merchant of Prato, did not learn to read till she was over thirty; her daughter, on the other hand, learned when still a child.[83] In any case we know that some girls went to school. Villani refers to 'boys and girls' learning to read in fourteenth-century Florence; it is too bad that this lover of statistics gives us no idea of the relative percentages. Again, we know that in sixteenth-century Milan, the Compagnia delli Servi, which was part of the Sunday-school system, taught girls as well as boys, but not what the proportion of pupils of each sex was. In Venice in 1587, the bishop's survey turned up 4,481 schoolchildren, of whom only twenty-eight were female, and 258 teachers, of whom only one was female, a certain Marieta.[84] This may be an underestimate: at all events, the Venetian censuses of the seventeenth century refer to women teachers. Two are mentioned in 1633, six in 1642 (not counting the twelve teachers at the Zittelle, a home for the daughters of prostitutes, whose names are not given), six more in 1670 – and this is an absolute minimum, since the records are incomplete and in any case list only heads of households. The laconic 'keeps a school' (*tien scola*) does not give very much away, but in two cases it is specified that the pupils are female, and in three cases that what is taught is reading.[85] In Rome in 1695, sixteen schoolmistresses are recorded, teaching reading and sewing.[86]

References to writing are rather more rare. Letters in the name of women do not prove that those women could write, since professional scribes were available. However, Alessandra degli Strozzi announces on one occasion that her letter was 'written with my spectacles on' (*questa mia é scritta cogli occhiali*), suggesting that she wrote for herself, while in the early seventeenth century the Genoese patrician Andrea Spinola, suspicious of literacy as he is, does allow women to write down expenses and draw up inventories.[87]

Having taken account of evidence like this, as well as of the handful of women who studied the classics or published books in this period, it still seems reasonable to suggest that women had little more than a toehold on literate culture. For them and for the illiterate majority of males as well, culture was essentially oral. The existence of this oral culture needs to be borne in mind as a corrective to the overemphasis on literacy encouraged by the survival of archives and libraries. All the same, I should like to suggest that writing was more important in daily life in Italy than in most parts of early modern Europe; that its importance was increasing steadily from the thirteenth century (if not before) to the seventeenth century (if not after); and that the uses of literacy diversified within each of the four domains discussed as new types of document proliferated. These suggestions cannot be proved, but the evidence discussed so far should at least make them plausible.

To this evidence should be added the fact that print multiplied texts of every kind from the later fifteenth century onwards. The effects of the new medium have generally been discussed from a literary point of view or in relation to cultural movements such as the Renaissance; there is more than a little to say, however, about the practical uses of print in the three public domains discussed above. In the sphere of business, one finds not only printed manuals for beginners but also printed forms for leases and IOU's, flysheets to advertise the sale of property and so on. In the religious sphere, one finds not only devotional treatises and manuals for confessors, but catechisms and broadsheets with prayers printed on them, some produced by order of the local bishop, while others have a less official character. There were printed forms for the parish priest to certify the good religious behaviour of orphan girls before they were married.

However, it is in the domain of politics that one finds the real invasion of printed matter in the course of the sixteenth and seventeenth centuries. Printed proclamations multiplied. They were still read aloud in the traditional manner but they were also posted up in public places. Laws were printed. News-sheets were printed: from the *avvisi da Roma* in the sixteenth century, which took the form of letters, to the first *gazzette* in the seventeenth century, with a format more like that of a modern newspaper. There was also a growing use of printed forms. By the middle of the seventeenth century, one even finds cardinals in conclave making use of such forms to elect a new pope. Forms were also employed in Venice by the census-takers to ensure that the information for each parish was organised in the same way. These forms are striking evidence of the numerate mentality, and they doubtless helped to spread this mode of thought throughout society. Like the self-consciousness engendered, or at least encouraged, by diary-keeping, the propensity to think in terms of precise figures should be reckoned as one of the most important consequences of literacy in early modern Italy, a consequence derived from its uses in practical contexts in this town-dominated society.

NOTES

[1] D. Lerner, *The Passing of Traditional Society* (Glencoe, 1958).

[2] J. Goody, *The Domestication of the Savage Mind* (Cambridge, 1977); *cf.* J. Goody and I. Watt, 'The Consequences of Literacy', *Comparative Studies in Society and History* 5 (1962–3), 304–45.

[3] C. Cipolla, *Literacy and Development in the West* (Harmondsworth, 1969).

[4] B. V. Street, *Literacy in Theory and Practice* (Cambridge, 1984).

[5] K. Basso, 'The Ethnography of Writing', in *Explorations in the Ethnography of Speaking*, ed. R. Bauman and J. Sherzer (Cambridge, 1974), Chapter 20; J. Szwed, 'The Ethnography of Literacy', in *Variation in Writing*, ed. M. F. Whiteman (Hillsdale, 1981), pp. 13–23. S. Scribner and M. Cole, 'Unpackaging Literacy', *ibid.*, pp. 71–87.

[6] R. Hoggart, *The Uses of Literacy* (London, 1957); P. Wormald, 'The Uses of Literacy in Anglo-Saxon England', *Transactions of the Royal Historical Society* 27 (1977), 95–114; M. T. Clanchy, *From Memory to Written Record* (London, 1979). K. V. Thomas's essay, 'The Meaning of Literacy in Early Modern England', remains unpublished at the time of writing.

[7] E. Johansson, 'Literacy Studies in Sweden' (1973), repr. in *Literacy and Development in the West*, ed. H. Graff (Cambridge, 1981), Chapter 8; R. S. Schofield, 'The Measurement of Literacy in Preindustrial England', in *Literacy in Traditional Societies*, ed. J. Goody (Cambridge, 1968), especially p. 321.

[8] A. Petrucci *et al.*, *Alfabetismo e cultura scritta* (special issue), *Quaderni Storici* 38 (1978).

[9] F. Villani, *Cronica*, ed. F. Dragomanni (Florence, 1845), Book xi, Chapter 92. See a recent discussion in C. Klapisch, 'Le chiavi fiorentine di Barbablù', *Quaderni Storici* 57 (1984), 775.

[10] Cipolla, *Literacy*, p. 59n; V. Baldo, *Alunni maestri e scuole in Venezia alla fine del xvi secolo* (Como, 1977).

[11] P. Morigi, *La nobiltà di Milano* (Milan, 1595), p. 299. G. B. Casale, a carpenter who became one of the 'coadjutors' of these schools in 1563, tells us us that he taught writing *gratis*; 'Giornale' (1552–98) in Milan, Biblioteca Ambrosiana, fondo Trotti, no. 413, ff. 7v and 10r.

[12] V. E. Giuntella, 'Documenti sull'istruzione popolare in Roma durante il "700" ', *Studi romani* 9 (1961), 553–60; A. Petrucci, *Scrittura e popolo nella Roma barocca* (Rome, 1982), nos. 42, 199.

[13] Vespasiano da Bisticci, *Vite di uomini illustri* [written in the late fifteenth century]; *cf.* H. J. Chaytor, *From Script to Print* (Cambridge, 1945).

[14] A. Petrucci, 'La scrittura tra ideologia e rappresentazione', *Storia dell'arte italiana* 9 (Turin, 1980), 5–123.

[15] C. Cipolla, 'The Professions', *Journal of European Economic History* 2 (1973), 37–52.

[16] Clanchy (*Memory*, p. 37), who thinks that the writer, Giovanni da Bologna, exaggerated the difference between the two countries.

[17] J. Fishman, 'Who speaks What Language to Whom and When', in *Sociolinguistics*, ed. J. B. Pride and J. Holmes (Harmondsworth, 1972), Chapter 1.

[18] These distinctions are clear in sixteenth-century writing manuals such as G. A. Tagliente,

La vera arte de lo excellente scrivere (Venice, 1536), and G. B. Palatino, *Libro nel quale s'insegna a scrivere ogni sorte lettere* (Rome, 1547).

[19] G. Rucellai, *Zibaldone*, ed. A. Perosa (London, 1960), p. 6. *Cf.* L. B. Alberti, *I libri della famiglia*, ed. R. Romano and A. Tenenti (Turin, 1969), p. 251.

[20] A. Spinola, *Scritti scelti*, ed. C. Bitossi (Genoa, 1981), pp. 220, 228–9.

[21] I. Origo, *The Merchant of Prato* (London, 1957).

[22] C. Bec, *Les marchands écrivains* (Paris and The Hague, 1967), pp. 49–50.

[23] R. Goldthwaite, 'Schools and Teachers of Commercial Arithmetic in Renaissance Florence', *Journal of European Economic History* 1 (1972), 418–33.

[24] An early printed example of a text-book with commercial applications is P. Borgo, *De arithmetica* (Venice, 1484).

[25] F. Ghaligai, *Summa de arithmetica* (1521; new edition, Florence, 1548); H. Tagliente, *Tesoro universale* (Venice, *c.*1530).

[26] Baldo, *Alunni*, p. 29.

[27] Paolo da Certaldo, *Libro di buoni costumi*, ed. A. Schiaffini (Florence, 1945), no. 251.

[28] R. de Roover, *The Rise and Decline of the Medici Bank* (New York, 1966), p. 125.

[29] A. degli Strozzi, *Lettere*, ed. C. Guasti (Florence, 1877), p. 345.

[30] A letter of 1540 in the Donà papers, quoted in F. Seneca, *Il doge Leonardo Donà* (Padua, 1959), p. 9.

[31] P. Ariès, *Centuries of Childhood* (1960; English translation, London, 1966).

[32] A. Luzio, *I precettori d'Isabella d'Este* (Ancona, 1887), pp. 37f.

[33] G. Pieraccini, *La stirpe dei Medici* (Florence, 1924), pp. 204, 218. The letters date from 1478 and 1485; the second is by Matteo Franco.

[34] Venice, Biblioteca Correr, Ms Donà 418, i, 5.

[35] L. Landucci, *Diario fiorentino*, ed. J. del Badia (Florence, 1883).

[36] B. Arditi, *Diario*, ed. R. Cantagallo (Florence, 1970).

[37] G. Priuli, *I diarii*, ed. A. Segre and R. Cessi (2 vols., Città di Castello and Bologna, 1912–37); G. Pallavicino, *Inventione di scriver tutte le cose accadute alli tempi suo*, ed. E. Grendi (Genoa, 1975); G. Nadi, *Diario bolognese*, ed. C. Ricci and A. Bacchi (Bologna, 1886); G. B. Casale, 'Giornale'.

[38] D. Velluti, *Cronaca*, ed. I. Del Lungo and G. Volpi (Florence, 1914).

[39] G. Morelli, *Ricordi*, ed. V. Branca (Florence, 1956), p. 81.

[40] Rucellai, *Zibaldone*, p. 2.

[41] P. da Certaldo, *Costumi*, nos. 136, 139.

[42] A. Murray, *Reason and Society in the Middle Ages* (Oxford, 1978), Chapter 7.

[43] J. Burckhardt, *Civilisation of the Renaissance in Italy* (1860; English translation, London, 1944), Chapter 2.

[44] T. C. P. Zimmermann, 'Confession and Autobiography in the Renaissance', in *Renaissance Studies in Honour of Hans Baron*, ed. A. Molho and J. Tedeschi (Dekalb, 1971), pp. 121–40; *cf.* M. Guglielminetti, *Memoria e scrittura* (Turin, 1977).

[45] G. da Sommaia, *Diario de un estudiante de Salamanca*, ed. G. Haley (Salamanca, 1977). Some interesting details have been omitted from this edition.

[46] R. Passegeri, *In artem notariae summule* (Venice, 1565).

[47] D. Hay, *The Church in Italy in the Fifteenth Century* (Cambridge, 1977), p. 56; C. Cairns, *Domenico Bollani* (Nieuwkoop, 1976), pp. 176, 199.

[48] P. Burke, *Popular Culture in Early Modern Europe* (London, 1978), p. 271; L. Allegra, 'Il parroco', *Storia d'Italia, Annali* 4 (Turin, 1981), 897–947.

[49] J. Goody, 'Restricted Literacy in Northern Ghana', in *Literacy in Traditional Societies*, ed. Goody (Cambridge, 1968), p. 202.

[50] *Documenti etnografici e folkloristici nei sinodi diocesani italiani*, ed. C. Corrain and P. L. Zampini (Bologna, 1970), pp. 36, 132, 147, 201, 282. *Cf.* G. Millunzi, 'Un processo di stregoneria nel 1627', *Archivio storico siciliano* 25 (1900), 253–377, from which the 'abracadabra' example comes, and M. R. O'Neil, 'Ecclesiastical and Superstitious Remedies', in *Understanding Popular Culture* (Berlin, 1984), Chapter 4. A good collection of magical recipes is to be found in Venice, Archivio di Stato, Sant'Ufficio, busta 55 (1585), the case of Annibale da Perugia.

[51] *Legenda et oratione di Santa Margherita* (Venice, *c.*1550). The instructions for use are to be found on the title-page.

[52] C. Ginzburg, *The Night Battles* (1966; English translation, London, 1983), p. 91.

[53] A. J. Schutte, 'Printing, Piety and the People in Italy', *Archiv für Reformationsgeschichte* 71 (1980), 5 19.

[54] A. Prosperi, 'Intellettuali e Chiesa', *Storia d'Italia, Annali* 4 (Turin, 1981), p. 195.

[55] C. Ginzburg, *Cheese and Worms* (1976; English translation, London, 1981).

[56] Venice, Archivio di Stato, Santo Ufficio, Processi, busta 55 (the case of Rinaldo Vio).

[57] E. Casali, *Il villano dirozzato* (Florence, 1982), pp. 72f.

[58] Baldo, *Alunni*, pp. 7f; A. Rotondò, 'La censura ecclesiastica e la cultura', *Storia d'Italia, Annali* 5 (Turin, 1973), 1397–1492; P. Grendler, *The Roman Inquisition and the Venetian Press, 1540–1605* (Princeton, 1977).

[59] F. Moryson, *Itinerary* (4 vols., Glasgow, 1907–8), vol. 1, p. 303.

[60] J. Goody, *The Domestication of the Savage Mind* (Cambridge, 1977), pp. 80f.

[61] J. F. D'Amico, *Renaissance Humanism in Papal Rome* (Baltimore and London, 1983), p. 36; C. Cipolla, *Literacy and Development in the West* (Harmondsworth, 1969), p. 58.

[62] D. Queller, *The Office of the Ambassador in the Middle Ages* (Princeton, 1967), p. 140.

[63] Among the best-known treatises are G. B. Palatino, *Dalle Cifre* (1540; English translation, Wormley, 1970); G. B. Bellano, *Novi et singulari modi di cifrare* (Brescia, 1553); G. B. Della Porta, *De furtivis literarum notis* (Naples, 1563).

[64] A useful selection in *Relazioni degli ambasciatori veneti al senato*, ed. A. Ventura (2 vols., Rome and Bari, 1980). The introduction discusses the history of the genre.

[65] D. Herlihy and C. Klapisch, *Les toscans et leurs familles* (Paris, 1978); the information is not available in the abridged English version of this study.

[66] C. Cipolla, *Public Health and the Medical Profession in the Renaissance* (Cambridge, 1976), p. 29.

[67] M. de Montaigne, *Journal de voyage*, ed. M. Rat (Paris, 1955), p. 80; P. Skippon, 'An Account of a Journey', in *Collection of Voyages*, ed. A. and J. Churchill (6 vols., London, 1732), vol. 6, pp. 502, 549, etc.

[68] M. E. Mallett and J. R. Hale, *The Military Organisation of a Renaissance State* (Cambridge, 1984), pp. 117, 123, 125, 127, etc.

[69] P. Pantera, *L'armata navale* (1614), quoted by Cipolla, *Literacy*, p. 23.

[70] N. Rubinstein, *The Government of Florence under the Medici* (Oxford, 1966), Chapters 1 and 2.

[71] J. C. Davis, *The Decline of the Venetian Nobility as a Ruling Class* (Baltimore, 1962), p. 19.

[72] P. Skippon, *op. cit.*, p. 491.

[73] Queller, *Ambassador*, p. 4; C. Caro Lopez, 'Gli Auditori Nuovi e il dominio di terraferma', in *Stato, società e giustizia nella repubblica veneta*, ed. G. Cozzi (Rome, 1980), pp. 259–316.

[74] F. McArdle, *Altopascio* (Cambridge, 1978), pp. 205f.

[75] A. M. degli Strozzi, *Lettere*, ed. C. Guasti (Florence, 1877), p. 540.

[76] M. Sanudo, *I Diarii*, ed. F. Stefani *et al.* (58 vols., Venice, 1879–1903), vol. 50, p. 500.

[77] C. Cipolla, 'The Professions', *Journal of European Economic History* 2 (1973), 37–52.

[78] The testimony is that of a vagabond called Girolamo in *Libro dei vagabondi*, ed. P. Camporesi (Turin, 1973), p. 357.

[79] Montesquieu, *Œuvres*, ed. D. Oster (Paris, 1964), p. 278.

[80] In Venice in 1711, a sea-captain named Angelo Boza declared nearly 1,000 ducats' worth of property but signed his declaration with a cross. Venice, Archivio di Stato, Dieci Savi alla Decima, Castello, no. 29.

[81] C. Klapisch, 'Chiavi', p. 776.

[82] Rome, Archivio di Stato, Tribunale Criminale del Governatore, Processi, seventeenth century, busta 18 (1602), f. 715 *et seq.*

[83] Origo, *Merchant*, p. 213.

[84] Baldo, *Alunni*, p. 21.

[85] Venice, Archivio di Stato, Provveditori della Sanità, buste 568–72, and Venice, biblioteca Correr, Ms Donà 351.

[86] Giuntella, 'Documenti', pp. 555f.

[87] Strozzi, *op. cit.*, p. 347; A. Spinola, *Scritti scelti*, ed. C. Bitossi (Genoa, 1981), p. 236.

3

PROVERBS AND SOCIAL HISTORY

James Obelkevich

Historians, G. M. Young once suggested, should go on reading till they can 'hear people talking'.[1] Good advice, of course, whatever their period or speciality, but for social historians of language not so much advice as part of the job description. To listen for the voice behind the text, to conjure orality out of literacy: that is one of our main tasks. Yet is it not often an impossible one? In what texts can we hear ordinary people talking in periods when most were unable to write? Not that sources are lacking entirely: from records of the Inquisition, and of civil courts relying on written evidence, Le Roy Ladurie and others have recovered something of the actual words of the people involved.[2] But in England, with nothing from the Inquisition and little from the courts of the common law, historians are not so lucky: there will never be an English *Montaillou* or *The Cheese and the Worms*.[3] Court records have their limitations in any event; to hear the voice of the people, in England and elsewhere, other sources and approaches are needed.

One alternative, as the work of folklorists and anthropologists has shown, is to study speech through its characteristic forms and genres – greetings, riddles, curses, jokes, tales and so on.[4] Unlike court records, which give us what one person said (perhaps under duress) on a unique occasion, they have the advantage of giving us what was said by many people on countless occasions in everyday life. Perhaps the most instructive of these is proverbs: they are old, they have been widely used, they embody popular attitudes and, not least, in a long line of printed collections, beginning in the sixteenth century, they have been recorded. Popular with speakers, they are also accessible to scholars.

Not until recently, however, have they had much attention from historians. (By contrast, the bibliographies of proverb research list thousands of works by literary scholars, folklorists and anthropologists.)[5] While the main reason for this has been a simple lack of curiosity about language in general – historians have been concerned with signifieds, not signifiers – there has also been a more specific difficulty. Proverbs have for some time been regarded by the educated classes with dislike, even disdain: proverbs, they feel, are old-fashioned, contradictory, impossible to take seriously. Yet if historians have only lately begun to free themselves from the anti-proverb prejudice, they are nevertheless the best equipped to show how it came into being and to trace its consequences. There are lessons for social history not only in the proverbs and their users, but also in those who have rejected them, and in the meaning of that rejection.

Easy to recognise, proverbs have been curiously difficult to define. But it would be generally agreed that they are traditional popular sayings which offer wisdom and advice in a brief and pithy manner.[6] Though much used in writing, they are primarily an oral genre, and an often witty and artful one at that, employing a wide range of poetic and rhetorical resources within their limited compass.[7] Metaphor, rhythm, alliteration, assonance, binary construction: these and other devices create in the form of the proverb an echo of the sense. (Not all are metaphorical: many are straightforward statements like *Absence makes the heart grow fonder*.) Compact and memorable, the proverb serves as the vehicle not only for moral but for practical wisdom, like occupational rules and weather lore.

What defines the proverb, though, is not its internal layout but its external function, and that, ordinarily, is moral and didactic: people use proverbs to tell others what to do in a given situation or what attitude to take towards it. Proverbs, then, are 'strategies for situations'; but they are strategies with authority, formulating some part of a society's common sense, its values and way of doing things. (They can therefore be distinguished from proverbial phrases, such as *to have an ace up one's sleeve*, and from conventional sayings like *I have other fish to fry*, which have an expressive rather than a moral purpose; this chapter is concerned with proverbs in the strict sense.)[8]

That air of authority is heightened by another feature, their impersonality. Offering stereotyped advice on recurrent problems, they take no notice of what individuals in a situation may feel to be unique or personal about it; and whether metaphorical or abstract, they make their point in an indirect, third person manner, leaving it to the hearer to draw his own conclusions. Anonymous, traditional, authoritative, they have an existence of their own, independent of authors, speakers and hearers alike. When a proverb is quoted it is often marked by some introductory formula ('As people say . . .') or by a change in the speaker's tone of voice: his words are not his own, but those of the community or common sense speaking through him.[9] Indeed, the authority of proverbs is rooted in the language itself. English proverbs, for example, form part of the English language in a way that other folk genres like riddles or folk tales do not; lists of proverbs still appear in dictionaries, and for centuries anyone studying a foreign language would learn its proverbs along with its grammar and vocabulary.

The charm and appeal of the 'old sayings' undoubtedly owes much to their aura of timelessness, of immutable truth about a static human nature. If they are not old, they seem old, and are sometimes archaic in their vocabulary or construction; they stand apart from catch-phrases, one-liners and other sayings of the moment – some of which may eventually become proverbs.[10]

Yet change there has been, both in the sayings themselves and in those who have used them. In this chapter, after a brief look at some of their characteristic users and uses, I shall examine first the question of proverb meaning and change of meaning, and then the major event in their history, their abandonment by the educated classes.

Users and uses

One of the oldest of folk genres and one of the most widely distributed geographically, proverbs have been used at one time or another by people in every class and group.[11] In early modern England, as we shall see, the educated classes were as addicted to them as anyone else. Perhaps the real question is, Who did *not* use them?

Certainly they have had their attractions for rulers as well as for ruled: political authority and proverbial authority have been allied since at least the time of Solomon. In England there was a medieval collection attributed to Alfred; the first printed collection was presented to Elizabeth; James I was partial to them. Would-be politicians studied their proverbs in Renaissance Europe as they still do in certain Third World societies of our own time; among the Merina of Madagascar, for example, it is expected that leaders should be orators and that orators should have vast numbers of proverbs at their command. And when rulers invent their own, the distinction between political slogan and proverb can easily be blurred: there is a political dimension to the proverbs of Solomon and a proverbial quality to the sayings of Chairman Mao.[12]

There seems little doubt, however, that in pre-industrial Europe it was the peasants, the majority of the population, who used proverbs most; with their oral culture and face-to-face social relations they have continued to do so down to the present day. Though proverbs are learned as well as popular in their origins, their content largely reflected peasant needs and realities: at any rate there seems to have been a saying, or several, for every contingency in agriculture and in life. Britain too had its proverb-wielding country folk. The Scots, in the early eighteenth century, were 'wonderfully given to this way of speaking', especially 'the better sort of the commonalty, none of whom will discourse you any considerable time, but he will confirm every assertion and observation with a Scots proverb'.[13] In the nineteenth century, the English equivalents of a peasantry, the small farmers, cottagers and farm labourers, also tended to be heavy users; Flora Thompson mentions that the labourers in her north Oxfordshire village had 'hundreds of proverbs'. Russia, the land with the most peasants, apparently had the most proverbs of all.

Proverbs and similar expressions have also been popular among the working classes in the towns. Robert Roberts describes working-class talk in pre-1914 Salford as 'peppered' with 'stale saws and clichés'; in inter-war Leeds, according to Richard Hoggart, working-class people were constantly quoting their favourite sayings, and if not all were standard proverbs they were used like proverbs.[14] Though the repertoire was a diminished one – many of the older sayings did not survive the journey from the countryside, and the new additions did not make up the losses – proverbs had their uses in the urban villages as well as in the rural ones left behind.

We should not assume, then, that proverbs simply wither away at the first exposure to modernisation. Indeed the evidence both from early modern Europe and from the Third World today suggests that it can have exactly the opposite effect. A recent study of the Igbo of Nigeria shows that when members of the elite learn English and adopt western ways, they do not give up proverbs but rather add English ones to their existing stock. It may be that in the long run proverbs are destined to decline: in the developed societies this appears to have taken place in varying degree in every social class. There are, however, exceptions. In contemporary Israel proverbs (not all of them from religious sources) are in frequent use by the highly educated. And they have kept much of their popularity and prestige in contemporary Russia, partly because the Soviet state has encouraged them (and other aspects of folk culture) for ideological reasons. Though the intellectuals do not often use proverbs, they know them and, because of their links with the people, respect them. Lenin and Stalin used them; Khrushchev's earthy sayings were those of a peasant; even the modern, sophisticated Gorbachev, visiting Britain in 1984, puzzled his hosts when he observed that 'If you send us a flea, we will put horseshoes on it.'[15]

The sparse European evidence on gender differences suggests that men tend to use proverbs more than women; this is consistent with the anti-female bias in the sayings themselves. In the urban working class, on the other hand, women appear to be the main users. As for age differences, the evidence suggests that proverbs are used most by old people, sometimes as part of an 'old people's ideology', and by children, with their own proverb-like sayings.[16]

Hardly less varied than the users is the ethnography of their uses and functions. Proverbs can be used in any mood, any situation; they cut across the normal boundaries of language registers and amount to a polyvalent, all-purpose register of their own. But it is the moral and educational role that comes first, whether they are used informally, in everyday life, or in formal instruction, as in the Elizabethan grammar schools or in the elementary schools of the nineteenth century. Through proverbs, social norms are internalised and – the distinction is not a rigid one – enforced. If we speak of social control it is not only because of the content and purpose of proverbs but because they are social or public in their mode of operation, employing shame and embarrassment rather than guilt; it is not only among the Maori that they appeal to the individual's 'self-esteem and his regard for his appearance in the eyes of others'.[17]

In situations of conflict, by contrast, proverbs are used less for their truth or wisdom than to take advantage of their impersonality; by expressing disapproval in an indirect manner, they draw the sting from criticism and make an angry response less likely. In some societies proverbs are a standard method of conflict management, helping people to cope with a chronic source of strain or tension; among the Igbo, the problems are those arising from the institution of polygyny; among the Zande, according to Evans-Pritchard, it is those arising from the master–subject pattern that is applied to all social relations. In certain societies proverbs have had a role in legal disputes: peasants used them in local courts in late medieval France, and among the Anang of Nigeria they are cited in judicial proceedings in place of precedents, with the case often won or lost on the choice of proverbs.[18]

At the opposite extreme are situations in which it is precisely the absence of conflict that proverbs give expression to; by swapping familiar proverbs, people indicate good will, reassure one another that they share common values, enjoy sociability for its own sake. The function of proverbs on such occasions is, to use Malinowski's term, phatic: to establish or restore a social relationship, to reinforce the solidarity of a peer group. Among older working-class women a ritualised exchange of proverbs can fill the greater part of a conversation, each piece of news receiving its consolatory stock response. According to Hoggart the 'phrases are used like counters, "click-click-click" ', and are 'drawn upon as a kind of comfort'; in a more recent study, also of the industrial West Riding, working-class women trotted them out every time they exchanged a few words, 'over back-yard walls and across doctors' waiting rooms' and in the shop or market. The rather stoic repertoire included *Good and bad go in cycles*; *Everything's for the best*; *It'll all come out in the wash*; *We take life as it comes*; *We must make the best of it*. In these sayings the phatic merges not only with the stoic but with the fatalistic, in an implicit code of endurance and survival.[19]

Finally, people may use proverbs because they sound good – because they enjoy their form and phraseology, their wit, imagery and verbal style. Among the Akan of Ghana their value is said to be primarily 'aesthetic or poetic'; they are judged by the 'quality of their imagery'.[20] Those who appreciate proverbs for their 'salt' as well as their sense may make them part of a way of speaking used in any and all situations. With proverbs everyone can have their share of good lines.

Meanings

What then do proverbs mean? Do they express a consistent outlook? What can they tell us about the attitudes and values of those who use them?

The answers, disappointingly, are less simple than might perhaps be supposed; the prospect of a social–historical short cut – with the mentalities in the proverbs and the proverbs in the books – turns out to be something of a mirage. In a given language there may be hundreds, perhaps thousands, of proverbs, saying a great many different things, some of them inconsistent or even contradictory. If they have anything in common it is not in their manifest but in their latent content – their anonymity, impersonality, appeal to tradition, and so on; at this level, at least, every proverb text carries with it a sub-text, and the medium itself has a message. But if the deeper meanings of proverbs are relatively clear, it is the surface meanings that interest users and historians, and it is there that the problems lie.

In the first place, as anthropologists remind us, the meaning of a proverb depends not only on the saying itself but also on the situation in which it is used; but about those situations our sources tell us disappointingly little. We have the texts but not the contexts, and without them some of the meaning is inevitably lost. And there are other difficulties. Proverbs with metaphors are inherently ambiguous (to take them literally may convert them into superstitions); variant forms – little studied, unlike those of other folk genres – may differ in meaning from the main form. Meanings have changed over time and can vary over space: *A rolling stone gathers no moss* is used in Scotland to encourage mobility, in England to deter it.[21] The meaning of a proverb cannot be read directly from the pages of the collections.[22]

Nor do the sayings form an undifferentiated mass; in the early modern period, for example, besides those which circulated generally, there were those with more limited constituencies. At the top end of the scale were sayings embodying official, orthodox values – straightforward statements, most of them, without metaphorical flourishes and hardly distinguishable from maxims. Despite, or because of, their dullness and lack of flavour, they have appealed to teachers, preachers and self-improvers in every age.[23]

At the opposite pole, among the common people (who also used the mainstream proverbial sayings), was a more subversive kind of wisdom. Sceptical of official pieties, though it rarely called for anything resembling political action, it was by turns cynical, amoral, coarse and obscene. (The clash between high and low wisdom provided the theme for the medieval dialogue of Solomon and Marcolf, Solomon's conventional pieties being capped by vulgar parodies from the rustic Marcolf.) With the coarser sayings rarely reaching print, proverbial wisdom can seem milder and tamer than it actually was. Proverbs on sex certainly existed, but apart from a single Russian collection, containing nearly 400, they have largely sunk without trace. Not only was there no room for the 'openly obscene' in John Ray's 1670 collection; when he included many of the 'homely and slovenly' (rough and lewd) – among them were 'a good number of the most witty and significant of our English proverbs' – these too gave offence, and he dropped them from the second edition. James Kelly, introducing his collection from early eighteenth-century Scotland, noted that there were 'very many openly obscene' ones, that they were 'apt and expressive' – and that he was leaving them out.[24] The authorities were also disturbed by what they regarded as cynicism; a medieval saying, *Young saint, old devil*, in the 'less orthodox' tradition of the ages of man, was a favourite with the people but was condemned by clerical moralists. A Danish study found that the proverbs taught in the schools were essentially copy-book maxims, but there was a 'bleak realism', even a 'rebellious temper', in those in the oral tradition.[25]

To some extent the contrast between high and low wisdom corresponds to that between national sayings and local ones. In nineteenth-century France there was a streak of coarseness (proverbs about farts, for example) in the regional collections; national proverbs, taught in the schools, were more refined, instruments in the civilising process. Another study concludes that regional sayings were more 'human' than national ones, with more indulgence towards physical beauty and more sadness about death. French research has also brought to light differences in outlook between regions. In proverbs relating to marriage, those from the south represented women as more secluded than those from the north, they associated marriage with grief and with male supremacy, and they asserted that supremacy in direct, straightforward terms, while the northern sayings did so metaphorically.[26]

As for national differences, it was Francis Bacon who first raised the question – 'The genius, wit, and spirit of a nation are discovered in its proverbs' – but not till the heyday of nationalism in the nineteenth century did it attract much interest. Too often, though, writers simply rehashed existing (and conflicting) stereotypes of national character, finding in proverbs exactly what they were looking for: the vanity and illusions of a nation are discovered in its writings about proverbs. The English, congratulating themselves on the manly and moral quality of their own sayings, found less to praise in other peoples': Italian proverbs, for example, were marked down for their cynicism, despite winning points for style.[27] Today, the experts are sceptical: national differences probably do not exist, and if they do they have not been demonstrated. Proverbial wisdom, we are told, is much the same from one country to another, with many sayings having direct parallels in several languages.[28] And yet anyone dipping into the big collections, first of one nation and then of another, is likely to find that each leaves a different aftertaste: impressionistic, no doubt, but if there are differences within countries there seems no reason why there should not also be differences between them.

With national character now in disrepute, certain anthropologists have tried an alternative approach, examining proverbs for their ethos and world view; taking as their corpus the proverbs of a nation, a region or even a single village, they seek to reconstruct their general conceptions of self and society, the broad assumptions that underlie hundreds or thousands of individual sayings.[29] Considered from this angle, proverbs have a cognitive, almost metaphysical character; their discourse on such matters as mind and body, stability and change, optimism and pessimism amounts virtually to a proverbial philosophy, though it might surprise many of their ordinary users. What these studies promise is an analysis of mentalities in the strong sense – nto only what but how people think, their basic mental categories, their structure of feeling; the danger is the creation of an analysts' artefact, remote from users, uses and actual situations. This approach may also overlook the fact that there are things in a people's experience, common sense and wisdom about life which leave no trace in their proverbs.[30] Among the English and French sayings, for example, there are many about wives but few about mothers (or husbands); they have little to say about religion, fear, or the passions; those of the seventeenth century are silent about witchcraft.[31] Proverbs can perhaps tell us a great deal – they do not reveal all.

But given their notorious propensity to contradict one another, can they tell us anything? For every *Out of sight, out of mind* is there not an *Absence makes the heart grow fonder*? In fact the contradictions matter less than is usually supposed. For they are after all non-antagonistic: in any such couplet, both sayings are true, but only one will be appropriate in a particular situation. To test proverbs for logical consistency as if they were propositions in a philosophical text is beside the point; their mode is oral, practical and *ad hoc*.[32] The real significance of contradictory proverbs is that they draw attention to situations causing difficulty and anxiety, or, occasionally, to conflicting social forces. In any case, they are not in fact very frequent; across a wide range of topics proverbs speak unequivocally, with hardly a contradiction in sight.

A good example can be found in a study of nineteenth-century French proverbs concerning the human body. Its physical functions, beauty, sexuality, diet, cleanliness, disease, the ages of life – on all its aspects and activities from the cradle to the grave they offer a coherent discourse, faithful to the realities of peasant life. On questions of religion, the English proverbs at any rate have little to say about the higher reaches of faith and doctrine but are consistent in their anti-clericalism. (In sixteenth-century Spain an entire collection was devoted to anti-clerical proverbs.) The law, in sayings from the early modern period, similarly comes in for harsh treatment: *Much law, little justice; One man had better steal a horse than another look over the hedge; The great thieves hang the little ones.*[33]

No less consistent, at least in European proverbs, is their hostility towards women, who are represented as nagging, scolding and generally talking too much: *Many women, many words; many geese, many turds; He that has a wife has strife; A husband must be deaf and the wife blind to have quietness; A woman's tongue is the last thing about her that dies.*[34] One of the few that are at all favourable to women is *What's sauce for the goose is sauce for the gander.* Perhaps the proverbs were right – perhaps women had indeed the quicker tongues, and could say what they wanted to without having to rely on ready-made proverbs. If a fictional character can be taken as evidence, Mrs Poyser (in *Adam Bede*) speaks with a splendid flow of imagery and salty wit, but of her many characteristic sayings, few are standard proverbs. Another possibility is that women's sayings did exist, but were never disclosed to the (male) collectors; anything on such matters as husbands' sexual inadequacies (until the nineteenth century it was popularly believed that women's sexual appetite was greater than men's) would have been even less likely to be recorded. At any rate it may be noted that many of the more misogynist sayings, current in the sixteenth and seventeenth centuries, have dropped out of use in more recent times.

In more general terms the outlook of proverbs is a familiar one. Things are what they are, what's done is past: *The leopard does not change its spots; Boys will be boys; Don't cry over spilt milk.* In an unpredictable, unfriendly world, prudence is vital: *Look before you leap; Prevention is better than cure; Don't put all your eggs in one basket; Don't count your chickens before they're hatched.* Words and promises are not to be trusted: *Actions speak louder than words; Fine words butter no parsnips; Great cry and little wool.* There is no alternative to self-reliance: *God helps them that help themselves.* Moderation is the rule whether in diet or in expectations: *Grasp all, lose all; Half a loaf is better than none; Enough is as good as a feast.* Realistic, unsentimental, suspicious of idealism and heroism, they call for a recognition of limits as the key to survival.

The question then is whether they do not overdo the point and breed pessimism, even fatalism? Russian proverbs, it is true, have been well known for their fatalism, but there appears to have been a good deal less of it elsewhere. In Finland it was balanced by anti-fatalism in the early modern sayings and has declined since then; a recent study of sixteenth-century French proverbs claims that it left few traces even then.[35] Where fatalism does occur in proverbs it can be seen as a response to the wider world beyond the speaker's control, where nature is unkind and society unfair and neither can be changed; this, however, is ordinarily combined with a call to action in one's immediate sphere where action brings results. If there is a social base corresponding to this outlook it is in the smaller peasants: distant from the notables above them but precariously close to the poor and the marginals below them, they have little hope of change for the better but will work hard to avoid sinking into destitution.[36]

For all their consistency, proverbs are far from static. Indeed they could not be, given the constant turnover in the sayings themselves; the western European languages not only inherited many from antiquity but have been renewing their stock ever since. It was probably the early modern period which saw the most new sayings added, and the proverb repertoires at their largest: there were 7,000 in Sebastian Franck's German collection of 1541, nearly 12,000 in Tilley's modern dictionary of English proverbs and proverbial phrases of the sixteenth and seventeenth centuries, over 20,000 each in two seventeenth-century German collections. Since then the curve has turned downward, the losses outnumbering the gains. Of the English proverbs current in the seventeenth century, the majority have fallen out of use and are now unfamiliar; today the total in active service probably does not exceed a thousand.[37]

New sayings, nevertheless, there have been, and they have brought with them both new meanings and new ways of producing meaning. Though little studied, changes in proverb form – in metaphors, rhythm and construction – have implications both for the history of the language and for the history of mentalities. Proverb content, better documented, has also changed with the times. A study of sixteenth-century French proverbs shows that they still preserved something of the medieval suspicion of riches and the belief that poverty could be virtuous – attitudes which did not survive into later periods. In seventeenth-century Russia proverbs began to reflect the growing conflict between landlords and peasants; between the sixteenth century and the nineteenth, Finnish proverbs changed both in their imagery and in their attitudes, becoming more tolerant and conciliatory, more humorous, less likely to ridicule the physically and mentally infirm. Eugen Weber's study of rural France in the nineteenth century shows that the new national proverbs, taught in the schools of the Third Republic, were not only less coarse than the regional and dialect sayings; they carried the novel (bourgeois liberal) message that everyone was free to choose for himself and that determination and deferred gratification would overcome all obstacles. Both spontaneously and by state action, proverbs have gradually been modernised.[38]

Though no comparable study exists for England, a start can be made by identifying the new sayings which became current in particular periods. (The modern scholarly collections give dates, in the manner of the *O.E.D.*, for the first recorded appearance in print of each proverb listed.)[39] Unfortunately, evidence about context is sparse, and a proverb could well have been current in speech some time before it first surfaced in print. Nevertheless, the findings suggest some of the ways in which proverbs in the last two or three centuries have reflected changes in English society.

In the eighteenth century, for example, some of the new sayings give expression to values associated with the expanding capitalist economy. More than ever before, 'economising' becomes the cardinal virtue: *Waste not, want not; Take care of the pence and the pounds will look after themselves*. The work ethic is reaffirmed: *If a thing is worth doing, it's worth doing well*; time itself, as Edward Thompson has shown, takes on a new value: *Time is money; Procrastination is the thief of time*. To be poor is to lose one's self-respect: *Empty sacks cannot stand upright*; money and market forces threaten to prevail over all else: *Every man has his price*. And for the private sphere, first recorded in a sermon by John Wesley, there was the indispensable *Cleanliness is next to godliness*.[40]

In the nineteenth century, despite claims that the age of proverb-making was past, the crop of new sayings was a large one, and they too reflect contemporary concerns.[41] In many of them we can catch glimpses of a certain strong-willed and hard-working Victorian culture hero: *Business before pleasure; You never know what you can do till you try; He who makes no mistakes makes nothing; Where there's a will there's a way; If at first you don't succeed, try, try again; Failure teaches success; Genius is an infinite capacity for taking pains; It's dogged as does it*. Work, achievement, optimism set the tone: *Nothing succeeds like success; Every cloud has a silver lining*. There was, however, a danger of overdoing it – *It's the pace that kills* (first used in hunting, then applied to work) – and only doubtful reassurance in the belief that *It's not work that kills but worry*. To the eighteenth-century valorisation of time the Victorians added a refinement – *Punctuality is the soul of business* – reflecting a more complex commercial world with meetings and appointments (and more clocks and watches). And as with time, so with space, which had its own equivalent to punctuality: what could be more evocative of Victorian values (and interiors) than *A place for everything and everything in its place*?

And yet with the deepening split between work and home, the cult of work was more than matched by the cult of domesticity: *There's no place like home*; *Home is where the heart is*; *East, west, home is best*. In the years before 1914 such sentiments were by no means limited to the middle classes; they could be found, written on pieces of coloured paper, attached to the walls in even the poorest working-class homes.[42] The implications for women were spelt out in *A woman's place is in the home*, first recorded in 1844, and, a few decades later, in *The hand that rocks the cradle rules the world*. Family and kinship, whether for working-class migrants 'claiming kin' or for the middle classes with their family firms, were perhaps more important in the nineteenth century than they had been previously; hence *Blood is thicker than water* and new statements of the influence of heredity: *Blood will tell* and *The apple never falls far from the tree* (the child inherits the characteristics of the parents). With home and family defined as the private sphere, its members were reminded that *Accidents will happen in the best regulated families* and that they should not *wash dirty linen in public*. There is even a new affirmation of the power of love itself. In earlier proverbs, it is true, love finds a way and surmounts obstacles, but the Victorians extend the point: *Love makes the world go round*. And whereas the older wisdom had concluded that *Out of sight, out of mind*, the Victorians, more sentimentally, decree that *Absence makes the heart grow fonder*.

Even in the proverb-phobic twentieth century certain catch-phrases have caught on and established themselves as proverbs. On themes relating to work, *A change is as good as a rest*, dating from the turn of the century, is still Victorian in spirit; in more recent sayings the moral certainties of the Victorians begin to crumble: *Work expands so as to fill the time available*; *If it works, it's obsolete*; *If anything can go wrong, it will*; *If you pay peanuts, you get monkeys*. (Where the work ethic survives, in *No pain, no gain*, its connexion is no longer with field or factory but with 'body work', the sweated labour of the exercise studio.) Other aspects of contemporary life find their proverbial reflections in *Small is beautiful*; *Garbage in, garbage out*; and, in a rare glimmer of optimism, *Life begins at forty*.

Proverbs and their meanings have a history, then, even if an elusive and slow-moving one. The history of their users, by contrast, is a more dramatic affair. It has a climax – the abandonment of proverbs by the educated classes – and an aftermath, in which proverbs became a source of division and conflict, the site of a 'struggle for meaning'. What was now at stake was not the meaning of this or that saying but the validity of proverbs as such.

Proverbs and the educated classes

In sixteenth-century England educated people studied, used and valued proverbs: by the twentieth century they had long since rejected them. In the history of that decline and fall – broken only by a temporary revival in the nineteenth century – lies both the transformation of elite culture and the breaking of its links with the culture of the people.

Elizabethan England, it has been said, was 'soaked in proverbs', and the educated classes, making constant use of them both in speech and in writing, were at least as immersed in them as anyone else.[43] In an age in which truth and wisdom ranked above facts and figures, proverbs had unquestioned authority; to educated people they were not folkloric curiosities but part of their cultural capital. Besides their English sayings, they studied Erasmus's great Latin collection, the *Adagia*; a set text in every grammar school and indeed one of the foundations of Renaissance culture. Schoolboys wrote both on proverbs and with them; as one of the standard 'figures' of rhetoric, recommended in all manuals on the subject, they were part of the training for any aspiring writer or fledgling orator. Along with maxims, 'sentences' and other short forms (from which they were not sharply distinguished) they were part of a writer's equipment, one of his bag of compositional tricks; they served to 'amplify' an argument and to give discourse the desired quality of *copia* – fluency and richness. Both as an instrument of persuasion and as an ornament of style they provided one of the ingredients of eloquence.[44]

Their purpose, then, was not only to instruct but to impress, and to bring credit to the writers who used them. (So that careless readers should not miss them, printers sometimes marked them typographically, with commas, inverted commas, italics or pointing hands in the margin.) A knowledge of proverbs was something to be proud of, and to show off; wherever they were used – in almanacs, advice books, polemical pamphlets, sermons and works of a more literary nature – they were sometimes overused as well. In 1601 an M.P. gave a speech in the House of Commons consisting almost entirely of proverbs; he was outscored, however, by an Italian writer, composing a literary letter in proverbs, whose total came to 381.[45] Yet what is striking about such exercises is not merely the quantities of proverbs involved but the quality of some of the writers taking part. Among the proverb virtuosi and their display pieces were Villon, with a 'Ballade en proverbes', and Rabelais and Cervantes, who filled whole chapters with them. In England too they were used by the great writers as well as the lesser lights. Chaucer had often used them to add a 'touch of sophistication'; there are more in the 'anti-popular' *Troilus and Criseide*, the 'most nearly perfect' of his works, than in any other. In the sixteenth century they appear in literary works of all types, including the highly wrought prose of Lyly, but are perhaps most striking in the drama, where proverb plays, illustrating and developing their proverb titles, formed a distinct genre; three superior examples were contributed by Shakespeare himself. Indeed in his use of proverbs Shakespeare has been ranked first among English poets, with only Chaucer as a rival: not just for the numbers he put into his works (though that is large enough, over 4,600 at the latest count) but for their poetic and dramatic purpose. Contrary to modern expectation, it is not only the rustic and comic characters who have proverbs in their lines but also the serious and tragic ones, and in the 'gravest and greatest' passages. In the best-known Shakespearian reference to a proverb, Lady Macbeth chides her husband for 'Letting "I dare not" wait upon "I would"', like the poor cat i' th' adage.' To Shakespeare's audience an allusion (*The cat would eat fish yet dare not wet its feet*) was sufficient; today it has to be explained by the learned editor in the notes.[46]

No mere survival, proverbs were if anything more in vogue at the end of the sixteenth century than at the beginning, and they highlight some of the characteristics of the learned and literary culture of the period. As a primarily oral form, yet one used constantly in written texts (long after the transition from script to print), they remind us of the important 'oral residue' in Tudor prose style. Not only was there a resemblance between the fluency of sixteenth-century writers, with their proverbs and commonplaces, and that of oral poets and story-tellers, with their stock epithets and formulae. There was also an oral quality to the very texture of Tudor writings: loose and informal, it had room for digressions and illustrations, proverbial and otherwise; it was closer in structure and spirit to the aggregative oral mode of the story-teller than to the tightly knit prose which would eventually triumph in the eighteenth century. (Even the punctuation of texts was 'elocutionary', based on the phrasing of oral delivery.) And proverbs, as ready-made expressions, are equally revealing in their very lack of originality. For this was a culture in which intertextuality was rampant; in which the notion of plagiarism (and the word itself) did not yet exist; in which there was no author's copyright, no property in ideas and no footnotes; in which, by the standards of Romanticism, there were no true authors, baring their souls in their works; in such a culture proverbs were a representative feature and to writers an indispensable one.[47]

In the second half of the sixteenth and early seventeenth centuries the vogue for proverbs was at its height, with more new sayings appearing than in any other period; it seems no coincidence that the golden age of proverbs was also the period of greatest exuberance and vitality for the language itself. Proverbs might turn up anywhere – not only in texts and in speech but in such improbable media as tapestries, plates, knife blades and sundials. They were also voluminously collected. Throughout Europe the manuscript lists of the Middle Ages were replaced by ever-expanding printed collections, the largest of which were not surpassed till the nineteenth century; John Ray, the botanist, who not only copied from previous works but obtained fresh contributions from local corre-spondents, produced the best English example.[48]

In the second half of the century, however, the educated classes' enthusiasm for proverbs began to wane. They largely disappear from the literature of the period, and by the early decades of the eighteenth century opinion was turning sharply against them. Though evidently still widely used in conversation, there too they came under attack; Swift pillories them, along with the trite witticisms and banal small talk of the day; other critics found them ostentatious, competitive, insincere – to use them was a 'sign of a coxcomb'.[49] Having dropped out of polite literature (and the manuals of rhetoric), they were then banished from polite conversation; by the 1740s, when Lord Chesterfield advised his son that 'a man of fashion never has recourse to proverbs or vulgar aphorisms', the process was complete. Chesterfield's anathema, conveniently set forth in such works as John Trusler's *Principles of Politeness* (12th ed., 1782), a reader's digest of the famous letters for the young upwardly mobile, was quickly installed as the new orthodoxy. In Richardson's *Clarissa* (1748), when the old-fashioned Lord M. writes to Lovelace, 'It is a long lane that has no turning,' he follows it with the plea 'Do not despise me for my proverbs.'[50]

In the general collapse of proverbiality, there were only two excep-tions. Biblical proverbs were still respected (though even they were to come in for rough handling from Blake), and what was too vulgar for the polite classes was still regarded as edifying for children: Trusler also published *Proverbs Exemplified, with Illustrations* (1790), to teach young people 'morality and a knowledge of the world'.[51] Not surprisingly, those who no longer used proverbs saw no point in collecting them; the blackout was nearly complete.

The expulsion of the proverb from learned culture is a landmark in social and linguistic history. How should it be interpreted?

In a narrow sense, first of all, as part of a change in upper-class manners. The old 'high' code of manners, with its aggressive sense of 'honour', had a conversational style to match, in which competition, 'railery' and display were the aims and proverbs one of the means; with the advent of a new social code, championed by Addison and Steele and others and closer to modern notions of good breeding, sincerity, 'modesty' and 'good nature' were the watchwords, and proverbs inevitably lost favour.[52] They were also affected by the withdrawal of the elite from its previous involvement in popular culture. No longer joining in the festivals and recreations of the people, the 'better sort' no longer wished to speak like the people; local accents were discarded in favour of what was now emerging as Received Pronunciation; proverbs, equally common, were also abandoned.[53] It is arguable that the importance of accents, significant only as class markers, has been exaggerated, while that of proverbs, which involve world view and mentalities, has been underestimated. At any rate, with the parting of the linguistic ways, a proverb gap opened up between the classes which has continued to the present.

Proverbs were put in a bad light by changes in learned culture itself – for example, by the emergence in the late seventeenth century of new models of literary prose style. Rhetoric as the guide to writing was replaced by grammar; metaphors were attacked, notably by the Royal Society, as emotional and untruthful; the ornate, 'cornucopian' style of the past, with its oral residue, gave way to a plain, clear, 'correct' and more 'written' style. (Even punctuation shifted from 'elocutionary' to 'syntactical'.) And when the bias of learned culture passed from wisdom to knowledge and from the Ancients to the Moderns, proverbs were left stranded. The Enlightenment did not venerate the past but wanted to break free from it; in the *Encyclopédie*, that compendium of progressive thought, there was little room for musty proverbs.[54] Their stoicism and pessimism, their assumption of 'limited good', were out of key with the official optimism of the period; their advice on damage limitation and on mere survival seemed irrelevant to those embarked on the pursuit of happiness. Static, stereotyped, incurably earthbound, they had no point of contact with the new conception of life as the unfolding of an individual destiny.

With the growing demand for 'originality', whether in language, literature or life, proverbs, unoriginal by definition, were again found wanting. It was now assumed that 'a man whose mind has been enlarged by education, and who has a complete mastery over the riches of his native language, expresses his ideas in his only words; and when he refers to any thing beyond the matter under his view, glances towards an abstract principle'. Needless to say, those 'riches' no longer included proverbs, fit only for the predictable 'vulgar man'. In literature the new outlook is set forth in Edward Young's *Conjectures on Original Composition* (1759). Like Chesterfield and the latter-day manuals of rhetoric, he warns writers to avoid expressions which are 'inelegant and obsolete' and 'tarnished by passing through the mouths of the vulgar', but he goes on to urge them to 'know' and indeed to 'reverence' themselves, to 'stand alone' and to trust their own 'genius', that 'God within'.[55] In this Romantic realm, with its apotheosis of the creative self, there is no role for the anonymous, impersonal proverb.

The new values left their mark not only on literary theory but on key words in the general vocabulary. 'Original' is applied both to persons and to works of art from the late seventeenth century; 'originality' takes on its modern meaning (that which is new, different, significant, etc.) in the eighteenth. But 'sententious', previously a term of praise (meaningful, intelligent, aphoristic), crosses over in the eighteenth century to become a term of abuse; 'commonplace' (as a noun) does the same – its negative sense is first recorded in 1745; 'hackneyed', a new word to disparage old ones, is first recorded in 1749, and 'platitude', similarly, in 1815.[56]

The proverb thus fell foul of virtually every major development in learned culture between 1660 and 1800; Renaissance humanism, which in some sense had been based on proverbs, was replaced by a culture – whether Augustan, enlightened or Romantic in emphasis – which was constructed on their rejection and absence.

What then was to take their place? One answer, best exemplified by William Blake's 'Proverbs of Hell' (from *The Marriage of Heaven and Hell*, 1790), was to retain the proverb form but to fill wit with a new, more personal content. In Blake's case the new proverbs, radical and anti-nomian in temper, attack the prudential wisdom of the old: 'The road of excess leads to the palace of wisdom'; 'The tygers of wrath are wiser than the horses of instruction.' (Though even Blake does not entirely avoid wisdom of a more conventional sort: 'The busy bee has no time for sorrow.')[57] But Blake's solution was exceptional. What was wanted was not a recycled or reinvented proverb but something different in style as well as content; and that meant an entirely new genre, the aphorism. Not surprisingly, the aphorism won favour just as the proverb was on the way out, in the second half of the seventeenth century, and was most in fashion, in the eighteenth century, when the proverb was most in disrepute. Despite the obvious similarities between the two forms, it is the differences that are the more revealing. There is the contrast between a primarily oral genre, used in a 'live' situation, and a purely literary genre, intended to be reflected on by the reader at his leisure, independent of any practical context. If proverbs have metaphors and other poetic qualities, the aphorism is usually abstract rather than metaphorical, and has the virtues of prose – the correct, classical and polished style which itself was perfected in the second half of the seventeenth century. Though both can be sceptical of official wisdom, the aphorism does so in a more aristocratic spirit, the proverb from the standpoint of common humanity. Whereas the proverb is anonymous and impersonal, aphorisms have authors, some of whom wrote entire books of them; and though cast as generalisations, universally valid, aphorisms reflect the outlook of their individual creators. In the transition from proverb to aphorism, wisdom became more abstract, yet more personal.[58]

After 1800, however, the intellectuals' anti-proverb consensus partly broke down, and the decline of the proverb was temporarily halted. There were still critics of proverbs, to be sure, as well as those who ignored them, but there were also those who rediscovered and to some extent rehabilitated them. And outside the ranks of the intellectuals, proverbs and proverb-like texts were cherished by serious-minded Victorians of all classes.

Indeed, wherever earnestness and respectability held sway there were likely to be proverbs and improving texts in the background. Upper-class children learned proverbs from their nannies; girls stitched them into their samplers; schoolchildren entered them into their copy-books, along with the much-derided copy-book maxims; schoolboys still swotted them when learning foreign languages. (The French returned the favour; a learners' collection of English proverbs, not all of them correctly worded, was prepared by the otherwise fastidious Mallarmé.) Framed proverbs and mottoes hung in parlours; Biblical texts appeared on the walls of churches and chapels. Yet at the same time proverbs lent themselves to more frivolous pursuits. Among parlour games, a favourite pastime in middle-class families, 'Proverbs' and 'Acting Proverbs' were two of the most popular. Edification also gave way to entertainment in Gilbert and Sullivan:

> Faint heart never won fair lady!
> Nothing venture, nothing win –
> Blood is thick, but water's thin –
> In for a penny, in for a pound –
> It's Love that makes the world go round![59]

To proverbs' critics, though, neither moral uplift nor operetta could justify them: indeed new and more serious charges were added to the indictment. Proverbs were not just vulgar: they actually did harm, narrowing and inhibiting those who used them, stunting their emotional growth. If proverbs were spared some of the critics' fire, it was only because maxims seemed even worse. To Coleridge, 'a man of maxims is like a Cyclops with one eye, and that eye placed in the back of his head'. An 'instinctive repugnance to the men of maxims', according to George Eliot, was shared by 'all people of broad, strong sense': they 'early discern that the mysterious complexity of our life is not to be embraced by maxims'. As for proverbs, 'cowardly' was Robert Louis Stevenson's word for them; they were 'conceived for the use of mediocre people' to 'console them in their mediocrity'. In a similar vein D. H. Lawrence lashed out at 'base-born proverbs, born in the cashbox', which 'hit directly against the intuitional consciousness'.[60] This essentially Romantic critique, more psychologically penetrating than any produced in the eighteenth century, still underlies the rejection of proverbs by the educated classes in our own time.

The nineteenth century also saw changes, and for similar reasons, in the taste for proverb substitutes. The aphorism, its classic, capsule wisdom now looking a little old-fashioned, had (apart from John Stuart Mill) few open admirers and (apart from Hazlitt) even fewer major practitioners; in England, if not on the Continent, its day had passed.[61] Instead, in the early nineteenth century, there was a vogue for a new genre, the fragment, which was both more discursive in form and more Romantic in feeling; with some of Coleridge's disciples producing entire books of fragments, it was among the younger Romantics, in England and Germany alike, that they had their greatest appeal. A fragment could contain a parable or a paradox, even an aphorism; often it expanded into a short essay; what was significant was that its open-ended form corresponded with a new Romantic conception of wisdom itself. Instead of delivering to the reader a closed, fixed truth from without, its aim was to stir up the powers of awareness that lay dormant within: true wisdom was not a finished product but an inward process, it was 'responsiveness itself'.[62]

But neither fragments nor aphorisms had much appeal outside narrow circles of literati. What new, post-proverbial wisdom was there for the middle classes? They knew their proverbs, but proverbs were not enough. For many Victorian philistines (as their highbrow critics called them) the answer was Martin Tupper's *Proverbial Philosophy* (1838); though one of the most parodied books of the century (and ridiculed by Marx), it was also one of the most popular (thirty-eight editions by 1860), a staple of birthdays and anniversaries and a favourite of the Queen herself. The title is misleading. Tupper's message, which no doubt deserves careful analysis, is sentimental rather than philosophical, and it is packaged not in proverbs but in rambling hexameters of free verse (which influenced Whitman!).[63] Another middlebrow alternative to the proverb, the great quotation, also emerged in these years, and like Tupper it represents a linguistic appropriation from other classes. In Tupper, the common proverb cuts its ties with the people and ascends into a kind of poetry; the quotation, conversely, is a downmarket version of the classical tag, that ornament and privilege of the elite. (Classical quotations were declining in any case; Gladstone's Latin tags were regarded as anachronistic.)[64]

If the quotations found favour in circles that sneered at Tupper – Matthew Arnold was in the habit of taking a single line of poetry and pondering it in the course of the day – they had a wider popularity as well, with anthologies of quotations finding an expanding market. More than fifty were devoted to Shakespeare alone; George Eliot, after dismissing the men of maxims, collaborated with the men of quotations on a substantial volume of *Wise, Witty and Tender Sayings in Prose and Verse* (1872) drawn from her works. But it was the dictionaries of quotations that truly enshrined the new genre; first appearing in the middle of the century – Bartlett's *Familiar Quotations* in 1855, Büchmann, the German equivalent, in 1864 – they have been going strong ever since.[65]

Like proverbs, quotations speak with authority, but whereas proverbs are usually anonymous and draw their force from the community, the authority of the quotation derives literally from its author; to cite a quotation is to identify with the genius of the author and to lift oneself above the common herd. (Hence the concern of Büchmann and other compilers for textual accuracy.) Not all quotations came from great writers. In an age of hero-worship – the National Portrait Gallery (1856) and the *Dictionary of National Biography* (1885–1901) are its monuments – when it was accepted that 'the trifling of a great man is never trivial', the anthologies made room for great men as well. Napoleon makes a strong showing, and even George III gets a look-in; *Short Sayings of Great Men* appeared in 1882, and there were collections of last words, chosen less for their piety than for their expression of individual character. For what was most prized in the sayings of the great was not their greatness, whatever that might be, but the 'stamp of a distinct personality'. Just as the aphorism was more personal than the proverb, and the fragment more so than the aphorism, so the sayings of the great men represent the most personalised form of wisdom yet, a wisdom that is equated with self-expression and self-realisation. ' "Know thyself!" was written over the portal of the antique world,' said Oscar Wilde; 'Over the portal of the new world, "Be thyself" shall be written.'[66]

Romanticism had exalted the words of the hero: it now helped, ironically, to rediscover the proverbs of the people; poetry and wisdom, after all, could be found in peasant communities as well as in the solitary genius. Not that the leading Romantic writers themselves were involved – Keats, to be sure, loved proverbs and often quoted them in his letters, but Wordsworth's attempts to render the 'real language of men' ignored all the proverbs and other conventional phrases that most men actually used. When the first step was taken it was not by a full-blooded Romantic but by one of their fellow-travellers (and an admirer of Blake), Isaac D'Israeli;

his pioneering essay on proverbs, appearing in 1823 in his popular *Curiosities of Literature*, did much to put them in a more favourable light. His first concern, inevitably, was to 'rescue' them from 'prevailing prejudices' – those associated with Lord Chesterfield above all – and he reminded his readers that men of fashion in earlier centuries, far from shunning proverbs, had used, studied and collected them. Characteristically, he recommended proverbs as 'neglected stores of curious amusement', but his main arguments were for their intrinsic truth and for their value as historical evidence: not much yet about their poetry. Their 'bold and concealed truths' give us 'a deep insight into domestic life, and open for us the heart of man'; they illuminate 'the manners of a people' and 'the genius of the age'. They are an indispensable source for 'what people think, and how they feel'. If they are 'no longer the ornaments of conversation, they have not ceased to be the treasuries of Thought'.[67]

Only a year later appeared the first substantial new collection in decades, *Select Proverbs of All Nations*, another challenge to anti-proverb prejudice. Its editor was the unexpected figure of John Wade, the radical journalist and compiler of the *Extraordinary Black Book*, and though he disappointingly leaves few traces of his politics, his enthusiasm for proverbs outdoes even D'Israeli's. He takes up Aristotle's view that through proverbs 'the wisdom of poets and philosophers became the every-day wisdom of the populace', but he also believes that they are 'founded on nature'; either way, they were the 'primitive language of mankind'. He is perhaps the first to note that they do a 'singular injustice to the fair sex', and suggests that they were 'made by the men'. Proverbs, he concludes, are the 'book of life, the salt of knowledge, and the gatherings of ages'.[68] Soon the reaction against Chesterfield spread even to the *Gentleman's Magazine*, which observed that 'the practice of abolishing from polite society the use of many good old English terms, as being vulgar, has been carried too far'; the 'copiousness' for which English had been celebrated was lost, among the middle and upper classes, by 'over-refinement'.[69]

Being unkind to Chesterfield, though, was only part of the story. What brought the revival to its ideological peak, R. C. Trench's still readable little book *On the Lessons in Proverbs* (1853), was the belated intervention of Romanticism, albeit with a dose of Victorian moralism. (A poet by avocation and linked with the Romantics by his friendship with Tennyson, Trench was also an Anglican parson, later becoming Dean of Westminster and Archbishop of Dublin.) Taking as his motto *Vox populi, vox dei* (also used by the seventeenth-century collector, James Howell), he makes the case for proverbs in terms of an aesthetic but non-political populism: 'whatever is *from* the people, or truly *for* the people' will have 'poetry' and 'imagination'. Full of praise for the 'bold imagery and striking comparisons' in sayings such as *Gray hairs are death's blossoms*, he is more responsive to the poetic qualities in proverbs than any previous writer. True also to his clerical calling, he devotes a chapter to the unlikely subject of 'The Theology of Proverbs', worrying in certain cases about their lack of moral tone; *Honesty is the best policy* disappoints him, even if its failure to appeal to higher motives does not rule them out. But he is relieved to conclude that 'in the main they range themselves under the banners of the right and the truth'.[70]

Even before Trench, proverbs had been taken up again by novelists, often merely to add touches of quaintness or low life, but occasionally to define characters whose shrewdness and understanding impress us in a more positive way. Sam Weller, from *The Pickwick Papers*, is the best example: acting as Dickens's 'surrogate' in the novel, its 'centre of intelligence', he puts much of his wisdom into his inimitable proverbs. Tolstoy goes even further, giving proverbs what can only be called an ideological role; himself a collector, he prized them as the expression of the peasant virtues which he admired, preached and sometimes imagined. In *War and Peace* – after finishing the first draft he considered changing the title to *All's Well that Ends Well* – Karataev, his great peasant character, has proverbs (and little else) for every situation; but all his exemplary unselfishness and acceptance of life are expressed in them, in contrast with the misguided characters vainly trying to control the course of events.[71]

With the rise of the folklore movement, the approach to proverbs, while still Romantic, became somewhat more scholarly, if not usually academic. Collectors joined in the hunt for proverbs from one end of Europe to the other, and the collections they produced are larger and more serious than anything from earlier centuries. In England, however, the results are thin and disappointing. Determined to uncover specifically local or county sayings – sensible enough in countries like France with more strongly developed regional cultures – the collectors often ignored the much more numerous and important national ones, and rarely placed them in the contexts in which they were used. Nevertheless, when the folklore movement declined, having failed to establish itself in the universities, intelligent curiosity about proverbs largely declined as well; what had been awakened by the Romantics failed to be taken up by the academics.

In the long run it was the critics of the proverb, not its defenders, who prevailed; once the effects of the Victorian revival wore off, the proverb resumed its decline, and today its reputation among educated people is lower than at any time since the seventeenth century. 'Wise-sounding but meaningless proverbs' – a topic set in *New Statesman* literary competitions – fairly reflects current attitudes.[72] Used in any straightforward way

– apart from the occasional allusion – proverbs are taboo.[73] Only when the old sayings can be made to say something new, whether by irony or by more drastic means, are they accepted, but in the process they cease to express the wisdom of the community and become raw material for the wit and originality of the individual speaker. Twisted, tampered with, turned upside down, they re-emerge as 'perverted proverbs' – 'Punctuality is the thief of time' (Oscar Wilde) or 'An apple a day keeps the doctor away, an onion a day keeps everybody away.' It is not new, this desire both to deflate the traditional proverb and to reinvent it, but it appears to be more widespread than ever before, and the results can be seen at every level of cultural activity, from graffiti ('Chaste makes waste') to advertising slogans ('Thirst come, thirst served', from a Coca-Cola campaign of 1932) as well as in literature. But the most radical assault on the proverb came at the hands of the surrealists; in order to get at what they believed were its deeper levels of meaning, they severed it from any external message or moral purpose, dislocated its language, and in the end turned it into a kind of nonsense. If this is an extreme case, it is only one in a long line of indignities visited upon the common proverb by an educated class which has rejected proverbs yet seems unable to leave them alone.[74]

Perhaps there is now something unacceptable in the very notion of collective wisdom: more to the modern individualist taste is Wilde's quip that 'a truth ceases to be true when more than one person believes it'. At any rate educated people have many reasons not to use proverbs, even if they rarely need to spell them out. That the purpose of life is to fulfil an inner potential, that happiness can be achieved and ought to be pursued, that in the process one becomes a unique individual – all of this clashes with one or another assumption implicit in proverbs. Proverbs put the collective before the individual, the recurrent and stereotyped before the unique, external rules before self-determination, common sense before the individual vision, survival before happiness. And with self-fulfilment goes self-expression: educated people make the further assumption that everyone has (or should have) their own unique, ever-changing experience of life, and that that experience should be expressed in freshly chosen words on every occasion. To use proverbs would deny the individuality of both speaker and listener. In this view, those who do use proverbs are either linguistically lazy or lacking in originality, their poverty of language reflecting poverty of experience and poverty of imagination. Proverbs are seen as part of a restricted code that encapsulates experience and imprisons it: they are conversation-stoppers. It does not matter that they can be used with a wit and subtlety unsuspected by their cultured despisers, nor that their critics may in practice tie themselves up in knots of jargon, or use fewer proverbs but more clichés; still less does it matter that in viewing proverbs as a linguistic 'other', associated with peasants, plebeians and the petty-bourgeois, they ignore their historic role in elite culture itself: the avoidance of proverbs remains one of the articles in the modern linguistic faith.[75]

In this century, moreover, the intellectuals have been avoiding the proverb substitutes as well. The aphorism tends to be regarded (if at all) as worthy but old-fashioned, the quotation as incurably middlebrow, almost as bad as the proverb itself; a psychoanalyst has suggested that reliance on quotations can be taken as evidence of a character disorder, caused by early restrictions on libido.[76] Notwithstanding the claims of the deconstructionists – that originality is impossible, that texts derive not from their nominal authors but from other texts and discourses – originality is still the order of the day.

And by the same token there is still the dread of unoriginality: what has changed in this century is that the object of that dread is less often the proverb or quotation than the cliché. Since the 1890s, when the term first appeared in English, clichés have been shunned by the man of taste in much the same way and for many of the same reasons that Chesterfield's man of fashion disdained proverbs. Indeed the modern, educated consensus has it that proverbs are no more than a variety of cliché – irritating, obsolete, with no redeeming literary or social value. Their poetry and wisdom unrecognised, they are a lost cause, consigned to the dustbin of sociolinguistic history.[77]

Conclusion

The proverb about appearances being deceptive can be applied to proverbs themselves. Taken at face value they seem safe and sensible, unproblematic constants of the human condition; looked at more closely, they turn out to be social and historical variables after all, a source of division and dispute, caught up in the language of politics and in the politics of language. Rarely questioned by the popular classes, they became the focus of a debate in the educated classes in which the nature and direction of elite culture itself was at issue.

But if that debate helps to give the common proverb a dignified intellectual history, it fails to throw much light on its social history; a great deal was said about the truth, poetry and morality of proverbs, frustratingly little – apart from complaints about their 'vulgarity' – about their users, uses and functions. This lack of curiosity about the things that interest us most can easily make us impatient – not only with the critics but with the defenders and, especially, the collectors, copying from other men's books instead of going into the field and doing their ethnographic duty.

Even so, the popularity of proverbs in traditional Europe is hardly in question. And not only proverbs: along with them were stock epithets, politeness formulae and the like, a wide repertoire of conventional phrases and sayings.[78] Proverbial phrases are a good example: so common were they in early eighteenth-century Scotland, according to Kelly, that to have written them all down would have been to transcribe 'a great share of the language used in that country'. Of course all language is conventional – a point usually limited to matters of grammar and vocabulary; what is striking is how stereotyped language has also been in its larger units and social uses.[79] Some of the missing links between linguistic structure and social structure may well be found amongst the oral genres and conventional phrases.

If no one has yet traced the consequences, it is not necessary to be a linguistic determinist to suppose that they have been considerable. As Ong remarks of learned culture in the early modern period, 'In formulas thought lived and moved and had its being.'[80] When people habitually use proverbs and similar expressions they will tend to think in terms of them and to act and live in accordance with them. If social life can be interpreted like a text, then as often as not it is the proverb or the stock phrase that provides the clue.

For historians concerned with meanings and mentalities, then, proverbs are a privileged source, a point of entry into the wider realm of the oral and the formulaic. And for all of us, immersed in print (and print-out), overimpressed by books, texts, script and scripture, prone to exaggerate their influence in everyday life, they are the classic corrective: proverbs, we may remind ourselves, 'existed before books', and it is 'not books, but the old sayings, which regulate human conduct'.[81]

NOTES

[1] Cited by W. D. Handcock, 'Introduction', in G. M. Young, *Victorian Essays* (London, 1962), p. 11.
[2] Emmanuel Le Roy Ladurie, *Montaillou* (Paris, 1975); Carlo Ginzburg, *The Cheese and the Worms*, trans. John and Anne Tedeschi (London, 1980). Of course, the Inquisition records are themselves Latin translations of testimony given in the vernacular; on this question see Natalie Davis, 'Les conteurs de Montaillou', *Annales E.S.C.* 34 (1979), 68–9.
[3] The depositions in the records of the English church courts have, however, been little used.
[4] See Roger Abrahams, 'A Rhetoric of Everyday Life: Traditional Conversational Genres', *Southern Folklore Quarterly* 32 (1968), 44–59.
[5] The most recent is Wolfgang Mieder, ed., *International Proverb Scholarship: An Annotated Bibliography* (New York and London, 1982); useful bibliographies also in Lutz Röhrich and Wolfgang Mieder, *Sprichwort* (Stuttgart, 1977).
[6] See, for example, Archer Taylor, *The Proverb* (Cambridge, Mass., 1931), p. 3; Roger D. Abrahams, 'Proverbs and Proverbial Expressions', in Richard M. Dorson, ed., *Folklore and Folklife: An Introduction* (Chicago and London, 1972), pp. 117–27; Alan Dundes, 'On the Structure of the Proverb', *Proverbium* 25 (1975), 961–73; Henri Meschonnic, 'Les proverbes, actes de discours', *Revue des sciences humaines* 41 (1976), 419–30.
[7] See Robert A. Rothstein, 'The Poetics of Proverbs', in Charles E. Gribble, ed., *Studies*

Presented to Prof. Roman Jakobson (Cambridge, Mass., 1968), pp. 265–74; Abrahams, 'Proverbs and Proverbial Expressions', pp. 119–21.

[8] 'Strategies for Situations': Kenneth Burke, *Philosophy of Literary Form*, 2nd ed. (Baton Rouge, La., 1967), p. 296; on the distinction between proverbs and proverbial expressions, Dundes, 'Structure of the Proverb', p. 972 n8; Röhrich and Mieder, *Sprichwort*, pp. 15–16; Abrahams, 'Proverbs and Proverbial Expressions', pp. 123–4.

[9] On impersonality, Abrahams, 'Rhetoric of Everyday Life', p. 48; on tone of voice, A. J. Greimas, 'Idiotismes, proverbes, dictions', *Cahiers de lexicologie* 2 (1969), p. 56.

[10] On archaic features, *ibid.*, p. 59.

[11] They are not universal, however; they have not been recorded among the Indians of North America nor in parts of Africa, otherwise rich in proverbs. Roger W. Wescott, 'From Proverb to Aphorism: The Evolution of a Verbal Art-Form', *Forum Linguisticum* 5 (1981), p. 213; Alfred Kroeber, *Anthropology*, new ed. (London, 1948), p. 544; B. J. Whiting, 'The Origin of the Proverb', *Harvard Studies and Notes in Philology and Literature* 13 (1931), pp. 61, 77.

[12] On the Merina, Maurice Bloch, 'Astrology and Writing in Madagascar', in Jack Goody, ed., *Literacy in Traditional Societies* (Cambridge, 1968), p. 293; on proverbs as an attribute of leadership, Joyce Penfield, *Communicating with Quotes: The Igbo Case* (Westport, Conn., 1983), pp. 70–1; on proverbs in contemporary political life, Röhrich and Mieder, *Sprichwort*, pp. 108–10.

[13] On the Scots, James Kelly, 'Introduction', *A Complete Collection of Scottish Proverbs* (London, 1721). Flora Thompson, *Lark Rise to Candleford* (Harmondsworth, 1973), p. 49. Also David Jenkins, *The Agricultural Community in South-West Wales at the Turn of the Twentieth Century* (Cardiff, 1971), p. 11.

[14] Robert Roberts, *The Classic Slum* (Harmondsworth, 1973), p. 177; Richard Hoggart, *The Uses of Literacy* (Harmondsworth, 1958), pp. 15–16 and *passim*.

[15] On the Igbo, Penfield, *Communicating with Quotes*, pp. 85–7. I am indebted to Mr David de Vries and to Dr Faith Wigzell for their observations on Israel and on Russia respectively; they bear no responsibility, however, for the use I have made of their advice. Gorbachev's remark: *The Observer* (23 Dec. 1984), p. 4.

[16] On the influence of age, Mathilde Hain, *Sprichwort und Volkssprache* (Geissen, 1951), p. 51; Démétrios Loukatos, 'L'emploi du proverbe aux différents âges', *Proverbium* 2 (1965), 17–26.

[17] Raymond Firth, 'Proverbs in Native Life, with special reference to those of the Maori', *Folk-Lore* 37 (1926), p. 147.

[18] On the uses of impersonality, Muriel Saville-Troike, *The Ethnography of Communication* (London, 1982), p. 36; on the Igbo, Penfield, *Communicating with Quotes*, p. 48; on the Zande, E. E. Evans-Pritchard, '*Sanza*, a Characteristic Feature of Zande Language and Thought', in *Essays in Social Anthropology* (London, 1962), p. 227; on France, Natalie Davis, 'Proverbial Wisdom and Popular Errors', in *Society and Culture in Early Modern France* (Stanford, Cal., 1975), p. 244; on Nigeria, John C. Messenger, 'The Role of Proverbs in a Nigerian Judicial System', *Southwestern Journal of Anthropology* 15 (1959), 64–73.

[19] On phatic speech, R. A. Hudson, *Sociolinguistics* (Cambridge, 1980), p. 109; Hoggart, *Uses of Literacy*, p. 16; 'a more recent study', Donald McKelvie, 'Aspects of Oral Tradition and Belief in an Industrial Region', *Folk Life* 1 (1963), p. 87, and McKelvie, 'Proverbial Elements in the Oral Tradition of an English Urban Industrial Region', *Journal of the Folklore Institute* 2 (1965), 249–50.

[20] Lawrence A. Boadi, 'The Language of the Proverb in Akani', in Richard M. Dorson, ed., *African Folklore* (New York, 1972), pp. 183, 185.

[21] On context and meaning, Barbara Kirshenblatt-Gimblett, 'Toward a Theory of Proverb Meaning', *Proverbium* 22 (1973), 821–7; Peter Seitel, 'Proverbs: A Social Use of Metaphor', *Genre* 2 (1969), 143–61. On variants, Vilmos Voigt, 'Les niveaux des variantes des proverbes', *Acta Linguistica Academiae Scientiarum Hungaricae* 20 (1970), 357–64; on *A rolling stone*, G. M. Milner, 'Quadripartite Structures', *Proverbium* 14 (1969), p. 380.

[22] Nor can the collections themselves be trusted. They omit a certain number of genuine

proverbs, and they also include items which were invented by editors and others in the hope that they would become proverbs, but which never did; some of the latter, copied in collection after collection, led a purely literary existence, never actually crossing anyone's lips. See Archer Taylor, 'How Nearly Complete are the Collections of Proverbs?', *Proverbium* 14 (1969), 369–71, and 'Problems in the Study of Proverbs', *Journal of American Folklore* 47 (1934), 1–21.

[23] An example from the early nineteenth century is John Clare, whose collection contains more maxims than true proverbs. MS. Book A-18, pp. 254, 270, 274–6; John Clare MSS., Peterborough Museum. I am indebted to Mr George Deacon for this reference.

[24] On Solomon and Marcolf, Davis, 'Proverbial Wisdom', p. 227; Russian collection, Claude Carey, *Les proverbes érotiques russes* (The Hague and Paris, 1972). John Ray, 'To the Reader', *A Collection of English Proverbs* (Cambridge, 1670); 2nd ed., 1678; Kelly, *Complete Collection* (unpaginated).

[25] J. A. Burrow, ' "Young Saint, Old Devil": Reflections on a Medieval Proverb', in *Essays on Medieval Literature* (Oxford, 1984), pp. 178, 184; on Denmark, Bengt Holbek, 'Oppositions and Contrasts in Folklore', in Venetia J. Newall, ed., *Folklore Studies in the Twentieth Century* (Woodbridge, 1980), p. 237.

[26] On nineteenth-century France, Eugen Weber, *Peasants into Frenchmen: The Modernization of Rural France 1870–1914* (London, 1979), pp. 420, 428; 'another study': Françoise Loux and Philippe Richard, *Sagesses du corps: la santé et la maladie dans les proverbes français* (Paris, 1978), p. 260; on marriage, Martine Segalen, *Love and Power in the Peasant Family*, trans. Sarah Matthews (Oxford, 1983), p. 170.

[27] For glib generalisations about national character in proverbs, Thomas Fielding (i.e. John Wade), *Select Proverbs of All Nations* (London, 1824), pp. x–xi. An exception is U. R. Burke, *Spanish Salt: A collection of all the proverbs which are to be found in Don Quixote* (London, 1877), p. xv.

[28] Taylor, *The Proverb*, pp. 164–8; Röhrich and Mieder, *Sprichwort*, pp. 70–1.

[29] D. B. Shimkin and Pedro Sanjan, 'Culture and World View: A Method of Analysis applied to Rural Russia', *American Anthropologist* 55 (1953), 329–48; Joseph Raymond, 'Attitudes and Cultural Patterns in Spanish Proverbs', *The Americas* 11 (1954), 57–77; Maureen J. Giovannini, 'A Structural Analysis of Proverbs in a Sicilian Village', *American Ethnologist* 5 (1978), 322–33. On ethos and world view, Clifford Geertz, 'Ethos, World View, and the Analysis of Sacred Symbols', *The Interpretation of Cultures* (New York, 1973), pp. 126–41.

[30] One example is superstition. Collectors like Ray and Kelly deliberately excluded sayings they regarded as superstitious, but these were probably not very numerous; superstitions and proverbs ordinarily deal with quite distinct sets of problems. Taylor, *The Proverb*, p. 69; Abrahams, 'Rhetoric of Everyday Life', pp. 45, 47–51.

[31] On fear, George M. Foster, 'Character and Personal Relationships Seen through Proverbs in Tzintzuntzan, Mexico', *Journal of American Folklore* 83 (1970), p. 305; on the passions, Jean-Louis Flandrin, *Les amours paysannes* (Paris, 1975), p. 15; on mothers, Martine Segalen, 'Le mariage et les femmes dans les proverbes populaires français', *Ethnologie française* 5 (1975), pp. 46, 77, 82.

[32] Jack Goody, *The Domestication of the Savage Mind* (Cambridge, 1977), p. 126; for a sensible observation by a philosopher, Renford Bambrough, *Reason, Truth and God* (London, 1969), p. 126. Also, Clifford Geertz, 'Common Sense as a Cultural System', *Antioch Review* 33 (1975), p. 23. On ideology in common sense, Antonio Gramsci, *Selections from the Prison Notebooks*, trans. and ed. Q. Hoare and G. Nowell-Smith (London, 1971), pp. 323, 326 n5.

[33] On the body, Loux and Richard, *Sagesses du corps*; on Spain, F. C. Hayes, 'The Collecting of Proverbs in Spain before 1650', *Hispania* 20 (1937), p. 91.

[34] Wade, *Select Proverbs*, p. xii; Daniel Rivière, ' "Qui plus a plus convoite": 60 proverbes pour une sagesse', *L'histoire* 25 (1980), p. 82 (on sixteenth-century France); Segalen, 'Le mariage', pp. 48, 124, 145; Michel Vovelle, *Proverbes et dictions provençaux* (Marseille, 1981), pp. 9–11; Shimkin and Sanjuan, 'Culture and World View', p. 329.

[35] On Russia, *ibid.*, p. 343; on Finland, Matti Kuusi, 'Fatalistic Traits in Finnish Proverbs', in Wolfgang Mieder and Alan Dundes, eds., *The Wisdom of Many: Essays on the*

Proverb (New York and London, 1981), pp. 281–2; on France, Rivière, ' "Qui plus a plus convoite" ', p. 81.

[36] Vovelle, *Proverbes*, pp. 12–13; Loux and Richard, *Sagesses*, p. 227.

[37] On the German collections, Röhrich and Mieder, *Sprichwort*, pp. 43–4; Morris Palmer Tilley, *Dictionary of the Proverbs in England in the Sixteenth and Seventeenth Centuries* (Ann Arbor, Mich., 1950); for contemporary English proverbs, J. A. Simpson, ed., *Concise Oxford Dictionary of Proverbs* (Oxford, 1982).

[38] On change in form, Taylor, *The Proverb*, pp. 151–2; on France, Rivière, ' "Qui plus a plus convoite" ', p. 82; on Russia, D. I. Raskin, 'Russische Sprichwörter als Wiederspiegelung der historischen Entwicklung der Ideologie des Bauerntums' (summary of article), *Russkih Fol'klor* 13 (1972), 308–9; on Finland, Matti Kuusi, 'Parömiologische Betrachtungen', trans. B. Assmuth, *FF Communications* 172 (1957), p. 39; Weber, *Peasants into Frenchmen*, pp. 427–8.

[39] Sources for this section, W. G. Smith and F. P. Wilson, *Oxford Dictionary of English Proverbs*, 3rd ed. (Oxford, 1970); Tilley, *Dictionary*; Simpson, *Concise Oxford Dictionary*.

[40] Scottish proverbs on dirt, some of them excusing it, are discussed by W. Motherwell, 'Preface', in Andrew Henderson, *Scottish Proverbs* (Edinburgh, 1832), pp. lxxvi–lxxvii.

[41] Age of proverb-making: Edward Tylor, *Primitive Culture* (London, 1871), vol. 1, p. 81.

[42] Roberts, *Classic Slum*, p. 53.

[43] Janet E. Heseltine, 'Introduction', W. G. Smith, *Oxford Dictionary of English Proverbs* (Oxford, 1935), p. xiv.

[44] On Erasmus, Margaret Mann Phillips, *The 'Adages' of Erasmus: A Study with Translations* (Cambridge, 1964); on grammar schools, T. W. Baldwin, *William Shakspere's Small Latin and Lesse Greeke* (Urbana, Ill., 1944), 2 vols., on composition, F. P. Wilson, 'Shakespeare and the Diction of Common Life' and 'The Proverbial Wisdom of Shakespeare', in *Shakespearian and Other Studies*, ed. Helen Gardner (Oxford, 1969); Walter J. Ong, 'Oral Residue in Tudor Prose Style', *PMLA* 80 (1965), 147–8.

[45] On typography, G. K. Hunter, 'The Marking of *Sententiae* in Elizabethan Printed Plays, Poems and Romances', *The Library,* 5th ser., 6 (1951), 178–88; on almanacs, Bernard Capp, *Astrology and the Popular Press: English Almanacs 1500–1800* (London, 1979), p. 229; on advice books, Louis Wright, *Middle-Class Culture in Elizabethan England* (Chapel Hill, N.C., 1935), Chapter 5; 1601 speech: Wilson, 'Shakespeare and the Diction of Common Life', p. 114; Italian letter: Charles Speroni, *The Italian Wellerism to the End of the Seventeenth Century* (Berkeley and Los Angeles, 1953), p. 3 n10.

[46] On Villon *et al.*, Rosalie L. Colie, *The Resources of Kind: Genre-Theory in the Renaissance* (Berkeley, 1973), p. 34; on Chaucer, Taylor, *The Proverb*, p. 172; B. J. Whiting, *Chaucer's Use of Proverbs* (Cambridge, Mass., 1934), pp. 49, 75; on proverb plays, Paula Neuss, 'The Sixteenth-Century English "Proverb" Play', *Comparative Drama* 18 (1984), 1–18; proverb count in Shakespeare: R. W. Dent, *Shakespeare's Proverbial Language: An Index* (Berkeley, 1981), pp. 3–4; 'gravest and greatest'; Wilson, 'Shakespeare and the Diction of Common Life', p. 119; *Macbeth* I.vii.44.

[47] On Tudor prose, Ong, 'Oral Residue', pp. 150–3; on punctuation, A. C. Partridge, *Orthography in Shakespeare and Elizabethan Drama* (London, 1964), p. 182; on plagiarism, Harold Ogden White, *Plagiarism and Imitation during the English Renaissance* (Cambridge, Mass., 1935), p. 202; on copyright, Lyman R. Patterson, *Copyright in Historical Perspective* (Nashville, Tenn., 1968); on medieval authors, H. J. Chaytor, *From Script to Print* (London, 1945), pp. 139–40.

[48] On the 'Golden Age', see also Röhrich and Mieder, *Sprichwort*, p. 33; on improbable media, Isaac D'Israeli, 'The Philosophy of Proverbs', *Second Series of Curiosities of Literature*, 3 vols. (London, 1823), vol. 1, pp. 426–7; Ray, *Collection*, 'To the Reader'.

[49] Jonathan Swift, *A Complete Collection of Genteel and Ingenious Conversation* (London, 1738; repr. 1963); this was largely written in the first decade of the century. 'Sign of a coxcomb': Samuel Palmer, *Moral Essays on some of the most curious and significant English, Scotch and Foreign Proverbs* (London, 1710), p. ix. Even the advocates of proverbs were now on the defensive: Oswald Dykes, *English Proverbs, with Moral Reflexions*, 2nd ed. (London, 1709).

[50] Lord Chesterfield, *Letters to his Son*, 2 vols. (London, 1774), letter dated 27 Sept., 1749, vol. 1, p. 464; Trusler, *Principles of Politeness*, 12th ed. (London, 1782), p. 20; Samuel Richardson, *Clarissa* (London, 1748, repr. 1962), vol. 2, letter 107. Allusions to proverbs and conventional phrases in eighteenth-century novels are discussed by Pat Rogers, 'Tristram Shandy's Polite Conversation', *Essays in Criticism* 32 (1982), 305–20.

[51] Biblical commentaries: Matthew Henry, *An Exposition of the Five Poetical Books of the Old Testament*, 3 vols. (London, 1725), vol. 3, p. 457; Bernard Hodgson, *The Proverbs of Solomon Translated from the Hebrew* (Oxford, 1788); Thomas Scott, *The Holy Bible, with Original Notes and Practical Observations* (London, 1792), vol. 2.

[52] On the 'high' manner, C. S. Lewis, 'Addison', in James L. Clifford, ed., *Eighteenth-Century English Literature: Modern Essays in Criticism* (New York, 1959), pp. 149–50; for 'raillery', sincerity, 'modesty' and 'good nature', Benjamin Stillingfleet, 'An Essay on Conversation', in *Collection of Poems by Several Hands* (London, 1748), vol. 1, pp. 173, 175.

[53] On the withdrawal of the elite, Peter Burke, *Popular Culture in Early Modern Europe* (London, 1978), pp. 270–81; on the rise of Received Pronunciation, Dick Leith, *A Social History of English* (London, 1983), p. 55.

[54] On changes in literary style, Morris W. Croll, 'The Baroque Style in Prose', in *Style, Rhetoric and Rhythm*, eds J. Max Patrick and Robert O. Evans (Princeton, 1966), p. 231; on the attack on metaphors, Joan Bennett, 'An Aspect of the Evolution of Seventeenth-Century Prose Style', *Review of English Studies* 17 (1941), 284–8; on punctuation, Partridge, *Orthography*, p. 182; on the *Encyclopédie*, Davis, 'Proverbial Wisdom', p. 253.

[55] 'A man whose mind': Motherwell, 'Preface', in Henderson, *Scottish Proverbs*, p. lxv; Young, *Conjectures on Original Composition* (London, 1759), pp. 13–14, 30–1, 36, 52–5.

[56] Changes in meaning have been traced in the *O.E.D.* On originality, see also Raymond Williams, *Keywords* (London, 1976), pp. 192–3 and Quentin Skinner, 'The Idea of a Cultural Lexicon', *Essays in Criticism* 29 (1978), p. 206.

[57] William Blake, *Complete Writings*, ed. Geoffrey Keynes (London, 1969), pp. 150–3; Harold Bloom, *Blake's Apocalypse* (London, 1963), pp. 83, 85.

[58] On contrasts between proverb and aphorism, see also John Gross, 'Introduction', *Oxford Book of Aphorisms* (Oxford, 1983), p. viii; Meschonnic, 'Les proverbes', p. 429.

[59] On nannies, Hugh Casson and Joyce Grenfell, *Nanny Says* (London, 1972); Jonathan Gathorne-Hardy, *Rise and Fall of the British Nanny* (London, 1972), pp. 330–6; copy-books: Anon., *Proverbs and Precepts for Copy Lines, for the Use of Schools* (London, 1850); Stéphane Mallarmé, 'Thèmes anglais', in *Œuvres complètes*, ed. H. Mondor and G. Jean-Aubry (Paris, 1945), pp. 1057–1156; B. J. Whiting, 'The English Proverbs of Stéphane Mallarmé', *Romanic Review* 36 (1945), 134–41; parlour games: Anon., *Acting Proverbs* (London, 1858); Alfred Elliott, *Within Doors: A Book of Games and Pastimes for the Drawing Room* (London, 1872), p. 32; W. S. Gilbert, 'Iolanthe', in *Selected Operas*, 2nd ser. (London, 1928), p. 133.

[60] S. T. Coleridge, *Specimens of the Table Talk*, 2 vols. (London, 1835), vol. 1, p. 69 (24 June 1827); George Eliot, *The Mill on the Floss* (London, 1860), Book 7, Chapter 2; Robert Louis Stevenson, 'Crabbed Age and Youth', *Virginibus Puerisque*, 2nd ed. (London, 1887), pp. 81–2; D. H. Lawrence, 'Introduction', *Paintings* (London, 1929), unpaginated.

[61] John Stuart Mill, 'Aphorisms', *Westminster Review* 26 (1837), 348–57; also John Morley, 'Aphorisms', *Studies in Literature* (London, 1890), pp. 54–102. Hazlitt's *Characteristics* (1823) was inspired by La Rochefoucauld.

[62] Robert Preyer, 'Victorian Wisdom Literature: Fragments and Maxims', *Victorian Studies* 6 (1963), 250–8. The best-known of the English fragment books is Augustus and Julius Hare, *Guesses at Truth* (London, 1827).

[63] On Tupper, Derek Hudson, *Martin Tupper: His Rise and Fall* (London, 1949), p. 43; a few examples of parodies in Walter Hamilton, ed., *Parodies*, 6 vols. (1884–9), vol. 6, pp. 88–91. For Marx, see *Capital*, trans. Ben Fowkes (Harmondsworth, 1976), vol. 1, pp. 758, 759 n; in a game of 'Confessions' Marx chose Tupper (along with violet powder) as his 'Aversion'; Marx and Engels, *Werke* (Berlin, 1965), vol. 31, photo facing p. 596. On

Tupper's influence on Whitman, Floyd Stovall, *The Foreground of 'Leaves of Grass'* (Charlottesville, Va, 1974), pp. 256–8.

[64] On the decline of classical quotations, George Watson, *The English Ideology: Studies in the Language of Victorian Politics* (London, 1973), p. 119.

[65] On Victorian anthologies, Michael Wheeler, *The Art of Allusion in Victorian Fiction* (London, 1979), p. 14.

[66] On Büchmann, W. Rust and G. Haupt, 'Die Geschichte des Büchmann', in G. Büchmann, *Geflügelte Worte*, 30th ed. (Berlin, 1961); 'trifling': Arthur Helps, *Thoughts in the Cloister and the Crowd* (London, 1835), p. 93. Samuel A. Bent, *Short Sayings of Great Men* (London, 1882); last words: Thomas H. Lewin, *Life and Death* (London, 1910); 'stamp of a distinct personality': Richard Holt Hutton, 'Sayings of Great Men', in *Brief Literary Criticisms* (London, 1906), p. 21. Wilde, 'The Soul of Man under Socialism', *Works*, ed. G. F. Maine (London, 1948), p. 1024.

[67] D'Israeli, 'Philosophy of Proverbs', pp. 416, 417, 480.

[68] Wade, *Select Proverbs*, pp. vii, viii, xiv. The volume was published under the name 'Thomas Fielding' but is attributed to Wade in the British Museum catalogue and in Samuel Halkett and John Laing, *Dictionary of Anonymous and Pseudonymous English Literature*, new ed. (Edinburgh, 1929), vol. 5, p. 216; for the latter reference I am grateful to Dr Masami Umekawa.

[69] Anonymous correspondent, *Gentleman's Magazine* 95 (1825), Part I, pp. 395–7.

[70] R. C. Trench, *On the Lessons in Proverbs* (London, 1853), pp. 71, 97, 100–1.

[71] Wellerisms, which existed long before Dickens, are much discussed in the literature on proverbs. On *Pickwick Papers*, Steven Marcus, *Dickens from Pickwick to Dombey* (New York, 1965), p. 34; on Tolstoy, Andrew Donskov, 'Tolstoy's Use of Proverbs in "The Power of Darkness" ', *Russian Literature* 9 (1975), p. 70. Karataev appears in *War and Peace*, Book 12, Chapter 3 and Book 14, Chapter 3.

[72] Weekend Competition, *New Statesman*, 5 Jan. 1979; also 1 Aug. 1980. Among the winners: 'Wise fish are never thirsty'; 'Age will come to those who wait.'

[73] But educated people who would never use proverbs in talking to others sometimes repeat them silently to themselves.

[74] On perverted proverbs, Susan Stewart, *Nonsense: Aspects of Intertextuality in Folklore and Literature* (Baltimore and London, 1979), p. 185; Wolfgang Mieder has collected 3,000 examples from German sources in *Antisprichwörter*, 2 vols. (Wiesbaden, 1983–5). 'Chaste makes waste': Jess Nierenberg, 'Proverbs in Graffiti', *Maledicta* 7 (1983), p. 50; 'Thirst come': Barbara and Wolfgang Mieder, 'Tradition and Innovation: Proverbs in Advertising', in Mieder and Dundes, *Wisdom of Many*, p. 313; on the surrealists, Thomas Ferenczi, 'Jean Paulhan et les problèmes du langage', *Cahiers dada surréalistes* 4 (1970), 45–63; Dominique Baudouin, 'Jeux de mots surréalistes: l'expérience du proverbe', *Symposium* 24 (1970), pp. 297, 301.

[75] Wilde, 'Phrases and Philosophies for the Use of the Young', *Works*, p. 1113.

[76] John Rickman, 'On Quotations', in *Selected Contributions to Psycho-Analysis* (London, 1957), p. 40.

[77] Proverbs as a variety of cliché: Anton C. Zijderveld, *On Clichés: The Supersedure of Meaning by Function in Modernity* (London, 1979), p. 16. The distinction is upheld by Paul Pickrel, 'Identifying Clichés', *College English* 47 (1985), p. 256.

[78] Besides the classic Roger Brown and Albert Gilman, 'The Pronouns of Power and Solidarity', in Thomas A. Sebeok, ed., *Style in Language* (Cambridge, Mass., 1960), pp. 253–76, there is, for example, Penelope Brown and Stephen Levinson, 'Universals in Language Use: Politeness Phenomena', in Esther N. Goody, ed., *Questions and Politeness* (Cambridge, 1978), pp. 52–289.

[79] On Scotland, Kelly, *Complete Collection*, 'Introduction'. On 'larger units', Florian Coulmas, 'On the Sociolinguistic Relevance of Routine Formulas', *Journal of Pragmatics* 3 (1979), 234–66.

[80] Ong, 'Romantic Difference and Technology', in *Rhetoric, Romance and Technology* (Ithaca and London, 1971), p. 275.

[81] 'Existed before books': D'Israeli, 'Philosophy of Proverbs, p. 417; 'not books': Wade, *Select Proverbs*, p. xix.

4

THE LANGUAGE OF QUACKERY IN ENGLAND, 1660–1800

Roy Porter

It is no accident that Apollo is god of both poetry and medicine, for the captivating power of song to move and soothe has always been seen to resemble the healing power of the word in sickness.[1] From Greek 'incubation' therapy (in which the god spoke to the sick in dreams), through the bedside manner of the traditional clinician right up to Freud's psychoanalytical 'talking cure', language has ever been crucial to the profession and practice of medicine.[2]

Yet the healing power of the word has often seemed to organised medicine an ambiguous gift, especially since the seventeenth-century Scientific Revolution embraced a philosophical nominalism which preached radical distrust of language. For the New Science's empirical epistomology denounced as a pernicious confusion that traditional marriage of words and things, names and power, endorsed by Scholasticism, by magic, and not least by Christianity itself ('in the beginning was the Word'). To prevent such contamination, indeed to prevent diabolism, reality and its verbal signs had to be systematically distinguished (so argued Bacon, Hobbes and Locke), otherwise truth and humanity would fall victims alike to the idols of the market place, tribe, cave and theatre. 'Words are wise men's counters,' pronounced Hobbes, 'they do but reckon by them; but they are the money of fools', a view echoed by the infant Royal Society's motto: *nullius in verba*, 'on the word [authority] of no-one'.[3]

Thereafter, the role of the healing word in medicine's armamentarium was always liable to suspicion, as Molière's anti-doctor satires show.[4] Therapies such as Mesmerism, relying on the physician's silver tongue, have continued to be suspect both to medical orthodoxy itself and to the public.[5] After all, if, as science teaches, Nature obeys the mechanical laws of cause and effect, mere words should not conquer diseases; and if they seem to, doesn't that betray a psychological sleight of hand, at best the work of 'imagination' or 'suggestion'?

In such a positivist intellectual climate, the proliferation of quacks ('swarms of pretended Physicians') in the century following the Restoration, was bound to fan controversy and scandal, for quacks (as even their name suggests) depended so heavily upon language, the gift of the gab, both for winning customers in the first place, and then for curing them (or at least producing the illusion of a cure). Quacks seemed to be making themselves heard everywhere (it was claimed in 1741, with some exaggeration, that no less than a quarter of the column inches of newspapers were filled with advertisements). Hence regular practitioners took it as their public duty – it was also, doubtless, their private interest – to mark out these empirics, 'advertising physicians' and 'pseudo-medici' as a public nuisance, indeed a health hazard. Luckily, physicians claimed, such cheats and frauds were instantly distinguishable from honest practitioners, for they condemned themselves out of their own mouths. They were indeed all 'mouth', blowing the gaff on themselves by vaporous rhetoric and gibberish. An exposé of this flummery, *The Cheats of London Exposed*, explained: 'They have nothing to recommend them but a consumate effrontery; and no other means of palming their pestiferous compounds upon the unwary, than groundless assurances and insolent detractions.'[6] Throughout the Georgian century, quack hunting continued, and it took as its targets the gamut of alleged evils created by these unlicensed practitioners (secret nostrums were dangers to health, quacks were profiteers who exploited sickness and undercut skilled practice, etc.). But the final indictment against the quack was always that he was *vox et praeterea nihil*, a windbag spouting what Ned Ward called 'senseless cant'.[7] In an age scandalised by how readily society was duped by all kinds of false appearances, by financial speculation and 'bubbles', by counterfeiting, by fashion, show, hypocrisy, and not least, royal 'pretenders', this was fearsome indeed.

Irregular practitioners answered back, of course. They did so not by celebrating the mystique of the word, but by shouting: *tu quoque*. Those really guilty of cashing in on the power of medical language to seduce the sick were (quacks argued) the pillars of orthodoxy themselves. Empirics never tired of lambasting pukka physicians for larding their speech with Latin and Greek mumbo-jumbo, or for their ancestor veneration for Hippocrates, Galen and other antique authorities invoked to bemuse the public (a trait of the 'homicides of Warwick Lane', satirised even by physicians themselves such as Samuel Garth, in his best-selling poem, 'The Dispensary').[8] Neither did surgeons escape more lightly. 'The greatest danger of his wound lies in the chirurgeon's hard words,' diagnoses Grimaldi in John Wilson's play *Belphegos*.[9]

Quacks, of course, made easy targets with their patter, showmanship and self-advertisement. But who could equal the faculty in ritual and palaver? Fashionable physicians themselves were sitting ducks with their rigmarole of coaches-and-six and running footmen ('a travelling sign post to draw in customers'),[10] and other devices for drumming up custom (the canny young physician, suggested Smollett, would be 'ordering himself to be called from church, alarming the neighbourhood with knocking at his door in the night, receiving sudden messages in places of resort, and inserting his cures by way of news in the daily papers').[11] Not surprisingly, therefore, for every anti-quack tirade, a squib was fired back against the ignorant learnedness of College hocus-pocus, such as *Medicina flagellata, or the Doctor Scarify'd* (1721), or *A Dose for the Doctor* (1759) by 'Gregory Glyster', with its 'analisation of such Aesculapian imposition' as 'large sounds with little meaning' and 'medical mystery'.

The faculty was thus hoist with its own petard. Its accusation that market-place medicine hinged on linguistic showmanship boomeranged. Indeed, the Augustan public was deeply cynical about official medicine's tricks with words. See, for example, how in his *London Tradesman* Robert Campbell offered a disillusioned 'receipt to make a modern doctor', stressing medicine's phoney front of jargon and glitter:

> To acquire this Art of Physic, requires only being acquainted with a few Books, to become Master of a few Aphorisms and Common-place Observations, to purchase a Latin Diploma from some Mercenary College, to step into a neat Chariot and put on a grave Face, a Sword and a long wig; then M. D. is flourished to the Name, the pert Coxcomb is dubbed a Doctor, and has a License to kill as many as trust him with their Health.[12]

– an account followed by an equally scathing unveiling of the cant of the apothecary, who 'must be able to call all the Army of Poisons by their proper Heathenish Names, and . . . must understand the Physical Cabala, the mysterious Character of an unintelligible Doctor's Scrawl.'[13] Or take depictions of physicians on the stage. George Bernard Shaw was not the first British playwright to expose the doctor's deceptions. In late eighteenth-century comedies such as Harry Rowe's *The Sham Doctor* or Peter Pinder's *Physic and Delusion*, it was regular doctors, not quacks, who were satirised as being all kill and no skill, and Rowe's doctor, Dr Potion, abused quacks simply because they threatened his livelihood:[14]

> Dearest, dearest Dr. Motion,
>   How these cursed Quacks increase!
> Oh that they were sunk i'th'ocean,
>   For they steal our golden fleece.

Or consider the scene in *Tom Jones* in which Fielding shows the surgeon, summoned to treat the hero after his fight with Northerton, being questioned by the lieutenant:[15]

> 'I hope, sir,' said the lieutenant, 'the skull is not fractured.'
> 'Hum,' cries the surgeon, 'fractures are not always the most

dangerous symptoms. Contusions and lacerations are often attended with worse phænomena . . .' 'I hope,' says the lieutenant, 'there are no such symptoms here.' 'Symptoms,' answered the surgeon, 'are not always regular nor constant . . . I was once, I remember, called to a patient who had received a violent contusion in his tibia by which the exterior cutis was lacerated, so that there was profuse sanguinary discharge; and the interior membranes were so divellicated, that the os or bone very plainly appeared through the aperture of the vulnus or wound. Some febril symptoms intervening at the same time (for the pulse was exuberant and indicated some phlebotomy), I aprehended an immediate mortification . . . But perhaps I do not make myself perfectly well understood?' 'No, really,' answered the lieutenant, 'I cannot say I understood a syllable.'

What these examples suggest is that Georgian opinion, while being angered by the hyperbole of irregular medicine, was no less aware that faculty physic could be tarred with the same brush: when the clap-cure surgeon John Marten accused his rivals of arrant quackery, one of them, John Spinke, retorted that this was a case of the 'pot calling the kettle Black A–e'.[16]

Here lies an important lesson. Historians of medicine have traditionally sided with regular medicine, deriding quacks as evil or absurd.[17] In linguistic terms, this would be the equivalent of implying that faculty physic spoke 'standard English' – that normal, perfect, translucent, neutral, objective medium of communication – whereas quacks used some degenerate argot or jargon (one hesitates to say quacks had their own pidgin). But this begs many questions. Faculty-talk and quackspeak need to be treated symmetrically. Both orthodox and irregular medicine generated their own linguistic sub-cultures, whose vocabulary, tones and speech mannerisms, though somewhat distinct, played similar socially and even therapeutically active roles.

Indeed, it is important not to view the regular and the quack medicines of two or three centuries ago as polar opposites. They were not white and black, nor even chalk and cheese. It is the similarities, indeed the overlap, between the practices which need emphasis. There is no room to clinch this point here, but a few examples may illustrate how the putative divides between regular and quack medicine often involve points of contact.[18] Quacks lived by nostrums, and elite physicians often attacked them. But plenty of orthodox practitioners lent their names to, or made money out of, patent medicines or proprietary pills made to secret formulae.[19] Dr Paul Chamberlain, F.R.C.P., sold teething necklaces, and Dr Robert James made his fortune from his best-selling febrifuge 'powders' for which Horace Walpole had such a 'superstitious veneration'.[20] Similarly, many quack and commercial preparations went under the names of great doctors, whether or not they profited from them personally. An anti-rabies preparation was called 'Dr Mead's powder', and a medicinal chocolate was known as 'Sir Hans Sloane's Milk Chocolate'.[21] Indeed, many regular doctors had no ethical qualms about nostrum-mongering. As John Hunter wrote to Edward Jenner about an emetic which Jenner had developed:

> Dear Jenner, – I am puffing of your tartar as the tartars of all tartars, and have given it to several physicians to make trial, but have had no account yet of the success. Had you not better let a bookseller have it to sell, as Glass of Oxford did his magnesia? Let it be called Jenner's Tartar Emetic, or anybody's else that you please. If that mode will do, I will speak to some, viz, Newberry, etc.[22]

What applies to nostrums applies to other spheres too, and it would be a forlorn and historically misguided enterprise, I suggest, to draw hard and fast lines between orthodox practitioners and quacks, using criteria such as integrity, scientific method or therapeutic efficacy. Of course, some practitioners were formally qualified and others were not; of course, certain therapies worked and some did not. But such litmus tests, far from revealing essential specific differences between distinct modes of practice, merely show how confused reality was, for it is not at all clear that certified doctors, or *London Dispensary* pharmaceuticals, enjoyed better success rates than their rivals. There were indeed different sorts of practitioners, but the differences were ones of style not kind; practitioners shade into each other along a continuum, and external markings bamboozle as much as they reveal. Take for example the question of qualifications.

Many quacks had no formal medical education, and some who styled themselves 'doctor' had no right to.[23] Yet other so-called quacks had an excellent medical training and title, John Pechey, for example, in the latter half of the seventeenth century, having received an apprenticeship from his father and being a graduate of Oxford and a licentiate of the College of Physicians – he noted how 'many men make it their business to ridicule the Public Way of Practice, because it thwarts their Private Interest'.[24] A century later James Graham (the future 'master-quack') studied at Edinburgh University under Cullen and Black. Indeed, exactly as with scores of regular practitioners, quacks such as William Brodum and Ebenezer Sibly bought their M.D.'s from St Andrews or Aberdeen University. In any case, are we to deny that Nicolas Culpeper or Dr Johnson's friend Robert Levet were medically competent merely because they lacked formal training? In many other ways it would be artificial to polarise quack and orthodox medicine: they overlapped and mingled.

A glance at the conditions of medical practice in seventeenth- and especially eighteenth-century England should make it clear why this was so.[25] Though regular medicine was legally recognised, and indeed institutionalised in the College of Physicians, the Incorporation of Surgeons and the Apothecaries' Company, it held no monopoly and its privileges were few. In the days before science and the laboratory transformed the organisation of medicine (through germ theory, diagnostic technology, and antiseptic surgery in the sterile hospital), educated laymen could speak man-to-man with their physicians, and (as Nicholas Jewson has stressed) patients who paid the piper called the therapeutic tune.[26] Given that traditional medicine's armoury had few counters to the major killing and crippling diseases, small wonder that patients shopped around in the medical market place, picking and choosing amongst the range of drug therapies on offer – regular, quack, popular and traditional.

It was thus rather a precarious milieu for the qualified practitioner. Few of his cures 'worked', in the sense of being sure to make the sick well.[27] Hence the physician fell back on other qualities; and so modes of address and skills in communication could thus be crucially important for the clinician. Polite society expected its physicians to behave and speak like gentlemen, which is why an Oxbridge education and familiarity with Classical culture and polite learning remained passports to success for the fashionable doctor, despite the fact that Oxbridge medical training was patently inferior to that given by Leiden, Edinburgh and elsewhere. And a good bedside manner – comforting and consoling where medicine could not cure – was, quite properly, as books of medical ethics and etiquette pointed out, the *sine qua non* of the humane as well as the fashionable clinician. The doyens of the profession in the late eighteenth century – men such as William Hunter, William Heberden, Matthew Baillie – were all admired for their culture and breeding.[28] The 'public relations' language of orthodox bedside physic is a subject that would richly repay study.

But in the rest of this chapter I shall explore the language of the quacks, by whom I mean those practitioners (honest or not, skilful or not) who practised principally in the open market, treating an anonymous clientele of patients by the sale of nostrums, and making themselves, their services and their medicines known through publicity; in other words, those (Oliver Goldsmith dubbed them 'the advertising professors')[29] who developed the entrepreneurial dimension of medicine. By exploring the linguistic sub-culture of this expanding sector, I hope to highlight the language of salesmanship and the culture of health in early modern

England. But I also aim to pinpoint the historical specificity of quackery, seen not primarily in terms of fraud or conspiracy, but as the business side of medicine, the rise of the medical market place. The history of quack medicine needs much rethinking and in-depth research, as indeed do medical entrepreneurship and medical economics in general.[30] Dispelling *canards* about quacks is not easy, however, for few private papers and business records survive. Most medical projectors can be approached only through their own self-constructed personae, or the jaundiced caricatures of others.[31] Hence in the body of this chapter I shall explore the social presence of quacks through analysis of their *language*, their own self-presentation in the public forum.

How are we to read quacks' own performance, their bid for the public ear and eye through oratory, handbills, broadsides, verse, street-theatre, and, increasingly, pamphlets and newspaper publicity? One wishes the ethnography of speaking would offer hints for such an analysis, but it is in fact of little help, on account of the preoccupations of the discipline.[32] For sociolinguistics has focused on community speech-patterns within linguistic sub-cultures, examining the conventions governing group use of patois and dialect, pidgin and creole, and probing tacit meanings in the dialectics of communication. Medical sociologists have rightly been eager to learn from the insights of such sociolinguistics, and fears about today's communications breakdown in clinical medicine have spurred research into the 'scripts' of doctor–patient interchange.[33] Drawing on ethnomethodology, studies have analysed the growing 'communications gap' between medical jargon and the vernacular within the hierarchical structures of professional medicine, sometimes harking back to a putative pre-industrial age when patients and doctors allegedly spoke the same language, and patients could negotiate their complaints on a linguistic par with their physicians.[34] Valuable though such medical sociolinguistics is, it is not, however, pertinent to the case in hand. For their concern with decoding doctor–patient dialogue is almost by definition inappropriate to the dynamics of market-place medicine. It is akin to a hermeneutics of chamber music, where what is here needed is a semantics of the solo.

For the speech of quackery is almost entirely one-way: a monologue, harangue, soliloquy, an act of salesmanship instilling confidence, exercising persuasion, disarming resistance.[35] Unlike group healing, psychoanalysis's talking-cure, or even routine clinical medicine, quackery supposes an audience of strangers which is relatively silent and passive – indeed, 'patient'. Though not 'captive', it is receptive (who doesn't want health?): its awed silence means consent. The quacks' clienteles are like the auditors of the demagogue, theatre-goers, or a preacher's congregation.[36] One-way speech of this kind has received little attention from sociolinguists or medical sociologists.

The words which quack doctors spoke were stage-managed within a larger performance. The traditional English quack, operating like his models, the Italian *ciarlatani*, in the market place, prefaced his act by establishing a public space (superior mountebanks had mobile stages or benches, whereas lesser charlatans just threw down their cloak on the highway).[37] He appeared in eye-catching garb, and was often accompanied by a stooge – a harlequin, clown, or zany – whose job it was to soften up the audience with fooling, dumb-show, doggerel, conjuring and tumbling. The act would be backed up by props such as cats, snakes, monkeys, and a gallimaufrey of gallipots, stuffed alligators, chemical or alchemical apparatus, surgical instruments, testimonials from satisfied customers and 'patents, certificates, medals and great seals, by which the several princes of Europe have testified their particular respect and esteem for the doctor'.[38] Some quacks did all the patter themselves. Others – especially foreigners with broken English – left the role of barker and the big-talk to their zany, and played the silent or mysterious sage. Like all the best circus acts, quack routines typically blended the familiar and time-honoured with the original and bizarre.[39] The audience was to be won over through a stylised performance which may have had its own therapeutic impact or placebo effect as a mini talking-cure.

The tricks of the quack doctors' tirade are familiar. They decried imposture and ineptitude, laid claim to infallible nostrums, and pledged to heal the incurable. Most had their gimmick: no cure, no money; bargain packs, free pamphlets with every purchase or a silver measuring spoon, sugar-coated pills, violin-shaped bottles,[40] treatment gratis for unfortunates or soldiers back from the wars, and so forth. Some performed dazzling stunts – their side-kicks would swallow 'poison', and then make miracle recoveries thanks to wonder antidotes. Others gave reassurance, promising confidentiality for those suffering from unmentionable disorders.[41] And above all they exploited the psychology of persuasion, mingling hard and soft sells, excitement and amusement, bathos, pathos, surprise, titillation. In playing on psychological susceptibilities, they did not miss a trick – witness, for example, this broadside publicising James Graham's lectures and healing acts:

NOW OR NEVER

You must come forward to hear and to see, and to receive what never more can be heard or seen in London, or in any other place, so long as the world endures.

GRATIS – LECTURES, and a Display of the Celestial

Brilliancy of the Temple of Health, before its final close and dissolution.

Dr. GRAHAM'S FAREWELL LAST BLESSING, and most PATHETIC EXHORTATIONS to the inhabitants of London and Westminster.

As the Sale of Dr. GRAHAM'S Furniture and Apparatus is to be next week, he desires respectfully to inform the Public, that THIS, and EVERY EVENING till the Sale, he will have the honour of delivering Gratis, a LECTURE on certain means (without medicines) of preserving life, till at least an hundred and fifty years of age. In the course of the Lecture, he will show mankind, how grossly they have been blinded and imposed upon, and robbed of their health, property, and lives, by the Physicians and Apothecaries.

The rooms are now crowded, and over flow every night more and more; as all London, especially the Ladies, seem determined to see this celebrated place – this enchanting elysium! in full glory, before its final dissolution – as it now exceeds in splendour, elegance, brilliancy and magnificence, every Royal Palace in the world.

Singing by a Young LADY.

†††Ladies are requested to come very early.

The Lecture begins at Half past Seven o'clock.

Free admission to the whole, to every Lady and Gentleman who purchases, price only one Shilling, The Guardian of Health, Long Life, and Happiness!

N.B. As the Temple has overflowed by several hundred persons, each of the three last nights, those Ladies and Gentlemen who wish earnestly to be admitted, must come, indeed, very early.[42]

– all of which bears out Dr Johnson's dictum in the *Idler* that 'promise, large promise, is the soul of an advertisement'.[43]

Quack doctors perfected the ringmaster's patter, what John Wilmot, Earl of Rochester, in self-parody called their 'damn'd unintelligible gybberish'.[44] Their cadences aimed at the heart, the pocket, the eye, and their skilful blend of the technical, the preposterous, and the humorous, are all parodied to a tee by Ned Ward in his *London Spy* vignette of the charlatan in full cry:

Gentlemen, you that have a Mind to be Mindful of preserving a Sound Mind in a Sound Body, that is, as the Learned Physician Doctor *Honorificabinitudinatibusque* has it, Manus Sanague in Cobile Sanaquorum, may here at the expence of twopence, furnish himself with a parcel, which tho' it is but small containeth mighty things of great Use and Wonderful Operation in the Bodies of Mankind, against all Distempers, whether Homogeneal or Complicated; whether deriv'd from your Parents, got by Infection, or proceeding from an ill Habit of your own Body.

In the first place, Gentlemen, I here present you with a little inconsiderable Pill to look at, you see not much bigger than a Corn of Pepper, yet in this Diminutive Pampharmica so powerful in effect, and of such excellent Vertues, that if you have Twenty Distempers lurking in the Mass of Blood, it shall give you just Twenty Stools, and every time it operates, it carries off a Distemper; but if your Blood's Wholesome, and your Body Sound, it will work you no more than the same quantity of Ginger bread. I therefore call it, from the admirable Qualities, *Pilula Ton Dobula*, which signifies in the Greek, *The Touch Stone of Nature*; For by taking of this Pill you will truly discover what state of Health or Infirmity your constitution is then under . . . [and so forth].[45]

Dissecting the quack's spiel more minutely, we find its appeal characteristically lies in a rhetoric combining flattery and assurance, hyperbole and bombast. Addressing the public, not his peers, the quack typically tried first to soften up his auditors with flattery: '*Beloved Women*, who are the *Admirablest Creatures* that ever God created under the *Canopy of Heaven*, to whom therefore, I have devoted my studies to the preserving of your Beauty, Health, Vigour, Strength and Long Life.'[46] He then needed to establish his own credentials, by stating his titles and boasting a roll-call of eminent cures. For example, though modestly denying being 'an infallible worker of miracles', James Graham offered himself not just as 'a graduate Physician of a British College, as an experienced and loving Minister of NATURE', but as 'a student of that university of truth . . . whose omnipotent Founder and eternal Chancellor is the infinitely glorious Creator and Preserver of the Universe'.[47] With an eye to the *ton*, John Taylor, self-styled 'chevalier', liked to fanfare himself as 'The Chevalier John Taylor, Ophthalminator, Pontifical, Imperial, and Royal, who treated Pope Benedict XIV, Augustus III, King of Poland, Frederick V, King of Denmark and Norway and Frederick Adolphus, King of Sweden.'[48]

Before the nineteenth century, however, quacks did not commonly 'graduate themselves',[49] that is, regale themselves with high falutin but phoney academic qualifications; Quacks' Colleges were a nineteenth-century invention. It was much more common – and clearly considered more impressive – to assume social rank or personal pre-eminence: hence quacks often portrayed themselves as experienced 'artists' and 'masters' of their arcana, having acquired profound wisdom through lengthy travels and by sitting at the feet of sages.[50]

Next they bragged of universal curative properties for their nostrums. John Newman's pills were 'never-failing',[51] and William Patence ('dentist and physician to several of the Royal family') similarly presented his 'Universal Medicine or Supreme Pills' as a panacea with the usual rigmarole of knock-down prices and 'money back if not satisfied' guarantees:[52]

> I shall offer no apology for my medicine, which is well-known to give ease and satisfaction in palsies, gout, rheumatism, piles, fistulas, cancers of any sort, King's Evil, hereditary infections, jaundice, green sickness, St. Anthony's Fire, convulsions, consumptions, scorbutic diseases, pains in the head, brain, temple, arteries, face, nose, mouth, and limbs, for which nothing upon the earth surer, softer or better.
>
> The Universal Medicine also restores lost hearing and sight, renews the vital and animal vitalities, gives complexion to the face, liveliness to the whole structure, and many times has given unexperienced relief on the verge of eternity . . . if they do not answer the end proposed, I will return the Money. The real *worth of a box is Ten Guineas*, but for the benefit of all, with proper directions, it is sold for three shillings; with personal advice, ten and sixpence.

And, of course, the brand-labels of the preparations were carefully chosen to evoke their promise. Certain names traded on the mystique of their begetter – Dr James's Powders, or Daffy's Elixir, immortalising a Stuart clergyman and still on sale this century. Most incorporated hyperbole, sailing under such flags as the 'Infallible Powder',[53] 'The Only True Plague Water',[54] 'The HERCULEON ANTIDOTE',[55] or the 'Sovereign Cordial'.[56] Or take 'Rose's Balsamick Elixir',

> The Most Noble Medicine that Art can produce . . . a signal Restorative for Consumptive persons and there is not such another preparation in the whole world . . .
>
> It cures the *English Frenchify'd* beyond all the other medicines upon the face of the Earth. It removes all pains in 3 or 4 doses and makes any man, tho' *rotten as a Pear*, to be *sound as a suckling lamb*.[57]

As a contemporary indictment, *The Modern Quacks*, remarked,[58] 'at the Head of each of these Remedies (being part of the Bait)',

> I find some very inviting Term, such as *Angelic, Royal, Incomparable, Odoriferous . . . Specifick*, (which is now become the universal Epithet, if it were but for a Remedy for broken-winded or founder'd Horses; so that in a little time we shall doubtless have *Specificks* to kill Rats and Mice (about which their Time and Medicines would be better employ'd) as there are already for Lice and Fleas) and most of them *Admirable, Infallible*, or *Never-failing*.

Alongside verbal magniloquence went the use of 'hard names'[59] – real or bogus jargon calling to mind scientific discoveries, the occult or the craft mysteries. This orotund cant, making free with neologisms, doubtless traded on the spell-binding associations of conjuring, the lure of the obscure, the magic of the arcane, while adding a bravura topping of sheer verbal pyrotechnics.[60]

> I am a High-German Doctor [announced a German quack of the seventeenth century] who, by the blessing of Aesculapius on his great Pains, Travels and Nocturnal Lucubrations, has attained to a greater share of knowledge than any person before him was ever known to do.
>
> IMPROMIS. Gentlemen, I present you with my 'Universal Solutive' which corrects all the Cacochymick and Cachexical Disease of the Intestines, Hydrocephalous, Epileptick Fits, Flowing of the Gall and many other distempers not hitherto distinguished by name.
>
> Secondly. My 'Friendly Pills' call'd the Never Failing Helogenes, which by dilating and expanding the Gelastick Muscles, first of all discovered by myself.
>
> They clear the Officina Intelligentiae, correct the Exorbitancy of the Spleen, mundify the Hypogastrium, comfort the Sphincter and are an excellent remedy against Prosopo Chlorosis or Green sickness.
>
> They operate seven several ways viz. Hypnotically, Hydrotically, Cathartically, Proppysinatically, Hydragogcially, Pulmatically, and lastly Synecdochically, by corroborating the whole Oeconomia Animalis.[61]

In their conviction that jargon was a crowd-winner, quacks clearly thought they were taking a leaf out of the book of orthodox physic, whose opaque verbiage was notorious. Witness the comment in Thomas Shadwell's play, *The Humourists*, where Crazy and Raymund have just been consulting with Dr Pullin, the orthodox French physician:

CRAZY: Is there any one symptom which I have not had? – Oh –
have I not had your carbuncula, acbrocordones, mermecii,
thymi, all sorts of ulcers superficial and profound, callous,
cancerous, fistilous.

RAYMUND: Hey-brave Crazy! Thou has terms enough to set up
two reasonable mountebanks.

CRAZY: Have I not had your pustulae, crustatae, and sine
crustis verucae, cristae, tophi, ossis, caries, chryonyatelephia,
disepulotica.

RAYMUND: What; art thou going to raise the devil with these
hard words?[62]

Within this rhetorical universe, quacks were deft at manipulating
allusions which carried 'pull' and prestige.[63] Many conspicuously
annexed the buzz-words of natural philosophy, aiming to blind with
science. Some boasted omniscience in the branches of natural philosophy, as for example Gustavus Katterfelto with his expertise in the
'Philosophical, Mathematical, Optical, Magnetical, Electrical, Physical,
Chemical, Pneumatic, Hydraulic, Hydrostatic, Proetic, Stenographic,
Blaenical and Caprimatic Arts'.[64] Brand names often drew on the
authority of seats of learning, such as the 'Oxon Pills' for scurvy (what
else?), or on the fame of top doctors and scientists: 'Dr Boerhaave's
Aurea Medicina', for example, could be bought alongside 'Dr Radcliffe's
Famous Purging Elixir'.[65] Similarly, the 'Chevalier' Taylor endlessly
name-dropped the geniuses he had met on his travels – Boerhaave,
Haller, Morgagni, Winslow, Monro, Linnaeus and the Hunters. He
dedicated his monograph, *An exact account of two hundred and forty-
three diseases to which the eye and its coverings are exposed* (1749), to the
Royal College of Physicians of Edinburgh, with gratitude for the
'Remembrance I have, of the Attention which some of your Body judged
me worthy of, by so frequently favouring me with their Presence at my
Lectures, and Method of Practice, and by their giving me such undeniable
Proofs of the good Opinion they have of me, from the many they have
recommended to my Care.'[66] Many nostrum-mongers thus sought cachet
by latching on to the lights of science and physic. The 'Pilula Salutiferens'
was claimed by its proprietor to have been prepared first by the 'famous
Dr. Sydenham for his own use, who afterwards prescribed it with
incredible success throughout the vast extent of his Laborious practice'.[67]
Another vendor traded on the prestige of Robert Boyle as 'the inventor
of an Effectual Pill': 'That the world may no longer be deceived by the
false and ignorant pretenders to Physick, of which this City has more than
enough; I present to all the ingenious, the most *Effectual Pills* of which
the ever-honoured Esquire Boyle was the Author.'[68] Dr Paul Chamber-

lain, marketer of a teething necklace for children, staked his claims to the secrets of dental health in 'a treatise dedicated to the Royal Society',[69] and Daffy's Elixir similarly bore a label attesting the blessing of 'Dr. King, physician to Charles II and the late learned Dr. Radcliffe'.[70] When early in his career he made great play of the vogue science of electricity (calling one of his medicines the 'electrical aether'), James Graham traced his own pedigree back to Cullen, Whytt, Priestley and Franklin.[71]

Passing off remedies in this way as the brainchildren of great minds was plausible because regular physicians themselves lent their names to market brands. And so the practice multiplied, with Dr Adair being outraged at the end of the eighteenth century to find that 'the names of FOTHERGILL, HUNTER and SOLANDER have been prostituted to those knavish purposes'[72] – and all of this exemplifying how a key strategy of 'the advertising professors' lay in appropriating the prestige of scientific discovery and progress. As argued below, the leading Stuart and Georgian quacks were not repudiating the physic of the orthodox, honoured and famous, but rather hoping to hitch their own wagon to it. This contrasts strongly with a key counter-current in the nineteenth century, when 'fringe' medicine repudiated the philosophy of orthodoxy and the values of polite, commercial society. Yet even in making use of the symbols of the New Science, empirics also clung, eclectically and opportunistically, to the selling-power of the traditional cosmology and arts of magic, alchemy and astrology; antagonisms between old and new learning were felt, if felt they were at all, only within the high temple of science proper.[73]

Take, for instance, quack medicine's manipulation of the 'natural symbols' of the material universe. Quacks needed to suggest they were masters of universal power, adepts at tapping the arcane forces of nature and distilling them into the compass of a pill.[74] Now hinting at the New Science, now harking back to old occultism, nostrum-mongers made great play with the associations of the elements and the precious metals. Mercury, a specific for syphilis, united the secrets of alchemy and astrology with the vaunted efficacy of the new 'heavy metal' medicines. Gold remained another potent icon of natural power, appearing, for example, in the form of Potable Gold ('aurum potabile') and in the best-selling 'Cordial Balm of Gold' manufactured by the late eighteenth-century Jewish vendor, Dr Solomon from Liverpool, who in his *Guide to Health* (dedicated to Lord Mansfield) described his Balm as 'extracted from the *seed of gold*, which our alchemists and philosophers have so long sought after in vain'.[75]

No less potent were the heavens. 'Solar' medicines enjoyed a great vogue, perhaps focusing the Enlightenment's fascination with light.[76] There were James Graham's pills, 'a pure extract drawn by the sunbeams',[77] Lyonel Lockyer's 'Pilulae Radiis Solis Extractae',[78] which Lockyer astutely stipulated were to be swallowed *before* one fell sick; 'England's Solar Pill against the Scurvy', Fletcher's 'Panacea', a 'medicine of a Solar (or Gold like) nature',[79] and, not least, Dr George Jones's 'Famous Friendly Pill', 'being the Tincture of the Sun, having dominion from the same light, giving Relief and Comfort to all mankind . . . a wonder among other wonderful medicines'.[80] Dr Ebenezer Sibly, empiric and mason, marketed a patented 'Solar Tincture', but probably made more money from his 'Lunar Tincture', which, with its hints at menstruation, was aimed at female complaints.[81]

The appeal to science was thus often complemented with the more traditional aura of the occult and of alchemy. Yet the 'advertising professors' clearly thought the kudos of science invaluable, for no proprietary drugs boasted of exploding the new-fangled heresies of modern science and physic. True, various remedies were still marketed whose allure was essentially homely, for example 'Mother Bedlicot's Drink for the Dropsy', or such folksy drugs (mocked in *The Modern Quacks*) as a 'Coal-heaver's Decoction, an Old-Woman's Plaister and Oyntment, a Tarpaulin's East India Oyl'.[82] But what is noteworthy, especially in contrast to Victorian popular medicines,[83] is the absence of a call to radical alternatives. Eighteenth-century proprietary medicines do not carry primitivist 'back to the earth', 'back to nature', backwoods purity crusades;[84] quite the reverse, for Georgian empirics and their nostrums basked in the cultural values of the Enlightenment.[85]

Eager for all kinds of legitimation, quack medicines also latched on to religion, or, as a critic succinctly put it, 'you will say you committed yourself to *Providence*, as well as *Prunes*'.[86] A small number of healers claimed a personal thaumaturgical mission, as perhaps James Graham, who in his later years styled himself 'Servant of the Lord, O. W. L.' (O Wondrous Love), or the theatrical designer Philip de Loutherbourg, who practised mesmeric healing and claimed to have 'received a most glorious power from the Lord Jehovah viz; the gift of healing all manner of diseases incident to the human body, such as blindness, deafness, lameness, cancers, loss of speach and palsies.'[87] Others appealed to Christian healing through charity, as for instance Henry Hippen, whose regular cures cost forty shillings but 'FOR THOSE THAT HAVE NO MONEY AND DESIRE IT FOR GOD's SAKE, HE WILL CURE GRATIS.'[88] But most common in nostrum publicity were verbal hints of supernatural qualities. Sometimes miracle cures were alluded to ('miraculous anodyne necklaces'); sometimes divine physic authenticated by the Bible, as in the many 'Balms of Gilead' on offer.[89] Often the religious overtone was ecumenical, and not even specifically Christian. Thus, for example, James Graham evoked pagan mythological healing with his

Temple of Health and Hymen, equipped with its Apollo Room, and with a priestess styled Hebe Vestina, The Goddess of Youth and Health (significantly Graham occupied the Adelphi Building off the Strand, designed by the Adam brothers, at the height of the vogue for Neo-Classical).[90] Perhaps surprisingly, even 'Mecca Pills' were on offer (marketed by the Jew, Dr Solomon);[91] here it was presumably the oriental rather than the specifically Islamic references that were meant to catch the eye.

What may be most intriguing in the nostrum trade's annexation of holiness is the range of references overtly to Roman Catholicism. Saints and Catholic worthies are commonly invoked, as for example in the 'Pulvus Benedictus' ('rather a miracle than a medicine'),[92] the 'Anodyne Necklaces' made from the bones of St Hugh,[93] and Fuller's Benedictine Pills;[94] but there is also Friar's Balsam, the 'Catholique Medicine' ('Catholique' having the connotation of 'universal'),[95] and most explicitly of all, Dr Trigg's 'Golden Vatican Pill', at two shillings a box.[96] Of course, healing and holiness are etymologically of a piece, and 'patter' comes from the *Pater Noster*, but the prominence of Catholic thaumaturgy is noteworthy in a land where 'No Popery' was belligerent. It was, indeed, a source of great anxiety, with the author of *The Modern Quacks* demanding that all such 'Popish Trumpery' be cast into the fire, and lamenting over the anodyne necklaces,

> Ah England! England! that it ever should be said of thee, that even the meanest *Masters* of thy Families (since *Popery* and *Superstition* have been banish'd hence) should permit, or the *Mistresses* thereof desire, such Childish *Trinkets* (fit only to amuse Ideots or Fools) to be brought in, or hung about their Children's Necks, in Expectation of Advantage by the same?[97]

The author feared that medicine chests would prove to be Trojan horses: unable to convert Britain by open proselytising, the Vatican was clandestinely infiltrating the nation through its ailments. A few eighteenth-century operators such as Joshua Ward did indeed have Jacobite sympathies, many had spent time travelling in Catholic Europe, and, of course, plenty of the quacks operating in England were natives of France and Italy, where it was routine to capitalise on the healing powers of hallowed waters, rosary-style beads and the laying on of hands. But, saddled with a confession which regarded the mystical and sacramental apparatus of healing as superstitious, vulgar and fetishistic, Protestant Englishmen had to quench their thirst for holy healing outside their own Church – either in the residual folklore of witchcraft and magic, or through the mystique of patent medicines. Such an interpretation, suggested by Keith Thomas,[98] in fact echoes the contemporary judgment of Lady Mary Wortley Montagu, that the relics of Popish superstition, expelled through the door, simply flooded back in again through the window, transmogrified into quackery:[99]

> The English are easyer tĥan any other Nation infatuated by the prospect of universal medicines, nor is there any country in the World where the Doctors raise such immense Fortunes. I attribute it to the Fund of Credulity which is in all Mankind. We have no longer faith in Miracles and Reliques, and therefore with the same Fury run after receits and Physicians. The same Money which 300 years ago was given for the Health of the Soul is now given for the Health of the Body, and by the same sort of People: Women and halfe-witted Men. In the countries where they have shrines and Images, Quacks are despis'd and Monks and Confessors find their account in managing the Fear and hope which rule the actions of the Multitude.

In addition to science and religion, medical entrepreneurs had an eye to the main chance of exploiting the suggestive power of language in other ways. Scores of seventeenth- and eighteenth-century nostrums and health advice pamphlets were marketed with brand-names, letterpress and tags in foreign tongues.[100] Of course, mirroring the kudos of orthodox physick, Latin was the favourite language, though a few, such as John Badger's 'Olbion' cordial, also squeezed in the occasional Greek maxim from Hippocrates. Nostrums whose very names were latinised include the 'Elixir Vitae' of Salvator Winter,[101] the 'Elixir Magnum Stomachicum' of Richard Stoughton,[102] Dr Pordage's 'Pilulae Anti-Scorbuticae',[103] Bromfield's 'Pilulae in Omnes Morbos',[104] Edward Jewel's 'Panaseton, or Extractum Humorale', Edward Andrew's 'Gremelli Pulmonates'[105] and Lyonel Lockyer's 'Pillulae Radiis Solis Extractae'.[106] There were numerous 'Aurum Potabile' and 'Aqua Coelestis' products, and one could also buy the 'Arcanum Magnum', the 'Solamen Miseris', the 'Arcanum Magnum', the 'Elixir Proprietatis', the 'Pilula Salutiferens', the 'Panchimagogum Febrifugum' and dozens besides.[107] Numerous quacks plumed themselves on their boasted classical erudition, John ('Chevalier') Taylor in particular claiming to lecture in 'the true Ciceronian, prodigiously difficult and never attempted in our language before'.[108] These pretensions were constantly ridiculed, as for example in an anonymous pamphlet of 1676, which accused the quack of engaging some 'friend that's Book-learn'd to correct the false English and sprucify the sence, and interlard it with Proverbial Latin and Cramp words, as a gammon of bacon is stuft with green herbs and cloaves . . .'[109] Throughout the century, in the endless pamphlet skirmishes involving quacks, many took great delight, not to mention inordinate space, in nitpicking rivals' French accents, Latin syntax and terminations.[110]

In wheeling in their batteries of classical technical terms, tags and proverbs quacks recognised that the medium was the message, and clearly hoped to have their cake and eat it. Conspicuous skills in learned languages would help to assimilate them to 'high medicine', while also commanding the awe of the ignorant. If the Classical words were all Greek to them, the *hoi polloi* would at least have to acknowledge that quack doctors belonged to the same stratum of society as genteel and learned professionals such as parsons and lawyers. In any case, it would be patronising to presume that none of the purchasers of proprietary medicines amongst the common people had any familiarity with Latin. And if a fair segment of quacks' clientele actually came from the more affluent and educated ranks – and some must have, for certain nostrums sold at prices up to half a guinea – Latin offered a cosy rapport between practitioner and customer, an earnest of ability.[111]

Classical tongues conjured up the mystique of venerable tradition. But hardly less common in quack medicines was an appeal to faraway places with strange-sounding names, peddled by practitioners claiming to hail from or to be steeped in the wisdom of distant parts. Pepys noted the xenophobia of the English: 'But Lord! to see the absurd nature of Englishmen, that cannot forebear laughing and jeering at anything that looks strange.'[112] Yet in medicine the foreign carried kudos, surely because so many of the leaders of the fine and performing arts in general in early modern England came from the Continent.[113]

There were indeed certain brews which traded on native loyalties, such as the 'Pilulae Londinenses', the 'British Pills',[114] the 'British Oil' and the 'Scots Pills' ('excellent after hard drinking');[115] but exoticism was seductive, and rich pickings lay in prospect for the foreign-born quack doctor coming from 'beyond the Seas' to do the English circuit. Up to the end of the seventeenth century, the Italian mountebank was perhaps most common, both in the flesh and caricatured in drama and satire. Generally licensed by the Crown, Italians such as Salvator Winter[116] – allegedly over ninety years old, and succeeded by his son – promoted elixirs of life, and, above all, poison antidotes, especially the 'Incomparable Orvietan',[117] the link with poisons being hardly surprising as Italy was synonymous in the public mind with Borgian skullduggery. French quacks were also much in evidence, offering themselves as non-pareil in treating the morbus Gallicus (or French pox) with remedies such as the 'Paris Pill';[118] but by the late seventeenth century, quacks seem to have hailed from all parts, High and Low Germans, and Germanic Jews, such as Dr Brodum and Dr Solomon, becoming common. A sprinkling of 'outlandish' cures even came from as far afield as Poland and Turkey, before the nineteenth century brought its massive invasion of alternative medical systems from the New World.[119]

Exotic tags for nostrums were clearly favoured as a selling feature. In 1698 Frederick van Neurenburg – 'just arrived'[120] – was offering a one-man Cook's tour round the pharmacopoeia, vending

> the *Persian Balsam* and Powder, which cures all Fluxe and sharp corrosive Humours in the Blood.
>
> The Asian Balm, the *American Balsam* and *Essence*, by the use of which the *Americans are generally strangers to the Gout*. The Japan Powder which expels all manner of worms. The Chinese Antidote for rheumatism. The *Empirical Pill* for the Ague. The *Grecian* and *Turkish Antidote* which prevents fainting. The *Arabian Antidote* that prevents and cures the Ptsick and Consumption. The *Balsam of Gilead* for internal pains . . . [etc.][121]

Trading on the mysteries of names, many quacks hinted that exotic wisdom had brushed off on to them on their serpentine travels, as for example:

> a most famous, German, Turkish and Imperial Physitian can shew his testimonials from Three Emperors, Nine Kings, as also from Seven Dukes, and Electoral Princes, as the Romish, Turkish, and Japanese Emperors; he can shew his testimonial in 36 languages, which no other doctor can shew, He hath cured the brother of the Turkish Emperor, which was blind thirteen years and hath obtained his natural sight again.
>
> This German Physitian has travelled through three parts of the world.[122]

It was, after all, the seventeenth and eighteenth centuries which saw the high-mark in European receptivity to the wisdom of the Asiatic civilisations.[123] Before the nineteenth-century Evangelical and Utilitarian new brooms, Europe was still reverential towards Semitic wisdom and the allure of the Levant and the Orient – a respect reflected in the marketing of proprietary medicines. Cagliostro touted 'Egyptian Pills';[124] powdered 'mummy' was a favourite long-life preparation, and inoculation was brought to England from Asia Minor, not long after those other health aids, coffee and the hummuns.[125] Some came from farther afield, such as the 'Indian Cattee' for scurvy.[126] Significantly, Bishop Berkeley chose to unfold the secrets of his tar-water nostrum in a work titled *Siris*, the old Ethiopian name for the Nile.[127] All the hullaballoo about 'Eastern promise' was, of course, an easy target for satirists and detractors. As *The Modern Quacks* put it:[128]

> we have *Salves* and *Waters* without Number, some of them as far
> fetch'd as *Jerusalem*, tho' they never travelled perhaps a Mile
> from the *Exchange* . . . for the *Toothache*, *Tinctures*, etc. and to
> whiten them *Dentifrices*, or *Powders* from *Morocco*, *China*, and
> *Japan*; for the *Mouth*, *Gargles* and *Washes*, many; for the whole
> *Face* and *Hands*, *Chymical Washballs*, besides *Pearls*, *Cream
> Balls*, *White-Pots*, and *Custards*, some from *Rome* and *Italy*,
> others from *Venice*.

Yet this manipulation of symbols surely shows medical entrepreneurs
trying to cash in on a cosmopolitanism in vogue in the Enlightenment.
Commercial medicine was not yet selling the line that healing, like
charity, began at home (a traditional view popular in the Victorian folksy
piety was that God had blessed each nation with cures for its own
diseases).[129]

One further source of prestige was tapped time and again in quack
medicine publicity and puffery: social cachet. The labels of proprietary
medicines read like a medical *Burke's Peerage*, echoing the titles of the
high and mighty. Alongside 'Sintelaer's Royal Decachor' one could try
James Graham's 'Imperial Pills' or Samuel Major's 'Imperial Snuff';[130]
then there was the 'Duke of Portland's Powder' for that aristocratic
disease, gout, 'Lady Moor's Drops' and 'the Countess of Kent's Powder'
for plague, tapping the traditions of Lady Bountiful as dispenser of
household medicine, and not least the 'Princesses Powder'.[131] And many
quack doctors cried up their (real or Mittyish) connexions with royalty.
Possessing a licence or patent or simply paying duty could be turned to
commercial advantage, for the royal seal could be made to imply royal
use or endorsement. So in 1695 Madam Gordan of Goodman's Fields
headed her medical bill 'By His Majesty's Authority' (a common head-
line) and rounded it off 'VIVAT REX';[132] and Cornelius à Tilbourg, the
Netherlandish itinerant, introduced himself 'By His Majesty's Special
License and Authority', claiming he was 'sworn chirurgeon to our
Sovereign Lord King William'.[133] Others had a juster title to plead royal
favour, witness Sir William Read's Bill (Plate 1), the lettering crowned by
the royal crest and a *Dieu et Mon Droit*.[134]

What's in a name? What has been shown by this brief survey of the
language and symbolism of mountebank medicines marketed in England
from the Restoration through to the end of the eighteenth century? At
the very least, it should have demonstrated that the vendors themselves
paid strenuous attention to the spoken and written word – to brand-
names, to advertising copy, to performance and patter, and of course to
the resonances of their publicity for image-creation. This point could be
further illustrated – space forbids it here – by examining their shrewd use

WILLIAM READ'S BILL

Plate 1 Sir William Read's bill, reproduced by kind permission of the Wellcome Institute Library, London.

of a widening range of publicity media, especially their pioneering role in the development of newspaper advertising.[135] Contemporaries were extremely well aware both of the high density of nostrum advertisements, from wall-posters and coffee-house bills to the saturation of newspaper columns, and of their innovative, eye-catching qualities. As Joseph

Addison remarked, the couplet 'Within this place, Lives Dr Case', made that clap-cure peddler more money than all his verse made for Dryden.

Much more research needs to be done before one can trace confidently how the trade in empirics' nostrums became big business. But, meantime, I shall suggest that the above survey warrants certain tentative conclusions, placing 'quacks' in context of the range of medical practice on offer, and highlighting certain features of the emergence of market-oriented consumer society.

Writing the history of irregular medicine poses tricky problems, since it is intuitively defined as a subject by its opposite – regular, orthodox, or faculty medicine. There is thus a considerable temptation to set about writing a history of a medical 'fringe' down the ages right up to today's alternative medical cosmologies and practices. To some degree traditional medical history always has done this, by regarding non-regular medicine as 'quackery', explicitly or implicitly fraudulent; or by automatically identifying the fringe as a 'lunatic fringe'. But the same sort of story could be told approvingly – heroically, even – as a history of radical, suppressed or 'heretical' systems, in which they either turned up therapeutic trumps in the end, or at least spoke in the authentic *vox populi* in an ongoing patrician *versus* plebeian *Kulturkampf*. There is clearly a certain truth in this account, at least for some groups at some periods: numerous medical sects did indeed sprout in the Victorian age, offering alternative cosmologies (e.g. homoeopathy) and explicitly pitting themselves against orthodoxy.[136] But my account above suggests that the emergence of a flourishing nostrum-vending sector in the eighteenth century does not fit into such a tale. For what analysis of the language of Georgian quack medicines suggests – and I believe further research into other areas of their marketing and public image would confirm it[137] – is that the empirics were not essentially repudiating orthodox medicine, and offering radical alternatives to it; rather they were an extra dimension of it, its penumbra, its commercial wing – even, maybe, its parasites, if one wishes to use such a term. And, to a surprising degree, they were operating in this way with the collusion of the regulars, numerous of whom were beneficiaries, directly or indirectly, from the sale of proprietary medicines. Certainly, regulars took hardly any legal action against the quacks. Nineteenth-century professional medicine, from Wakley's *Lancet* to the Royal College of Physicians, chose to see professional and ethical medicine battling tooth and nail against shop and street-corner medicine (though, as Jeanne Peterson notes, even then this vision was often a matter more of ideals and rhetoric than of reality).[138] Yet such a contrast would be utterly misleading for the Georgian period, when relations between regulars and irregulars are better described as collusion rather than collision.

Second, attention to the language of eighteenth-century quackery will help illuminate wider aspects of the development of English market society. Economic history has recently been insisting that a key factor – maybe even the *primum mobile* – in eighteenth-century economic growth (and hence, by implication, in the Industrial Revolution) was played by rising personal demand, by the extension of commercialisation and of market mechanisms, and by the cultivation of the consumer and consumerism.[139] Marketing, the service sector, shopping and distribution all grew in socioeconomic importance. From razor strops to Wedgwood porcelain, brand-name products became conspicuous features of the market, beneficiaries of advertising, fashion, emulative spending and consumer psychology. The enormous increase in the sales of nostrums in this period represents the medical dimension of these developments, indeed the commercialisation of medicine. It was an age when (as Dr James McKitterick Adair put it) it had become fashionable to be ill, 'sick by way of amusement', and when fashion led people to choose their illnesses, their doctors, and their medicines.[140] Not surprisingly, a highly organised medical service industry emerged, equipped with manufacturing depots, warehouses, nation-wide wholesale and retail marketing facilities and mass advertising. Brand-name medicines, I suggest, became amongst the earliest nationally advertised and nationally marketed products. A full century before Pears Soap, washstand closets contained their shots of Dr James's Powders. To grasp the rise of consumer society, we must understand the key role played by the language of salesmanship, with its implied soft-sell collusion between marketer and customer. And an early, important and abundant source for that is the history of medical nostrums, the world of healers and dealers.

NOTES

[1] See the useful discussion in D. C. Goellnicht, *The Poet–Physician, Keats and Medical Science* (Pittsburgh, 1984), pp. 166f.

[2] See P. Lain Entralgo, *The Therapy of the Word in Classical Antiquity* (New Haven, 1970); C. McCabe, ed., *The Talking Cure* (London, 1981).

[3] See R. F. Jones, *Ancients and Moderns* (St Louis, 1936); B. Willey, *The Seventeenth Century Background* (London, 1934); B. Shapiro, *Probability and Certainty in Seventeenth Century England* (Princeton, 1983), pp. 21–8.

[4] J. Starobinski, 'Molière and the Doctors', *Ciba Symposium* 14 (1966), 143–8; I. P. Couliano, *Eros et magie* (Paris, 1984).

[5] See J. Martin, *Animal Magnetism Examined* (London, 1790), p. 45.

[6] [Anon.], *The Cheats of London Town Exposed* (London, 1766). Quacks were perceived as being on the increase. According to an anonymous satire of 1676, 'A quack doctor is one of the Epidemical Diseases of this age'. Quoted in C. J. S. Thompson, *The Quacks of Old London* (London, 1928), p. 78. See also Irvine Loudon, 'The vile race of quacks with which this country is infested', in W. F. Bynum and Roy Porter, eds., *Medical Fringe and Medical Orthodoxy* (London, 1986), pp. 106–28.

[7] For 'senseless cant', see Ned Ward, *The London Spy*, ed. K. Fenwick (London, 1955), p. 104.

[8] R. I. Cook, *Sir Samuel Garth* (Boston, 1980), p. 77. Warwick Lane was, of course, the site of the College of Physicians. Thomas Beddoes was another regular who attacked the quackery and corruption of the profession. See D. Stansfield, *Thomas Beddoes* (Dordrecht, 1984).

[9] H. Silvette, *The Doctor on the Stage* (Knoxville, Tennessee, 1967), p. 259.

[10] T. Smollett, *Ferdinand Count Fathom*, ed. D. Grant (London, 1971), p. 258.

[11] *Ibid.*, p. 260. See also J. Keevil, 'Coffee house cures', *Journal of the History of Medicine* 9 (1954), 191–5, W. Wadd, *Mems., Maxims and Memoirs* (London, 1827) and [W. MacMichael], *The Gold Headed Cane* (London, 1854) which abound with tales of the commercial astuteness of orthodox doctors. For the personal display of orthodox physicians and quacks alike, see P. Cunnington and C. Lucas, *Occupational Costume in England* (London, 1967). For Smollett, see G. S. Rousseau, *Tobias Smollett, Essays of Two Decades* (Edinburgh, 1982); R. Hambridge, 'Empiricomany, or an Infatuation in favour of *Empiricism* or *Quackery*. The Socioeconomics of Eighteenth Century Quackery', in S. Soupel and R. Hambridge, *Literature and science and medicine* (Los Angeles, 1982), pp. 47–102. See also the judgment of Jeremiah Jenkins, *Observations on the present state of the profession and trade of medicine* (London, 1811), p. 7:

> The physicians of that period were pompous, conceited, and overbearing, and as much acquainted with the mean artifices of imposing on the credulous public, as the most impudent advertising quack of the present day. The bushy wig, the golden-headed cane, the grave countenance, and an ostentatious show of learning, were certainly well calculated in those days of ignorance and credulity to inspire confidence, and so are false promises of the quack.

[12] R. Campbell, *The English Tradesman* (London, 1947), p. 41.

[13] *Ibid.*, p. 64. For the quackery and imposture of *all* professions, see C. Probyn, 'Swift and the Physicians', *Medical History* 18 (1974), 249–61; S. La Casce, 'Swift on Medical Extremism', *Journal of the History of Ideas* 31 (1970), 599–606; G. Hatfield, 'Quacks, Pettifoggers and Parsons: Fielding's Case against the Learned Professions', *Texas Studies in Literature and Language* 9 (1967), 69–83.

[14] Harry Rowe, *The Sham Doctor* (n.p., n.d., but late eighteenth century), p. 58; see also Silvette, *op. cit.*

[15] Henry Fielding, *The History of Tom Jones* (Harmondsworth, 1975), p. 347.

[16] J. Spinke, *Quackery Unmasked* (London, 1709), p. 47.

[17] For standard hostile histories, see E. Jameson, *The Natural History of Quackery* (London, 1961); P. Taylor Barnum, *The Humbugs of the World* (London, 1866); A. D. Crabtre, *The Funny Side of Physic* (Hartford, 1874); B. Hill, 'Medical Imposters', *History of Medicine* 2 (1970), 7–11; L. Harris and L. Knowles, 'The Golden Days of Dr Quack', *History of Medicine* 6 (1975), 76–81; H. Burger, 'The Doctor, the Quack and the Appetite of the Public for Magic in Medicine', *Proceedings of the Royal Society of Medicine* 27 (1933), 171–6; H. Silvette, 'On Quacks and Quackery in Seventeenth Century England', *Annals of Medical History*, 3rd ser., 1 (1939), 239–51; G. Williams, *The Age of Agony* (London, 1975), Chapter 7; J. Camp, *Magic, Myth and Medicine* (London, 1973); M. Fishbein, *Fads and Quackery in Healing* (New York, 1932); E. Maple, *Magic, Medicine and Quackery* (London, 1968); *varii*, 'Quacks and Quackery', *British Medical Journal* 1 (1911), 1217–96; H. B. Wheatley, 'The Company of Undertakers', in *Hogarth's London* (London, 1909), pp. 223–31; S. H. Holbrook, *The Golden Age of Quackery* (New York, 1959); A. D. Wright, 'The Quacks of John Hunter's Time', *Transactions of the Hunterian Society* 11 (1952–3), 68–84; somewhat more substantial are A. Corsini, *Medici ciarlatani e ciarlatani medici* (Bologna, 1922), and Grete de Francesco, *Die Macht des Charlatans* (Basle, 1937), but these say little about England.

[18] William Hogarth illustrates this point. His engraving, *The Company of Undertakers*, pointedly juxtaposes three of the most notorious quacks of his age, Chevalier Taylor, 'Spot' Ward and Sally Mapp, with a covey of anonymous regular physicians: 'et plurima imago mortis'. As Roger Cowley has recently emphasised, the point about the 'quack' V.D. practitioner in Scene 3 of *Marriage à la Mode* is that he – nominally Dr Pillule – is

actually Dr J. Misaubin, licentiate of the College of Physicians: *Marriage à la Mode* (Manchester, 1983). For other exemplifications, see P. Brewster, 'Physicians and Surgeons as Represented in Sixteenth and Seventeenth Century English Literature', *Osiris* 14 (1962), 13–32; M. Yearsley, *Doctors in Elizabethan Drama* (London, 1933).

[19] Thompson, *Quacks of Old London*, p. 327. Here, as in many places, Thompson drew upon the unrivalled British Library collection of quack handbills, advertisements, etc. Where Thompson quotes from these, I give the page references to his book.

[19] J. Crellin, 'Dr James's Fever Powder', *Transactions of the British Society for the History of Pharmacy* 1 (1974), 136–43.

[20] M. H. Nicolson, 'Ward's Pill and Drop and Men of Letters', *Journal of the History of Ideas* 29 (1968), 173–96, p. 196. Walpole recommended James's powders 'for cough – for gout – for smallpox – for everything'. Another example would be the surgeon, Sir Charles Blicke, who used as a specific against cancer a proprietary mixture called 'Plundet's Caustic', which was chiefly composed of white oxide of arsenic. See also Thompson, *The Quacks of Old London*, p. 327.

[21] See the trade card reproduced in E. St J. Brooks, *Sir Hans Sloane* (London, 1954), p. 88:

> Sold here Sir Hans Sloane's Milk Chocolate. Made (only) by William White, successor to Mr. Nicholas Sanders, No. 8 Greek St., Soho, London. Greatly recommended by several eminent physicians, especially those of Sir Hans Sloane's acquaintance, for its lightness on the stomach and its great use in all consumptive cases. N.B. what is not signed with my name and sealed with my arms is counterfeit.

[22] See S. Paget, *John Hunter* (London, 1897), p. 165. Newbery was a leading publisher and distributor of commercial medicines.

[23] For the argument that medical qualifications meant little in any case at this period see G. Holmes, *Augustan England: Professions, State and Society, 1680–1730* (London, 1982). Take the Elizabethan practitioner, Simon Forman; he had no formal medical training, and was hounded by the College of Physicians; subsequently, through having friends in high places, he obtained a licence from Cambridge.

[24] Thompson, *The Quacks of Old London*, pp. 132f.

[25] For the sociointellectual context of medicine in early modern England, see L. S. King, *The Road to Medical Enlightenment* (London, 1970); *idem*, *The Medical World of the Eighteenth Century* (Chicago, 1958); W. F. Bynum, 'Health, Disease and Medical Care', in G. S. Rousseau and Roy Porter, eds., *The Ferment of Knowledge* (Cambridge, 1980), pp. 211–54; G. S. Rousseau, 'Psychology', in *ibid.*, pp. 143–210; R. S. Roberts, 'The Personnel and Practice of Medicine in Tudor and Stuart England', *Medical History* 6 (1962), 363–82; C. Webster, ed., *Health, Medicine and Mortality in the Sixteenth Century* (Cambridge, 1979); Holmes, *op. cit.*

[26] N. Jewson, 'Medical Knowledge and the Patronage System in Eighteenth Century England', *Sociology* 8 (1974), 369–85; for general socioeconomic background to England as an emergent market-oriented opportunity society, see A. Macfarlane, *The Origins of English Individualism* (Oxford, 1978); C. B. MacPherson, *The Political Theory of Possessive Individualism* (Oxford, 1962); Derek Jarrett, *England in the Age of Hogarth* (London, 1974); H. Perkin, *The Origins of Modern English Society* (London, 1969); J. Thirsk, *Economic Policy and Projects* (Oxford, 1978).

[27] In contemporary parlance, a remedy worked not when it cured but when it achieved its expected short-term effect – e.g. a purge opened the bowels. See the discussion in Andrew Wear, 'Puritan Perceptions of Illness', in Roy Porter, ed., *Patients and Practitioners: Lay Perceptions of Medicine in Pre-Industrial Society* (Cambridge, 1985), pp. 55–99.

[28] See Roy Porter, 'William Hunter: A Surgeon and a Gentleman', in W. F. Bynum and Roy Porter, eds., *William Hunter and the Eighteenth Century Medical World* (Cambridge, 1985), pp. 7–34.

[29] O. Goldsmith, *Citizen of the World* (Everyman ed., London, 1934), letter 24, p. 63.

[30] There is an extensive recent literature discussing new perspectives in the history of medicine. See M. Pelling, 'Medicine since 1500', in P. Corsi and P. Weindling, eds.,

Information Sources in the History of Science and Medicine (London, 1983), pp. 379–410;
C. Webster, 'The Historiography of Medicine', in *ibid.*, pp. 29–43; M. MacDonald,
'Anthropological Perspectives on the History of Science and Medicine', in *ibid.*, pp. 81–
98; and L. J. Jordanova, 'The Social Sciences and History of Science and Medicine', in
ibid., pp. 81–98. Unfortunately none of this touches much on 'quacks'. One suspects they
are not thought serious enough.

[31] On historical approaches to decoding images see R. Barthes, *Mythologies* (London,
1972).

[32] For introductions, see J. B. Pride and J. Holmes, eds., *Socio-Linguistics* (Harmondsworth, 1972); P. P. Giglioni, ed., *Language and Social Context* (Harmondsworth,
1975); R. Bauman and J. Sherzer, *Explorations in the Ethnography of Speaking*
(Cambridge, 1974).

[33] For introductions, see D. Locker, *Symptoms and Illness: The Cognitive Organization of
Disorder* (London, 1981); A. Cartwright, *Patients and their Doctors* (London, 1967); M.
Balint, *The Doctor, the Patient and his Illness* (London, 1957); P. M. Strong, *The
Ceremonial Order of the Clinic* (London, 1979); D. Pendleton and J. Hasler, eds.,
Doctor–Patient Communication (London, 1983); D. Armstrong, *The Political Anatomy
of the Body* (Cambridge, 1983); E. Cassell, *Talking to Patients*, 2 vols. (Cambridge,
Mass., 1985).

[34] See N. Jewson, 'Medical Knowledge and the Patronage System in Eighteenth Century
England', *Sociology* 13 (1974), 369–85; Roy Porter, 'The Doctor and the Word', *Medical
Sociology News* 9 (1983), 21–8.

[35] Oddly, the historical language of selling has been little studied. For an introduction, see
N. McKendrick, 'George Packwood and the Commercialization of Shaving: The Art of
Eighteenth Century Advertising, or "The way to get money and be happy" ', in N.
McKendrick, J. Brewer and J. H. Plumb, *The Birth of a Consumer Society* (London,
1982), pp. 146–96.

[36] For the seventeenth- and eighteenth-century trope that life was theatre and all the world
was a stage, on which men were constantly performing, see R. Paulson, *Popular and
Polite Art in the Age of Hogarth and Fielding* (Notre Dame, 1979); and for a rather more
formally dramaturgical approach, R. Isaac, *The Transformation of Virginia* (New York,
1982). For pulpit oratory, see Horton Davies, *Worship and Theology in England*
(Princeton, 1975). For contemporary comment on the theatre of quackery, see *The
Modern Quacks* (London, 1724), p. 147, which speaks of the quack's 'gawdy Tinsel
Appearance, like the strolling Comedians, to amuse your outward Senses, whilst with his
poor dull Rhetorick, he is flourishing you out of your inward, I mean your Intellects, in
order to put off a Parcel of most unwholsome Trash, made up into Packets'.

[37] See Thompson, *The Quacks of Old London*, *passim*; De Francesco, *op. cit.* It must be
noted that such mountebanks remained long in evidence. In the mid-eighteenth century
Thomas Turner, the Sussex shopkeeper, noted that a local village was visited weekly by a
'Mountebank'. D. Vaisey, ed., *The Diary of Thoms Turner* (Oxford, 1984), pp. 11, 208.

[38] Quacks proclaimed the authenticity of their testimonials. Thus, see Graham's advertisement in the *Morning Herald* of 5 June 1781: 'N.B. A pamphlet is now published, (by
permission) with the particulars of several hundred cures in confirmed diseases, lately
performed at the Temple of Health, with the names and residence of the patients, at their
own particular desire, to be had of the porter at the Temple, price only 3d.' Their
opponents claimed they were frauds. Thus J. McK. Adair, *Essays on Fashionable
Diseases* (London, 1790), p. 259: 'Whilst other great men depend on contemporaries or
posterity for the celebration of their worth, the quack doctor is his own historian, and
publishes in every pamphlet and newspaper, cases of cures never performed, and copies
of affidavits never sworn to; whilst great and small vulgar give them entire credit for their
candour, and their veracity, all of which are equally respectable.'

[39] For a wealth of evidence from handbills, see the British Library Collection of Quack
Medicine Advertisements (C.112, f9), many of which are digested in Thompson, *The
Quacks of Old London*. For satire against a quack's broken English see *The Modern
Quacks* (London, 1724), pp. 128f.

[40] Thompson, *ibid.*, p. 121. Turlington's Balsam was sold in violin-shaped bottles.

41 Thompson, *The Quacks of Old London*, pp. 42, 47.
42 There is a fine collection of Graham's newspaper advertisements in the library of the Wellcome Institute for the History of Medicine, MS 73143; some are reproduced in F. Grose, *A Guide to Health, Beauty, Riches and Honour* (London, 1796). For a contextual approach to Graham, see Roy Porter, 'The sexual politics of James Graham', *British Journal for Eighteenth Century Studies* 5 (1982), 199–206; see also C. J. S. Thompson, *Mysteries of History* (London, 1928), pp. 259–77; W. I. Whitwell, 'James Graham, Masterquack', *Eighteenth Century Life* 4 (1977–8), 47–8.
43 For Johnson (whose dictum appeared in the *Idler*, no. 40) and advertising, see Roy Porter, *English Society in the Eighteenth Century* (Harmondsworth, 1982), pp. 206, 240.
44 T. Alcock and J. Wilmot, *The Famous Pathologist or the Noble Mountebank*, ed. V. Da Sola Pinto (Nottingham, 1961); W. O. Ober, 'Noble Quacksalver: the Earl of Rochester's Merry Prank', *History of Medicine* 5 (1973), pp. 24–6.
45 Ned Ward, *The London Spy*, ed. K. Fenwick (London, 1955), pp. 101–2. John Corry in his *A Satirical View of London* (London, 1803), p. 104, argued that the total obscurity of Dr Brodum's language constituted a supreme instance of Burke's category of the 'sublime'.
46 Thompson, *The Quacks of Old London*, pp. 214–15: the patter belonged to Stephen Draper.
47 James Graham, *Address to the Public in General* (handbill).
48 Taylor styled himself on the title page of his autobiography:

> Chevalier JOHN TAYLOR, OPHTHALMIATER; Pontifical – Imperial and Royal – The Kings of Poland, Denmark, Sweden, The Electors of the holy Empire – The Princes of Saxegotha, Mecklenberg, Anspach, Brunswick, Parme, Modena, Zerbst, Loraine, Saxony, Hesse, Cassel, Holstein, Salzburg, Baviere, Leige, Bareith, Georgia, etc. Pr. in Opt. C. of Rom. M.D. – C.D. – Author of 45 Works in different Languages: the Produce for upwards of thirty Years, of the greatest Practice in the Cure of distempered Eyes, of any in the Age we live – Who has been in every Court, Kingdom, Province, State, City, and Town of the least consideration in all Europe, without exception. Written by HIMSELF.

'Chevalier' Taylor, *The History of the Travels and Adventures of the Chevalier John Taylor* (3 vols., London, 1760–2).
49 Smollett, *Ferdinand Count Fathom*, p. 253.
50 Thus, for example, Katterfelto, whose newspaper advertisements commonly stressed aristocratic connexions. See E. Jameson, *op. cit.*, p. 63, who notes that the *Morning Post* of 16 September 1781 reported that 'Mr Katterfelto was honoured this week with the Duke of Montagu, Lords Cholmondeley, Abergavenny and Ashby, General Johnson, Sir J. Stepney, and several other ladies and gentlemen of distinction.'
51 Thompson, *The Quacks of Old London*, p. 221.
52 Thompson, *The Quacks of Old London*, p. 343. Illuminating here is B. Cottle, 'Names', in L. Michaels and C. Ricks, eds., *The State of the Language* (Berkeley, 1980), pp. 98–107.
53 Thompson, *The Quacks of Old London*, p. 156.
54 *Ibid.*, p. 218.
55 *Ibid.*, p. 169.
56 *Ibid.*, p. 218.
57 *Ibid.*, p. 188. 'Frenchify'd' meant poxed.
58 [Anon.], *The Modern Quacks* (London, 1724), p. 11.
59 *The Modern Quacks*, p. 3.
60 For seventeenth- and eighteenth-century language as a palimpsest of associations, see J. Arthos, *The Language of Natural Description in Eighteenth Century Poetry* (New York, 1949); D. Davie, *The Language of Science and the Language of Literature 1700–1740* (London, 1963); W. K. Wimsatt, *Philosophical Words* (New Haven, 1948); S. Tucker, *Protean Shape* (London, 1957).
61 Thompson, *The Quacks of Old London*, p. 142.

[62] Quoted in Silvette, *op. cit.*, p. 189.
[63] Thus the language of atomism turns up in the claim that a cure removed 'all venerial Atomes'; Thompson, *The Quacks of Old London*, p. 254.
[64] Quoted in J. Money, *Experience and Identity: Birmingham and the West Midlands, 1760–1800* (Manchester, 1977), p. 140.
[65] For 'Oxon Pills', see *Medical Advertisements* (British Library, 551 a 32).
[66] See W. Ober, 'Bach, Handel and "Chevalier" John Taylor, M.D., Ophthalmiator', *New York State Journal of Medicine* 69 (1969), 1797–1806. This practice was attacked by Jeremiah Jenkins in his *Observations on the Present State of the Profession and Trade of Medicine* (London, 1810), p. 106:

> It is a common practice with venders of patent medicines, to bring out a medicine under the sanction of the name of an emiment practitioner, immediately after his dissolution: thus we have Dr. Fothergill's Nervous Drops; Dr. Warren's Stomach Pills; Dr. Hugh Smith's Bilious Pills; thus are those respectable names handed down to posterity in the schedule of the act of parliament for regulating the duty on quack medicines, as patronising the most infamous traffic existing in human nature. If the College of Physicians connive at such disgraceful practices, they may . . . join in the chorus 'Tanta-rara-rum, quacks all! quacks all!'

[67] Thompson, *The Quacks of Old London*, p. 224.
[68] *Ibid.*, p. 223.
[69] *Ibid.*, p. 212.
[70] *Ibid.*, p. 255.
[71] See Porter, *op. cit.*
[72] J. McK. Adair, *Essays on Fashionable Diseases* (London, 1790), p. 193.
[73] Recent scholarship in any case tends to stress the congruity of old and new science, not their conflict, in the seventeenth and eighteenth centuries. See S. Schaffer, 'Natural Philosophy and Public Spectacle in the Eighteenth Century', *History of Science* 21 (1983), 1–43; *idem*, 'Natural Philosophy', in G. S. Rousseau and Roy Porter, eds., *The Ferment of Knowledge* (Cambridge, 1980), pp. 53–92.
[74] *Cf.* D. Outram, 'The Language of Natural Power: The Eloges of George Cuvier and the Public Language of Nineteenth Century Science', *History of Science* 16 (1978), 153–78.
[75] Thompson, *The Quacks of Old London*, p. 329.
[76] R. Paulson, *Literary Landscape, Turner and Constable* (Hew Haven, 1982), pp. 90f.
[77] James Graham, *A New and Curious Treatise* (London, 1780), p. 27.
[78] Thompson, *The Quacks of Old London*, p. 109; J. K. Crellin and J. R. Scott, 'Lionel Lockyer and his Pills', *Proceedings of the XXIII International Congress of the History of Medicine* (1972), pp. 1182–6.
[79] Thompson, *The Quacks of Old London*, p. 229.
[80] *Ibid.*, p. 154. For 'England's Solar Pill' see *Medical Advertisements* (British Library, 551 a 32).
[81] See A. G. Debus, 'Scientific Truth and Occult Tradition: The Medical World of Ebenezer Sibly (1751–1799)', *Medical History* 26 (1982), 259–78; A. Comfort, *The Anxiety Makers* (London, 1967). For other 'female pills', see P. S. Brown, 'Female Pills and the Reputation of Iron as an Abortifacient', *Medical History* 21 (1977), 291–304, and A. Maclaren, *Reproductive Rituals* (London, 1984).
[82] *The Modern Quacks*, p. 9.
[83] See J. Whorton, *Crusaders for Fitness* (Princeton, 1982); G. Risse, ed., *Medicine Without Doctors* (New York, 1977); A. C. and M. Fellman, *Making Sense of Self* (Philadelphia, 1981); R. Wallis and P. Morley, eds., *Marginal Medicine* (London, 1976); J. V. Pickstone, 'Establishment and Dissent in Nineteenth Century Medicine', in W. J. Sheils, ed., *The Church and Healing* (Oxford, 1982), pp. 165–90, and L. Barrow, 'Anti-Establishment Healing: Spiritualism in Britain', in *ibid.*, pp. 225–48.
[84] E. J. Trimmer, 'Medical Folklore and Quackery', *Folklore* 76 (1965), 161–75.

[85] A good wider example of which is Mesmerism. See R. Darnton, *Mesmerism and the End of the Enlightenment in France* (Cambridge, Mass., 1968).

[86] *The Modern Quacks*, p. 183. For medicine and religion, see W. Sheils, ed., *The Church and Healing* (Oxford, 1982). Note Wadd's sour comments, in *Mems., Maxims and Memoirs* (London, 1827), p. 67: 'The distinguishing characteristics of the Quacking Fraternity are, *promising largely*, *lying stoutly*, and *affecting sanctity*. The pretended piety of Quacks is very effective. All their bills and books attest a variety of cures done partly by their medicines, and partly by the blessing of God. This is very emphatical and very effective in this age of cant.'

[87] Thompson, *The Quacks of Old London*, p. 337; R. Altick, *The Shows of London* (Cambridge, Mass., 1978).

[88] Thompson, *The Quacks of Old London*, p. 29.

[89] *Ibid.*, p. 253.

[90] For some of the connotations of classical mythological names, see D. Brooks-Davies, 'The Mythology of Love: Venusean (and related) Iconography in Pope, Fielding, Cleland and Sterne', in P. G. Boucé, ed., *Sexuality in Eighteenth Century Britain* (Manchester, 1982), pp. 176–97.

[91] Thompson, *The Quacks of Old London*, p. 330.

[92] Thompson, *The Quacks of Old London*, p. 205.

[93] *Ibid.*

[94] F. S. Brown, 'Medicines Advertised in Eighteenth Century Bath Newspapers', *Medical History* 20 (1976), 152–68.

[95] An invention of Rochester's; see note 44.

[96] Thompson, *The Quacks of Old London*, p. 94; J. G. Matthews, 'Licensed Mountebanks in Britain', *Journal of the History of Medicine* 19 (1964), 26–45.

[97] *The Modern Quacks*, pp. 14–15.

[98] K. V. Thomas, *Religion and the Decline of Magic* (London, 1971).

[99] Quoted in M. H. Nicolson, *op. cit.*, p. 132.

[100] For suggestive remarks on the differential power of language in a polyglot world, see P. Burke, *Popular Culture in Early Modern Europe* (London, 1978); D. Leith, *A Social History of English* (London, 1983); R. Paulson, *Popular and Polite Art in the Age of Hogarth and Fielding* (London, 1979).

[101] Thompson, *The Quacks of Old London*, p. 95.

[102] *Ibid.*, p. 100.

[103] *Ibid.*, p. 180.

[104] *Ibid.*, p. 195.

[105] *Ibid.*, p. 136.

[106] *Ibid.*, p. 108.

[107] *Ibid.*, pp. 108, 117, 229, 224, 232.

[108] See Ober, *op. cit.*

[109] Thompson, *The Quacks of Old London*, p. 80.

[110] See the attack on John Marten's Latin in J. Spinke, *Quackery Unmasked* (London, 1709).

[111] During the seventeenth and eighteenth centuries, for example, London street signs and trade plates still commonly contained some Latin. See B. Lillywhite, *London Signs* (London, 1972). In Sheridan's *The Rivals* the servant girl Lucy mistakes *sal volatile* for the name of a novel; but that is part of a mask of 'simplicity' which profits her handsomely. For quack medicine prices see Roy Porter, 'Lay Medical Knowledge in the Eighteenth Century: The Evidence of the *Gentleman's Magazine*', *Medical History* 29 (1985), 138–68, pp. 166–8.

[112] Robert Latham and W. Matthews, eds., *The Diary of Samuel Pepys* (11 vols., London, 1970–83), vol. 3, 27 November 1662.

[113] The lure of exoticism is well brought out in R. Altick, *The Shows of London* (Cambridge, Mass., 1978).

[114] Thompson, *The Quacks of Old London*, p. 193; *cf.* Brown, *op. cit.*

[115] Thompson, *The Quacks of Old London*, p. 256.

[116] L. C. Matthews, 'Licensed Mountebanks in Britain', *Journal of the History of Medicine* 19 (1964), 28–45.

[117] Thompson, *The Quacks of Old London*, p. 165; Silvette, *op. cit.*, p. 74.

[118] For fun with quacks' broken English, see *The Modern Quacks* (London, 1724), p. 127:

> . . . He puts on his *Conjuring Cap*, lifts up the Urinal, shakes his Head, and begins very gravely his Speech, *Dis Person very bad*; Yes, indeed Doctor replies the old Woman, so *he* is: Hence he gathers it is a Man's Water, and goes on; *Dis be de Man's Water, good Woman is it not?* Yes, Sir, answers the Messenger. Then very demurely looking thereon again, he runs over his common Catalogue us'd at all times, as thus: *Here be much Pain in de Head*, then looking wishfully in the Woman's Face, to see if she contradicts him, if she say, not much, Sir, in the Head, *then here be great Pain in de Breast*: Very much indeed, Sir, replies old Nurse: *Me see here be very great Disorder in de Breast, and also in de Stomaach.*

For Shadwell's French Dr Pullen, see Silvette, *op. cit.*, p. 187, with his 'syringin English' (= surgeon's English).

[119] Thompson, *The Quacks of Old London*, pp. 328–9. Brodum was dubbed 'an aspiring little Jew', in J. Corry, *The Detector of Quackery* (London, 1802), p. 22; guilty of 'pseudology', he was as 'profoundly obscure' as an 'advertising physician' and 'miracle monger'.

[120] Thompson, *The Quacks of Old London*, p. 163.

[121] *Ibid.*, p. 168.

[122] *Ibid.*, p. 170.

[123] P. J. Marshall and G. Williams, *The Great Map of Mankind* (London, 1982); J. Elliott, *The Old World and the New* (London, 1965).

[124] G. de Francesco, *The Power of the Charlatan* (New Haven, 1939), pp. 209–13.

[125] Genevieve Miller, *The Adoption of Inoculation for Smallpox in England and France* (Philadelphia, 1957).

[126] A. Ellis, *The Penny Universities, a History of the Coffee Houses* (London, 1956). *Medical Advertisements* (British Library, C.112, f9).

[127] M. H. Nicolson and G. S. Rousseau, 'Bishop Berkeley and Tar Water', in H. K. Miller, ed., *The Augustan Milieu* (Oxford, 1970), pp. 102–37.

[128] *The Modern Quacks* (London, 1724), p. 7.

[129] G. Risse *et al.*, eds., *Medicine Without Doctors* (New York, 1977).

[130] F. Grose, *A Guide to Health, Beauty, Riches and Honour* (London, 1796), p. 1.

[131] W. Besant, *London in the Eighteenth Century* (London, 1902), p. 98; *cf.* C. Webster, *The Great Instauration* (London, 1975), p. 255; *Medical Advertisements* (British Library, C.112, f9).

[132] Thompson, *The Quacks of Old London*, p. 152.

[133] *Ibid.*, p. 89.

[134] *Ibid.*, p. 278.

[135] On the rise of newspapers, see G. A. Cranfield, *The Developmemt of the Provincial Newspaper 1700–1760* (Oxford, 1962); R. McK. Wiles, *Freshest Advices* (Columbus, Ohio, 1965); for quacks and publicity, see J. H. Young, *The Toadstool Millionaires* (Princeton, 1961); *idem*, *The Medical Messiahs* (Princeton, 1967); for advertising, see M. Nevett, *Advertising in Britain: A History* (London, 1982); F. Prestbury, *The History and Development of Advertising* (New York, 1929); E. S. Turner, *The Shocking History of Advertising* (London, 1953); T. Vestergard and K. Schroder, *The Language of Advertising* (Oxford, 1985).

[136] For sensitive studies of Victorian fringe marginal medicine, see above, note 83.

[137] Many are the areas of the operation of empirical medicine in the eighteenth century about which little is yet known. One is its organisation as a manufacturing and distributing industry. The role of the provincial newspaper in this has been admirably surveyed recently in J. J. Looney, 'Advertising and Society in England, 1720–1820: A Statistical Analysis of Yorkshire Newspaper Advertisements' (Princeton University Ph.D. thesis, 1983). Another is the question of patients' opinions and choices. Pre-

cisely who took proprietary medicines, or made use of the services of itinerants and mountebanks? Some material is contained in Roy Porter, ed., *Patients and Practitioners: Lay Perceptions of Medicine in Preindustrial Society* (Cambridge, 1985). I explore some of these issues in 'Before the Fringe', in R. Cooter, ed., *Alternatives* (London, 1987).

[138] J. Peterson, *The Medical Profession in Mid-Victorian London* (Berkeley, 1978), is illuminating on the question of how Victorian physicians simultaneously pursued medical entrepreneurship while wearing an ethical professional disinterest. For the lasting involvement of eminent practitioners in marketing commercial medicines, see F. C. Tring, 'The Influence of Victorian "Patent Medicines" on the Development of Early 20th Century Medical Practice' (University of Sheffield Ph.D. thesis, 1982).

[139] For the interface of economic change and culture, see N. McKendrick, 'The Consumer Revolution of Eighteenth Century England', in N. McKendrick, J. Brewer and J. H. Plumb, eds., *The Birth of a Consumer Society* (London, 1982), pp. 9–33; J. R. Millburn, *Benjamin Martin, Author, Instrument Maker and 'Country-Showman'* (Leyden, 1976); Roy Porter, 'Science, Provincial Culture and Public Opinion in Enlightenment England', *British Journal for Eighteenth Century Studies* 3 (1980), pp. 20–46; J. H. Plumb, *The Commercialization of Leisure in Eighteenth Century England* (Reading, 1973); *idem, Georgian Delights* (London, 1980); H. Cunningham, *Leisure in the Industrial Revolution* (London, 1980); S. Rosenfeld, *The Theatre of the London Fairs in the Eighteenth Century* (Cambridge, 1960).

[140] For contemporary comment, see J. McK. Adair, *Essays on Fashionable Diseases* (London, 1790), pp. 188f; for analysis, see Roy Porter, 'The Rage of Party: A Glorious Revolution in English Psychiatry?', *Medical History* 27 (1983), 35–50; G. S. Rousseau, 'Nerves, Spirits and Fibres: Towards defining the Origins of Sensibility, with a Postscript 1976', in *The Blue Guitar* 3 (1976), 125–53; E. Fischer-Homberger, 'Hypochondriasis of the Eighteenth Century: Neurosis of the Present Century', *Bulletin of the History of Medicine*, 46 (1972), 391–401; G. S. Rousseau, 'Science and the Discovery of the Imagination in Enlightenment England', *Eighteenth Century Studies* 3 (1969), 108–35. Foucault argued that health became to the bourgeoisie what blood had been to aristocrats: see 'Introduction', M. Foucault, *A History of Sexuality* (London, 1979), vol. 1.

5

VERBAL INSULTS IN EIGHTEENTH-CENTURY PARIS

David Garrioch

Insults may shock; they may entertain or amuse. A perennial product and indicator of human conflict, they are present in every culture and language, sometimes colourful, often repetitive, tired expressions whose original meaning is only remotely remembered. Yet insults are a fertile source for the sociolinguist and for the social historian. Even the weariest clichés, when looked at in context, can be vibrant with meaning.

For insults, like other forms of speech, are a product of the society in which they are aired. The central tenet of sociolinguistics is that speech is an act whose significance goes far beyond the literal, dictionary definition of the words used. No communciation, whether verbal or non-verbal, can be understood without reference to the social context within which it is produced. Furthermore, there are in each context coherent conventions, both grammatical and social, which govern linguistic behaviour. These are crucial notions for the historian, who like the social anthropologist is to some extent a traveller from one culture to another, concerned to describe and understand a society to which he or she does not belong.

Nowhere are these observations more essential to understanding than in the case of verbal insults. This is obvious as soon as we attempt to define what constitutes an insult. In any culture there are many words and imputations which are potentially insulting – indeed almost any expression is – but they do not actually become so until used in a particular way. Calling someone a thief, for example, may convey real information about a convicted robber who is being led from the dock: it is not insulting. Between friends, jocular epithets lose their literal meaning and express familiarity: their context renders them harmless. Thus groups of black youths in various American cities use ritual insults regularly, with no offensive content.[1] The very same terms used against a social superior, a stranger, or an enemy, on the other hand, may become deadly insults. In French the use of the familiar 'tu', normally an indication of closeness and friendship, is highly insulting if used to a stranger, a person of higher rank, or to anyone else who would normally be addressed with the more formal 'vous'. Who the speakers are, and the relationship between them, thus helps to define what constitutes an insult and what does not. But

104

there is more to context than this. Words spoken in private may be acceptable, whereas the same words used between the same people, but publicly, become insulting. We must also take into account the way words are said: spoken angrily, with obvious intent to insult, they are understood that way; articulated quietly, or in a playful tone, they might be taken quite differently. A great many variables come into play.

But the 'meaning' of insults goes much further, for their use is often very subtle, their significance highly complex. There are, for example, degrees of insults. Again context is vitally important. Depending on who the speaker and the victim are, and on the relationship between them, the same words can carry more or less weight. According to the tone used, they may express impatience, hatred or simple disapproval. Shouted in anger in the heat of a quarrel, or by someone who is drunk, they may be more forgivable than when pronounced with apparent self-control. The literal meaning of the words used may affect their gravity, and in any individual case particular epithets are chosen in preference to others: some are stronger and can cause greater offence. Some are better adapted for use against certain sorts of people. They may be used exclusively or primarily against men or against women. Certain insults may be inappropriate against members of the same family: Y. Castan notes that in eighteenth-century Languedoc some insults were less often heard in family fights because outsiders might misinterpret them.[2]

Many factors, therefore, determine the 'meaning' of insults and the reaction they provoke. There is no absolute scale, no way of measuring the weight of each variable, for all vary from one culture to another, in different languages and over time. In each case, however, the variations reflect the functioning of a particular society, and in some sense mirror its values, its conventions of behaviour, the character and weight of certain relationships. The following pages seek to illustrate this by examining the 'meaning' of verbal insults in a particular society at a particular time: popular society in Paris in the second half of the eighteenth century. Certain concepts of sociolinguistics are particularly applicable here, notably the ideas of social meaning, of different levels of communication, and of behavioural and linguistic codes.[3]

The source used is the archives of the *commissaires au Châtelet*, the local police officials of eighteenth-century Paris, and primarily the numerous complaints that these men received.[4] People came to complain about all sorts of things: about fraud, ranging from the sale of an underweight loaf of bread to the extraction of large sums of money under false pretences; about usury; about abuses by the officials of the corporations; about water (or the contents of chamber-pots) thrown out of upper-storey windows. But most of all they came to complain about insults: by neighbours and colleagues, by friends and acquaintances, sometimes by relatives or by strangers. Despite the fact that a formal complaint was expensive – two or three days' wages for a labourer – a wide social range is represented, from noblemen to day labourers, even prostitutes. But the people who came most frequently were those who were most numerous in the city: shopkeeepers, artisans (both masters and journeymen), and their wives.

The insults they came to complain about are usually faithfully and indignantly reproduced, often in hilarious detail. The plaintiff describes the context in which they occurred, emphasises the most damaging ones, explains his or her motives for making a formal complaint. Where both parties come to the *commissaire* a comparison is often revealing. The complaints are, of course, gloriously biased, this in itself telling us much about people's values and mentality.

Each complaint was, of course, written down by a scribe, yet ensconced among the judicial formulae are popular expressions, and, of course, the insults themselves, essential evidence in case of further judicial proceedings. This, the wealth of irrelevant detail, and the afterthoughts added at the end or jotted down in the margins, indicate that the scribe was for the most part copying what people actually said, although writing it in the third person. The presence of the *commissaire* remains a distorting factor, of course, making people present themselves as they wished to be seen, and in some cases pay lip-service to what they thought to be the values of the authorities. On the whole this does not pose a serious problem for the analysis of the insults themselves, however, for the most striking and in the plaintiff's opinion the most damaging ones are reproduced verbatim.

More of a problem in assessing the 'meaning' of insults in a historical context is the fact that we cannot observe their intonation or their non-verbal accessories, factors which, as I have suggested above, may affect their overall message. Furthermore, our information on the circumstances of the exchange and on other aspects of the context is often incomplete, dependent on the inevitably partial reports of witnesses or more often of the victim. It is frequently very difficult to assess the exact relationship between speaker and victim, and we rarely know much about their wealth, age or place of origin. This naturally limits our ability to relate language to particular social factors. On the other hand the reports we receive are those of people who belonged to the culture we are studying, and who were therefore best able to pick out the facts and circumstances which were most important to those involved. We have both a description of behaviour, for the benefit of the magistrate who was not present, and a commentary on that behaviour.

A further limitation must also be recognised: we are dealing only with

certain types of insults, those taken to the police. There were undoubtedly others which could not be reported, perhaps because they were felt
to be too infamous, certainly if they were too mild to be taken seriously
(although these are sometimes mentioned as minor aggravations).

The source remains, however, an extremely valuable one for the social
history of language. The following pages look first at the vocabulary of
insults and at their literal meaning, seeking to explain why particular
themes and expressions were chosen in preference to others, and to relate
them to social conditions. The second part studies the context in which
insults were used, and the effects of this on their 'meaning': that is, on the
total information that they conveyed.

The most common way of insulting someone is to call them names. In
eighteenth-century Paris it was equally insulting to cast aspersions on
their close family: spouse and children, parents, nephews and nieces, less
frequently cousins and in-laws. The epithets used are bewildering in their
richness and diversity but concentrate on two main themes, those
guaranteed to have maximum effect in the conditions prevailing in
eighteenth-century Paris. The first was sexual, used almost entirely
against women and playing primarily on the themes of sexual promiscuity, prostitution and venereal disease. Thus a baker called the wife of a
chirurgien (barber–surgeon) 'cul pourri' (rotting arse) and shouted out
that her son 'n'étoit pas de son mary, mais bien un bâtard' (was not her
husband's but a bastard). Someone else said of a woman that 'elle avoit
affaire à plusieurs prêtres de St Médard . . . qu'il ne voudroit pas que son
chien habitât avec elle parce qu'elle luy donneroit la vérole' (she was
carrying on with several priests from St Médard, and he wouldn't want his
dog to live with her because she would give it the pox).[5] Such insults seem
to have been used equally by men and women.

The second main theme, used against both sexes but more often
directed against men, was that of various kinds of dishonesty and criminal
activity, most commonly theft: 'le plaignant receloit ce qu'il voloit' (he
sold off things he had stolen); 'il avoit volé tout son bien' (he had stolen
everything he owned); 'te voilà donc gueux et voleur' (there you are you
scoundrel, thief).[6] Women were often accused specifically of stealing
clothes.[7] Whenever possible the accusation of theft was linked with a
suggestion of infidelity: 'les maisons qu'il avoit achetées c'étoit avec le
bien qu'il avoit volé chez ses maîtres' (the houses he had bought from
profits made out of stealing from his masters). Even more commonly
evoked was dishonesty in business: 'vendeur à faux poids' (seller by false
weights) was a common insult. A woman spread the rumour that a milk-
seller in the Rue St Denis put water in her milk. Those in business were
accused of fraud and of bankruptcy: 'voleur et banqueroutier' (thief,
bankrupt); 'mauvais payeur' (poor debt-payer). A journeyman baker

claimed that his former employer 'avoit fait de faux billets en Bavière' (had written false IOU's in Bavaria).[8]

Another favourite technique was to call someone by the name of a well-known criminal – Jean Diau, Raffiat, Cartouche – or to suggest some criminal association: 'reste de Bicêtre' (left-over from Bicêtre, a notorious prison for convicted criminals), 'reste de gibet' (scaffold left-over). 'Si son mary avoit ce qu'il méritoit il seroit au carcan' (if her husband got what he deserved he would be in shackles); 'il y avoit des personnes que l'on pendoit à la Grève qui ne le méritoit pas tant' (they hanged in the Place de Grève people who deserved it less).[9] Then there were open accusations of criminal convictions: 'il avoit été affiché' (he had been publicly shamed); '[il] avoit été fouetté et marqué' (he had been whipped and branded). Such accusations against women were much less frequent, although they did occur. A female fruit-seller, for example, complained that a rival in the Rue de Vaugirard had called out that she had been whipped and branded back in her own province.[10] Here, as in Castan's Languedoc, it is the punishment which defines the criminal, rather than the crime itself.

Closely related to these insults were accusations, primarily against men, of practising a dishonourable profession, such as 'maquereau' (pimp) and 'souteneur de bordel' (brothel-keeper), which of course lent themselves to combination with an attack on the man's wife: 'il étoit le macreau [sic] de sa femme' (he was pimp to his wife). Inherent in such expressions was a sense of dishonest and shady activity, and this was also evoked in insults like 'rôdeur de nuit' (night-prowler), 'espion' (spy), and towards the end of the ancien regime 'mouchard' (police spy).[11]

These are overwhelmingly the most common insults, and only occasionally do other themes appear. Rare instances occur of attacks based on someone's geographic origins: an ironmonger told a *marchand tapissier* 'qu'il n'étoit pas françois et qu'il déshonoroit la société' (he was not French and dishonoured society), although this is reported by a witness and is not among the insults retained by the plaintiff. Urban or northern snobbery very occasionally appears: the wife of a dancing-master called a domestic servant 'cambrousse' (country bumpkin), and a *marchand de vin* (proprietor of a wine shop) told another man that he was a 'f[outu] Gascon' [fucking Gascon].[12] Accusations of homosexuality are extremely rare, and I have come across only one use of 'sorcière' (witch/sorcerer), an insult fairly common against both men and women in early seventeenth-century French Canada.[13] There are only very occasional references to religion, unlike in the early years of the eighteenth century in Paris, when blasphemy was systematically invoked in complaints. One particularly colourful insult, used by an animal-breeder against a baker's wife, dubbed her 'une âme damnée qu'elle sera accrochée derrière la porte de l'enfer, et que l'enfant dont elle est enceinte n'est point un Chrétien mais un chien' (a damned soul who would be nailed up behind the door of hell, and the child she was pregnant with was not a Christian but a dog). Another, totally unexpected and quite foreign to the values encouraged by the authorities, was the accusation that a woman was 'une bigote qui alloit tous les jours à confesse aux Carmes' (a bigot who went to confession every day at the Carmelite monastery), to which was added, for good measure, that she was a prostitute, an 'excroqueuse' ('con-woman'), and that she was not really married![14]

Other themes which might be expected to occur are absent. There is no trace of accusations of having abandoned children. Nor was abortion used, its appearance in a single example apparently being simply a disguised way of accusing an unmarried woman of sexual promiscuity. Suggestions of infanticide and of incest, which were quite common in French Canada in the late seventeenth and early eighteenth centuries, are missing from the Parisian repertoire.[15] Personal hygiene is not invoked, except for venereal disease in women, and physical features or deformities do not provide the stuff of insults as they did in Languedoc at the same period. Nor is cuckoldry an explicit theme, although it is implicit in suggestions of female infidelity, especially where insults against a man's wife are among those levelled at him. Accusations of drunkenness are rare and little emphasised, and greed, much used against women in eighteenth-century Languedoc, never appears as an insult.[16] And whereas in the small English village of Ryton in the late sixteenth and early seventeenth centuries accusations of slovenly housekeeping were commonly made against women, such calumnies are absent from the Parisian abusive repertoire.[17] Finally, and surprisingly in a society dominated by artisanal work, no aspersions are ever cast on an individual's professional competence: insults emphasise fraud and bad faith, never lack of skill (see Table 1).

A limited range of themes was therefore used, the variety of insults arising from the inventive skill of the speaker in embroidering on a given pattern. Unfortunately the information available in each case does not allow a detailed analysis of the factors which determined an individual's choice, from this semantically limited repertoire, of particular words and expressions. Adjustments were certainly made according to who the victim was, with references to names and places from their past, to their age or profession, or occasionally to their physical appearance. The theme of sexual promiscuity was varied slightly depending on whether a woman was married or not, and it was presumably less available for use against old women. Variation according to the identity of the speaker is much harder to detect, although there were no doubt preferences for particular words and expressions among people from different places,

Table 1. *Sample of insults from the Grève and Faubourg St Antoine quarters, 1752*

	Grève	Faubourg	Total
Sexual			
Whore (putain, raccrocheuse, etc.)	22	25	47
Kept woman (femme entretenue)	1	1	2
Has had illegitimate child	1		1
Has V.D.	1	2	3
Adulteress	1		1
Followed by soldiers	1	—	1
	27	28	55
Dishonesty in trade			
Bankrupt	2	2	4
Makes counterfeit IOU's	1		1
Uses false weights	1		1
Doesn't pay debts	1	—	1
	5	2	7
Criminal			
Thief	11	10	21
Called by name of well-known criminal	2		2
Poisoner	1		1
Has been in prison	2	1	3
Sells stolen goods	2	2	4
	18	13	31
Suspect			
Night prowler (rôdeur de nuit)	1		1
Spy (espion)	1		1
	2		2
Dishonourable profession			
Pimp	2	2	4
Brothel-keeper	1	—	1
	3	2	5
Physical appearance			
Ugly hag (guenon)	1		1
Ugly (vilain)	1	1	2
	2	1	3
Miscellaneous			
Jean-foutre (good-for-nothing)	6	12	18
Bougre, bougresse (rascal)	7	6	13
Gueux, gueuse (beggar, rogue)	4	7	11
Coquin, coquine (knave)	5	4	9
Fripon, friponne (rogue)	4	1	5
Misérable	2		2
Chien (dog)	1	1	2
Insolent, impertinent, affronteur (impudent)	3	1	4
Canaille (rabble)	1	1	2
Pouilleux (lousy)		1	1
Croc (meaning unclear)	1		1
Drôle (peculiar)	1		1
Mangeur de biens (spendthrift)		1	1
Overall totals	92	81	173

generations or socioeconomic backgrounds. There may also have been a hierarchy of insults on the same theme, some milder than others, although this is not distinguishable from the reactions of plaintiffs and witnesses. Of course, mild insults were less likely to be reported. Most of these variations, however, did not change the literal meaning of the insults, or, as we shall see, the social information they conveyed.

The fact that particular themes appear in the Parisian vocabulary of insults, while others do not, or that some were more popular than others, is not a matter of chance. For the themes which people drew on reflect the principal fears and obsessions of eighteenth-century Parisians. They were haunted by the possibility of theft: there was little that people could do to protect their belongings, for locks were easily opened and there were not many hiding places for valuables. There were no banks for cash, and quite large sums were often left under a mattress or in a chest of drawers. For people close to the bread-line even a small theft could have disastrous consequences.

In business, too, there was little security. Agreements were often verbal, credit was used extensively, and innumerable complaints of fraud indicate the unreliability of the system of *billets* and even of bills of exchange. The slightest rumour of fraud, therefore, was worrying, and the constant fear of bankruptcy, evoked in the *cahiers de doléances* of 1789, was all the greater for the artisan or small shopkeeper who often relied on the payment of a debt owed to him in order to satisfy his own creditors.

Principal tenants and house-owners, too, were obsessed by fear of losing their rents. With payment being made at the end of the *terme* (rent period) and not in advance, clandestine moves by indigent tenants gave rise to many complaints. For the principal tenant, who still had to pay the owner whether he received the rent from his sub-tenants or not, the end of the *terme* was a worrying time, and hearing claims that someone had never paid their rent, or that they were in any way dishonest, was not likely to reassure him.

Another obsessive fear in Paris and elsewhere, as G. Lefebvre showed in his study of 'la Grande Peur', was that of vagabonds and brigands.[18] Insults such as 'rôdeur de nuit' (night prowler), 'gueux', 'fripon' (rogue), and the socially equivalent female ones 'gueuse', 'putain', 'coureuse' (female rogue, whore) played on the themes of rootlessness and lack of scruples. 'Espion' awoke fears of denunciation. It is not clear to what extent ordinary Parisians shared Mercier's obsession with the police presence, but there is a very noticeable upsurge of such fears in 1789, when 'mouchard' (police spy) became a standard insult.[19] At other times there was more danger of denunciation to the officials of the trades corporations, to one of the numerous *régies* holding monopolies over various products, or to either religious or civil authorities during Lent, when the smuggling of meat became a major industry.[20] Insults played ruthlessly on all of these fears.

The difference in the epithets and abuse directed against men and women reflects their different social roles. Men were more often in trade than women, hence the more frequent accusations of professional dishonesty. The greater use against men of suggestions of criminal activity or convictions, and against women of petty theft and above all of sexual deviance reflects, possibly the real distribution of criminality between the sexes, but certainly the judicial one: relatively few women were tried for or convicted of major offences.[21] More importantly, it defines the forms of delinquency in which men and women were thought most likely to be involved, and thus reflects contemporary stereotyping.

Here a comparison with J. A. Sharpe's work on slander in York is interesting. In cases of defamation brought before the church courts there in the 1590s, sexual slander against men was common. Indeed, allegations of begetting illegitimate children were made equally against men and women, although accusations of fornication were twice as frequent against women. However, by the 1690s sexual slander against men was markedly less frequent, although it still occurred. Sharpe's suggestion that this reflects the growth of the double standard is supported by the evidence from eighteenth-century Paris.[22] It may be that this evolution is paralleled by a change in the economic and social position of women. Certainly the concentration on sexual behaviour in insults against women in Paris reflects their place in that society in a wider sense. The opportunities open to an unmarried woman who got pregnant were extremely narrow. For a married woman, who, as O. Hufton has shown, was more often than not the one who held the family together and who kept it afloat economically, loyalty to her husband and children was vital for the survival of all.[23] Whether married or unmarried, therefore, her sexual fidelity was seen as a guarantee of a wider constancy. A man's behaviour had no such symbolic quality and he was not the one who, literally, was left holding the baby.

Certain other characteristics of the Parisian vocabulary of insults may also be explained by local conditions. References to provincial origin, for example, were very risky in an environment where a large proportion of the onlookers was likely to be from somewhere else. Abortion and abandonment of children were possibly so frequent as to have become morally neutral, and they were certainly not the subject of official concern and public debate that they were to become at the end of the nineteenth century. The infrequency of accusations of greed, so often directed against women in eighteenth-century Languedoc, perhaps arises from the fact that in rural areas people stored their own food, which it was the woman's job to guard, and this may also account for the absence in Paris of accusations of poor housekeeping. Drunkenness seems, at least in popular circles, to have been socially acceptable, not sufficiently open to condemnation to be used to blacken someone's character. It could, indeed, be used as an excuse for unacceptable behaviour. Witchcraft, if it had ever been used as an insult in Paris, was definitely out of date by the eighteenth century. This, together with the paucity of insults accusing lack of religion – in marked contrast to the early years of the century, when references to blasphemy are frequent in complaints – suggests the progress of secularisation in the city during the eighteenth century. The absence of attacks on professional skill is less easy to explain: was professional incompetence considered less blameworthy than deliberate fraud, or did people hesitate to accuse others of lack of skill through fear of being thought jealous?

What is clear, however, is that the values reflected in insults were essentially those necessary for survival in the particular social and economic context in which people found themselves, and if the listeners actually believed the accusations then the victim's livelihood would suffer. This is a possibility frequently evoked in complaints. A journey-man baker, insulted in the street by the wife of a nearby innkeeper, said that her calumnies could prevent him from finding work in future because of the impression they might make on people who didn't know him well. Public insults against a tailor were likely, he claimed, to make him lose most of his clients.[24] Insults thus served to enforce the dominant value system. At the very least they were a form of socialisation, a way of teaching that value system, and of compelling, if not real observance, at least lip-service to it.

Yet the literal meaning of insults is only significant up to a point, for there was clearly a strong element of rhetoric and show. Furthermore, many of the insults most frequently used, like 'coquin', 'gueux', 'jean-foutre', retained little of their original meaning. 'Gueuse' and 'putain' were the standard insults used against women, and must have been recognised as such by the onlookers. In many cases they were obviously not to be taken literally, and we should not make too much of the actual words used.

Of course, epithets and insinuations were not the only form of insults available. The use of the familiar 'tu', when the relationship required 'vous', was highly insulting. As in modern French, 'vous' was the form used between strangers, neighbours and acquaintances. It was used between master craftsmen and journeymen, and might even prevail between close relatives: we find the mother and brother of a waiter in a café both writing to him as 'vous'.[25] 'Tu' was employed by close friends, by lovers, and within many families (at least between siblings and between husband and wife). Usage was very variable and subtle, and 'tu' was not necessarily the pronoun of solidarity, as has been argued.[26] Enormous solidarity, based on mutual respect, could exist within families, between neighbours or between masters and journeymen who normally called each other 'vous'. It is true, however, that the use of 'tu' by one party and of 'vous' by the other expressed an unequal relationship: that between adults and children, and between employers and their servants. It defined a relationship of authority/submission and of respect/familiarity. For this reason the use of 'tu' where etiquette required 'vous' was a sign of contempt, an assumption of superiority by the speaker which normally drew a sharp reaction. It was a frequent device used in disputes, along with epithets, and is often pointed out by witnesses as an indication of aggressive intent. Thus we find, for example, the keeper of a wine shop picking a fight with a journeyman nail-maker and addressing him as 'tu', while the latter, not wanting to fight, continues to say 'vous'.[27] Here again, therefore, it was the relationship between individuals, and the normal expression of that relationship in day-to-day speech, which determined what constituted an insult.

Closely related to the use of the second person pronoun were tone and manner. Everyday courtesy dictated a polite approach, a particular intonation and degree of warmth in expression. A scarcely definable departure from this pattern indicated aggressive intent and constituted a very subtle form of insult which the interlocutor, although not necessarily the witnesses, was quick to pick up. A master gilder, coming to pick a fight, used 'un ton impérieux et insolent' (an imperious and insolent tone). A *huissier* came looking for someone with an 'air insolent'.[28]

Also available as insults, of course, were gestures: showing someone two fingers or making horns at them; baring one's bottom at someone (apparently only used by men, and mostly against women); shaking a fist at someone; taking them by the collar. There was a whole vocabulary of gestures which could be used alongside verbal insults, some of them adapted for use from a distance and thus equivalent to shouted insults, some employed at closer range. These fall outside the scope of this essay, but had a grammar and code of their own.

All of these insults were, furthermore, supplemented by other forms of verbal attack, most commonly threats. There was a parallel and likewise thematically limited repertoire of threats, often made to a third person in advance of an open quarrel, but sometimes used in a face-to-face encounter. Promises to 'lui couper le visage' (to cut him/her across the face) evoked the marking of a criminal. More straightforward were threats to 'lui donner son affaire' (give him what he deserved), and the bloodthirsty 'il ne mourra que de sa main', which Castan records as a common threat in Languedoc.[29]

Yet another form of verbal attack is totally absent from eighteenth-century Paris: cursing. Never are curses against a person or their family reported, either by plaintiffs or by witnesses. The absence of such imprecations, like that of accusations of witchcraft and sorcery, perhaps testifies to an increasingly secular approach. People apparently did not perceive the supernatural as a potential tool for striking at their enemies, an indication of declining belief in divine or satanic involvement in human affairs.

Verbal insults, therefore, were only part of an arsenal of devices available for attacking an enemy. Like gestures and threats, they contained a strong theatrical element which becomes obvious if we look at the context in which all of these weapons were used. Most commonly they appear as part of a longer dispute. As tempers flared the protagonists would raise their voices and deploy a range of minor insults: expressions of contempt such as the use of 'tu' and of insolent tone and manner, perhaps accompanied by gestures. Verbal insults of the sort we have considered were generally the next step, accompanied by a further rise in volume and by movement, if necessary, into a public place. Sometimes the parties actually came to blows, but on other occasions they did not go beyond a shouting match, often quite protracted.

If we examine the identity of the participants in such quarrels and the relationship between them with as much precision as the available evidence allows, further patterns emerge. The vast majority of the insults recorded were exchanged between people who knew each other, most often as neighbours or colleagues, sometimes both. They were nearly always of similar rank, and very rarely was either in a position of dependence on the other (as a servant, for example). A similar consistency appears in the locations of insults. They were usually used outside: in the street in front of the house where one or both parties lived, or in the courtyard. Sometimes they were shouted out on the stairs, or spoken in the semi-public environment of the wine shop. The audience – and there was always an audience – was therefore composed principally of neighbours and workmates, family and friends. The publicity of insults is constantly emphasised in complaints: they were spoken 'publiquement dans la boucherie', 'crié à haute et intelligible voix en présence d'un grand nombre de personnes' (publicly in the abbatoir, called out in a loud and clear voice in the presence of a large number of people). And invariably they were repeated loudly.[30]

In this overall context the insults, whichever ones were chosen, fulfilled several essential functions. If a serious grievance underlay the dispute the insults could be an appeal for public mediation: there are examples of neighbours attempting a reconciliation after a dispute. Alternatively, public abuse challenged the adversary to justify his or her position or else to offer concessions: 'il est impossible au plaignant,' said a tailor, 'de supporter davantage les injures dudit Richer sans s'exposer à se faire passer pour un homme de mauvaise foi' (it is impossible for the plaintiff to tolerate the said Richer's insults any longer without running the risk of appearing to be in bad faith).[31] If the opponent did not join battle the insults proclaimed the victory of the insulter and the public shaming of the victim. It is here that creative skill became important, in fashioning new variations on given themes. Well-chosen insults were appreciated by an attentive audience: 'elle ne devoit pas y avoir de regret, qu'elle l'avoit bien assaisonné' (she shouldn't have any regrets, she had given him a good telling off) was a spectator's comment to a participant in one colourful contest.[32] There is very rarely any suggestion in the statements of witnesses that insults could rebound on the aggressor. And because in most cases the participants and the audience knew each other well, the victory was to some extent converted into social precedence, creating a pecking order in which one person was considered more formidable, the other less worthy of consideration. The efficacy of insults in eighteenth-century Paris, as elsewhere, largely depended on the existence of a local, neighbourhood community. Honour was important because it gave people a place within that community – it was not a value which in some way 'filtered down' from the upper classes.[33]

If this public and local context was the most common, it was, nevertheless, not the only one. Family disputes, of which a certain number were reported to the police, generally took place inside, in private. The neighbours usually knew all about them, walls being thin and houses crowded, but it was not normal for them to be aired publicly. The insults used were much the same, but their meaning was in this context somewhat different. They remained expressions of antipathy and contempt, but did not have the same significance in shaming the victim. They were not normally directed to an audience and did not invite intervention. Occasionally, it is true, they did occur more publicly and in this case might constitute an attempt by one party to bring public pressure to bear to force the other to behave differently. Occasionally, too, local knowledge of supposedly private quarrels was used as justification for a woman to leave her husband, and in this case the insults used may have been to some extent deliberately designed to inform the neighbours of what was happening.

Insults between strangers were also slightly different, almost always being outside the neighbourhood where one or both of the parties were known. In this case the shame of being insulted was not so acute because the opponent and the audience might well not be there the next day to rub it in. There was less likelihood of permanent loss of face. This explains why disputes between strangers were not usually reported unless one side was seriously injured and therefore demanded compensation. Between people who did not know each other, too, the insults could not be as well adjusted to the opponent and were therefore more likely to be standard epithets chosen somewhat more randomly.

The context could therefore change the social meaning of insults considerably, quite independently of their literal meaning. Nevertheless, in certain types of disputes there could also be an interplay between vocabulary – the words chosen – and context, which would affect the information they conveyed. For example, a common source of disputes was money which had been borrowed, one side claiming to have paid the debt and the other maintaining that it was still outstanding. Here the subject of the quarrel made it likely that the insults used would concentrate on the theme of theft. They were therefore conveying the information that the borrower was generally untrustworthy and undesirable, that the lender had a grievance which the public were called upon to witness and to judge, and at the same time that the offender really was a thief. The literal meaning was, therefore, in this context, part of the message, and understood as such by the audience, whereas had the dispute been over something different the epithet of 'thief' could be understood in a more general sense.

In all of this an important prerequisite for the use of insults to convey a range of information is thus, as certain sociolinguists have emphasised, the existence of a behavioural and linguistic code. Certain words and imputations are understood to be insulting, and when used in a certain way have a conventional significance which is recognised by speaker, victim and audience alike.

What this chapter has explored, then, is the code of insults in eighteenth-century Paris and the cultural determination of that code. We have seen, in studying the literal meaning of insults, that the behaviour they condemned was that most inimical to survival in the social and economic context of eighteenth-century Paris. Thus when people called someone a thief or a whore they were reaffirming the basic values whose general, if not necessarily universal, observance was essential both to individual survival and to that of the community in its existing form.

At the same time, the context of insults, the way they were used and the variety of information that context conveyed were also culturally determined. In their most common use – at least in the source I have used – insults were tools for use against an opponent, a symbolic rejection, a means of forcing him or her to give way by public shaming. They made possible the expression of grievance in a local forum where the matter could be resolved with a minimum of damage. The social function of insults was adapted to the social structure and conditions of a particular society at a particular time.

Despite their apparent triviality, therefore, insults can tell the historian quite a lot. Because linguistic behaviour plays a central role in social interaction, where the documentary evidence exists it is a valuable source of information about social relations. Like any behaviour it conforms to norms which reflect the social condition of those concerned. Looking at who the actors are, at their relationship to each other, and at the way they express themselves, can tell us about relations between social inferiors and superiors, between men and women, or between supplier and client, to choose some obvious examples. Conformity to different norms in varying contexts, or among different sorts of people, illustrates the social distinctions which were perceived and observed at the time. In a more general sense, too, studying the way words were used enables us to some extent to enter the mental world of people in the past. The way they expressed themselves reflects their preoccupations and reveals much about the dominant models and articulated values (although we must not assume that these fully reflect private behaviour).

I have relied heavily on the concepts of sociolinguistics, extremely useful analytical tools for the historian. Indeed, not only do they provide a fruitful approach to language in a historical context but they also furnish an analytical framework for comparison between different places and periods. There is, however, another side to historical sociolinguists. If social anthropologists and sociologists can profitably study language in order to explore society, so too can linguists employ social information in order to explain language. Indeed much work in sociolinguistics has been in this direction. Most of it, however, has been synchronic, concerned with variations in a given language at a particular time. The case of insults suggests, however, that social factors can also help to explain changes over time. Admittedly, the present study looks exclusively at vocabulary and not at syntax or style, and even then concentrates on nouns and adjectives. Nor have I given more than one or two examples of changes in the vocabulary of insults. But there is an implicit comparison with the twentieth century, and in analysing the choice of semantic themes for insults I have mentioned other places at other times. If the words chosen are closely related to political, social, and economic conditions, and the way they are used – their social function – similarly reflects the forms of social organisation, then there is no such thing as a universal insult. From one place to another, and in different centuries, changes in conditions and in social organisation will lead to transformations in the vocabulary and use of insults, and in their overall meaning. One of the most fertile areas for future research, therefore, lies in applying the concepts of sociolinguistics to the historical study of language, and in seeking to explain not only how social factors affect language, but how cultural and social change transform it.

NOTES

1 W. Labov, 'Rules for Ritual Insults', in D. Sudnow, ed., *Studies in Social Interaction* (New York, 1972), pp. 120–69.
2 Y. Castan, *Honnêteté et relations sociales en Languedoc* (Paris, 1974), p. 217.
3 See the essays in P. P. Giglioli, ed., *Language and Social Context* (Harmondsworth, 1972).
4 Archives nationales, Paris, Y10719–16022.
5 Y10994, 23 Nov. 1752, witness 5. Y12597, 5 Sept. 1752, wit. 6.
6 Y15350, 3 Aug. 1752. Y15100, 25 Nov. 1788, wit. 2. Y10994, 1 Nov. 1752.
7 Y13290, 14 Oct. 1788. Y12596, 29 June 1752. Y12597, 19 Sept. 1752, wit. 4. Y13290, 6 Sept. 1788, wit. 5.
8 Y10994, 31 July 1752. Y15350, 31 Aug., 1 July 1752. Y10994, 20 Sept., 16 Oct. 1752.
9 Y11239, 13 Oct. 1752. Y10994, 16 July, 29 Sept. 1752. Y14436, 4 Oct. 1788. Y15350, 24 Nov. 1752, wit. 3. Y11239, 28 Dec., 30 Apr. 1752.
10 Y13290, 15 June 1788, wit. 8. Y15117, 13 June 1788. Y10994, 27 Sept. 1752. Y12596, 2 July 1752.
11 Y10994, 29 Nov., 29 Sept. 1752. Y15100, 1 Dec. 1788. Y15117, 16 June, 31 July 1789.
12 Y14436, 21 July 1788, wit. 1; 13 July 1788. Y14078, 1 Aug., 30 May 1752.
13 P. Moogk, ' "Thieving Buggers" and "Stupid Sluts": Insults and Popular Culture in New France', *William and Mary Quarterly* 36, no. 4 (1979), 524–47, p. 540.
14 Y14078, 12 Sept. 1752. Y11239, 20 May 1752. Y14436, 4 Aug. 1788. Y11705, 3 Feb. 1775.
15 Moogk, ' "Thieving Buggers" ', p. 535.
16 Y11239, 8 Sept. 1752. Y. Castan, *Honnêteté*, pp. 170–1, 287–8.
17 M. Chaytor, 'Household and Kinship: Ryton in the Late Sixteenth Century and Early Seventeenth Centuries', *History Workshop Journal* 10 (1980), 25–60, p. 26. See also E. Ross, 'Survival Networks: Women's Neighbourhood Sharing in London before World War I', *History Workshop Journal* 15 (1983), 4–27, p. 14.
18 G. Lefebvre, *La Grande Peur* (Paris, 1932), Chapter 3.
19 L. S. Mercier, *Tableau de Paris*, 12 vols. (Amsterdam, 1782–8), vol. 1, pp. 192–6.
20 Y15350, 'procès-verbal cartes à jouer', 1752. Y14078, 'procès-verbaux des visites du gras défendu pendant le Caresme', 1752.
21 N. Castan, *Les criminels de Languedoc* (Toulouse, 1980), pp. 26, 34–5. P. Petrovitch, 'Recherches sur la criminalité à Paris dans la seconde moitié du XVIIIe siècle', in *Crimes et criminalité en France sous l'Ancien Régime* (Paris, 1971), pp. 187–261, pp. 234–5.
22 J. A. Sharpe, 'Defamation and Sexual Slander in Early Modern England: The Church Courts at York', University of York, *Borthwick Papers*, no. 58 [1980], pp. 10, 16, 27–8.
23 O. Hufton, 'Women and the Family Economy in Eighteenth-Century France', *French Historical Studies* 9 (1975), 1–22.
24 Y10994, two complaints of 28 Feb. 1752.
25 Y11239, 26 Jan. 1752, wit. 7, 9. Y13751, dossier of interrogations, 19 Sept. 1746, no. 14. Y14484, 3 Oct. 1789, wit. 2. Y16003, dossier Quatremer, letters of 9 Feb. 1779, 27 Jan. 1780.
26 Y15100, 25 Nov. 1788, wit. 6. Y11706, 26 Aug. 1775, wit. 1, 2. Y14436, 3 May 1788. Y14484, 4 April 1789, wit. 3. Y15350, 3 Dec. 1752. R. Brown and A. Gilman, 'The Pronouns of Power and Solidarity', in T. A. Sebeok, ed., *Style in Language* (Cambridge, Mass., 1960), pp. 253–76.
27 Y13290, 8 Sept. 1788, wit. 9. See also Y14078, 23 Dec. 1752, wit. 9.
28 Y11239, 17 Oct. 1752. Y14078, 21 Mar. 1752.
29 Y11239, 16 June 1752. Y12596, 16 May 1752. Y10994, 16 June 1752. Y14436, 7 Feb. 1788. Y. Castan, *Honnêteté*, p. 167.
30 Y12597, 17 Oct. 1752. Y11239, 16 May 1752.
31 Y10994, 28 Feb. 1752.
32 Y12597, 19 Sept. 1752, wit. 1.
33 These points are developed in D. Garrioch, *Neighbourhood and Community in Paris, 1740–1790* (Cambridge University Press, 1986). On the function of ritual insults in establishing position among peers, see W. Labov, 'Rules for Ritual Insults'.

6

LE LANGAGE MÂLE DE LA VERTU: WOMEN AND THE DISCOURSE OF THE FRENCH REVOLUTION

Dorinda Outram

The history of the French Revolution used to be dominated by studies of class struggle, *crises de subsistances*, war and terror. But it is now increasingly recognised that it is impossible to understand the revolutionary phenomenon itself without examining the very special political discourse which it generated.[1] For François Furet in particular, that discourse is the central motor of the Revolution:

> Since the people alone had the right to govern – or at least, when it could not do so, to reassert public authority continually – power was in the hands of those who spoke for the people. Therefore, not only did that power reside in the word, for the word being public, was the means of unmasking forces that hoped to remain hidden and were thus nefarious; but also power was always at stake in the conflict between words, for power could only be appropriated through them, and so they had to compete for the conquest of that evanescent yet primordial entity, the people's will. The Revolution replaced the conflict of interests for power with a competition of discourses for the appropriation of legitimacy . . . Revolutionary activity *par excellence* was the production of a maximalist language through the intermediary of unanimous assemblies mythically endowed with the general will. In that respect, the history of the Revolution is marked throughout by a fundamental dichotomy. The deputies made laws in the name of the people, whom they were presumed to *represent*; but the members of the *sections* and of the clubs acted as the *embodiment* of the people, as vigilant sentinels, duty-bound to track down and denounce any discrepancy between action and values, and to reinstate the body politic at every moment . . . the salient feature of the period between May–June 1789 and 9 thermidor 1794, was not the conflict between Revolution and counter-revolution, but the struggle between the representatives of the successive assemblies and the club militants for the dominant symbolic position, the people's will.[2]

The nature of revolutionary politics, in other words, made political discourse central, and political discourse shaped the very motor of revolution itself. The Revolution was the first point in French history where persuasion of a mass audience was crucial and an integral part of the political phenomenon. Words, as Furet argues, were power. At the same time, the collapse not only of the institutions of the Old Regime, but also of its ideological legitimation, meant that a desperate need existed to create a new discourse of validation for the new State, and for the groups which competed for this control. Control of the discourse of the Revolution gave access to opinion, to the general will, and conferred the power which came from successful representation of that general will to itself.

We need to explain further why this discourse was capable of playing this role. The answer comes from the Revolution's rejecting and contorted attitude to power. Many writers have stressed the extent to which, in this discourse, power as such was seen as evil and contaminating, in other words was approached almost entirely in moral terms. Politics and morality were completely conflated.[3] Under the Revolution, claims to power thus came from the denunciation of power; but now, the denunciation of power had to be carried out in the name of a pure and undivided general will. Thus, what the Revolution *used* as its political discourse does not fulfil what Pocock has described as the minimum criterion that a discourse *be* regarded as political, that it should 'consist in the utterance of essentially disputed propositions'.[4] It contained no means of admitting that political morality might be variable, and it contained no way of discussing conflicting sectional interests which undermined its ideal of the endless, unbroken harmony of the general will, from which all revolutionary legitimacy stemmed. As Roger Barny has put it, 'Les théories politiques bourgeoises . . . évacuait les rapports sociaux concrets . . . [et] ne pouvaient pas se plier aux nécessités d'une lutte politique exprimant, dans son fond, la lutte des classes.'[5] Thus the discourse of the Revolution was an object of competition because it offered the false, though convincing, promise that it was not a political discourse at all, and thus that it guaranteed the purity and hence the legitimacy of its users.

How is this revolutionary discourse to be recognised? Firstly, by its ritualised invocation of absolute, moral concepts, of which the most important was that of 'virtue', as the guarantors of the integrity of the Revolution. Such concepts, like the 'general will', are hypostazied entities, hardly ever receiving described real embodiment; for if the nation is as one in its general will, and that general will is the guarantor of the legitimacy of the Revolution, sectional interests do not exist, and there are therefore no precise descriptive words for them. It is not surprising that this discourse is also full of human reference figures turned into embodied universals. To take only the most famous – and for our purposes, most significant – figure, that of the elder Brutus, we find that the political discourse of this period abounds in shorthand references to Brutus as the embodiment of virtue, a man who put the safety of the state above private emotion and the destruction of his family: 'virtue' and 'Brutus' are virtually reciprocal referents.[6] This is also a discourse which proceeds by the ritual invocation of polarities: vice and virtue, aristocrat and people. This is the reason that the exclusionary power of this discourse is so strong. He who is not with us is against us. And this is why struggle for appropriation of this discourse could literally take on a life and death character. Furet is surely correct to see this form of political discourse, which leaves no middle ground open for debate and negotiation, as one of the explanations of the high turnover of ruling groups in revolutionary politics.[7]

But we can take the description of revolutionary discourse further than Furet does, and ask other questions about it. First of all it is clear that in spite of its maximalist claims to embody the people's will, that discourse never replaced many other sorts of discourse which were used, when convenient, for political ends. Many of the key words of the discourse of the Revolution, such as 'virtue', also had powerful resonances in completely other discourses, and in particular in that discourse on feminity to which the eighteenth century had added so much elaboration. Such facts are crucial in women's encounter with the public language of the Revolution. In particular, the conflation of morality and politics within the discourse of the Revolution made the barriers between that, and the discourse on femininity, a highly permeable one.

We can also ask of this discourse, as we would of any other, where are its weaknesses and stresses? Furet's account shows us a monolithic discourse terrifying in its capacity to aid and initiate proscription and Terror. Yet it was also a discourse able, if necessary, to abandon its circular, self-consistent character, and ruthlessly to appropriate other discourses to itself. It was also a treacherous discourse. It posed more problems to the majority of its users than Furet admits, for there is no discourse which causes so many problems to its users as that one whose control is a life and death matter, which is itself a validation of the power to speak at all, but which is useless for the negotiation of their sectional interests. In the case of the bourgeoisie, we may concur with Patrice Higonnet's argument that this characteristic of the discourse accounts for the incoherence of bourgeois aims in the Revolution up to 1794, and for the length of time which it took them to gain unchallenged control of the revolutionary movement. In other words, to pursue sectional interests through a universalistic rhetoric may be necessary, but it is also inefficient and dangerous, even for social classes which *have* actual control of the political process, and even more for excluded groups. This is a problem which affects women's use of the 'revolutionary discourse' to the highest degree.

Women's use of and response to the discourse of the Revolution, and male reactions to their attempt to appropriate that discourse, is a topic which broadens our perspective on the nature and uses of political language. As an excluded sectional group *par excellence* women had to struggle for their own interests through the medium of a political discourse unsuited to their needs, as it was to the needs of every other excluded sectional group. But surprisingly enough even the simultaneous recent increase of interest both in the language of the Revolution and in women's participation in the Revolution has not resulted in any study of women's reaction to that discourse. Public utterances by women using the 'revolutionary discourse' have been the subject of great attention from feminist historians, but they have almost all concentrated on the message, the explicit content of their utterances, to the exclusion of the problems posed for women by the nature of the discourse itself. This partly stems from the Whig orientation of much of women's history, which leads it to concentrate on demands which can be seen as foreshadowing later and more successful 'feminism'. This approach leaves on one side the entire problem of the structure of public utterance itself, and what it tells us about the position of women in relation to the public sphere. If we knew more about that, then we might also be able to say more about the reasons for women's failure to achieve demands for political equality in this period.[8]

Feminist historians have also paid very little attention to the non-public relations of women in this period. Autobiographies, private letters and private diaries rarely figure in their accounts of the female response in this period, and with this omission we lose an essential alternative register to the political, public voices which were often as wrapped up in the revolutionary discourse as any man's. Once again, this failure to utilise private documentation reflects a tendency to stay within the canon of 'founding mothers', which, as has been frequently remarked, forms at once one of the strengths and the weakness of much women's history. It is certain, however, that concentration on continuous retelling of the acts of a small band of female activists such as Théroigne de Méricourt means that women's history in the revolutionary period may well continue to be curiously isolated from that of the general history of the Revolution, and that mainstream history will accordingly take little account of women's history. It is significant both of this isolation, and of this lack of sensitivity to the problem of women's response to the revolutionary discourse, that, for example, Régine Robin's analysis of public utterances by revolutionary leaders should not only ignore the whole issue, but also tacitly exclude public utterances by women from her analysis.[9] I would argue here for the use of a far wider selection of material produced by women than has usually been the case, for it is largely in informal, private writing that explicit comments on the use of language in public surroundings seem to occur. There is also the methodological point that far more interesting sorts of queries can be answered about language if different sorts of discourse can be identified and their uses contrasted with each other. The success of Paul Fussell's analysis of stresses in 'official' discourse through their reflections in such private discourses as soldiers' letters home and private diaries, is a continuous reminder of how the historian of discourse can proceed only if he has at his disposal that *variety* of registers which Furet has christened the 'dual keyboard' of utterance. Only thus can the historian become aware of the rules governing the use of different types of discourse, of their permeability to each other, and the tensions between them.[10]

The invisibility of the problem of women's encounter with public discourse is also encouraged by the state of contemporary sociolinguistics, which seems determined to provide as few models as possible to the historian. Contemporary sociolinguistics commits the reverse sin from that of the feminist historians of the Revolution, and tells us little if at all about women's speech outside the private realm, the home, and little too about how women talk to each other. In other words, it replicates the still persistent myth of women as private beings, creatures of an interior. There is as far as I know, no study of women's use of public discourses, let alone of the problems they might encounter in such use.[11] What follows can only be a tentative attack on the problem, but it is clear that this topic would tell us not only a great deal about women's political difficulties under the Revolution; it would also tell us much about the stresses within that revolutionary discourse of which Furet has given us so monolithic a picture.

Problems in the use of a specific discourse may also arise not simply from the inner character of that discourse, but also from the way it is socially inserted, its resonances against the rest of speech. Revolutionary discourse was not sex-neutral. Its main emotive words, such as 'virtue', were ones which had a long history behind them, not only in the tradition of civic humanism, but also of weighing more heavily on the female sex than on the male. All sectional groups were disadvantaged by this discourse, but at least the dispossessed, the 'people' at large, could claim to be the general will, *le souvereign*, and thus to embody political virtue. The fact that it was difficult to identify the sovereign and its will, and that the bourgeois leaders of the Revolution assumed control of that definition for their own purposes, should not lead us to overlook the fact that in the interior of that discourse *le souvereign* was automatically Good.[12] Women as such, in this bi-polar world of reference, were Bad. To a very

large extent, the influence of women was seen as the defining characteristic of the corruption of power under the Old Regime. Boudoir politics,
the exchange of political gifts for sexual favours, are seen both as causes
of the weakness of the Old Regime, and as the justification of the
Revolution. Perhaps the most telling example of this occurred during the
trial of Marie Antoinette, the deposed Queen of France, in 1793. The
'political' counts against her – of aiding the King's flight to Varennes, of
plotting the invasion of France – were inseparable from, and bolstered
by, the accusations of sexual perversion and incest which accompanied
them. In 'corrupting' the Dauphin, the heir to France, with sexuality, her
accusers implied that she had corrupted the body politic at one and the
same time as she had corrupted the actual physical body of her son.[13]

As Furet remarks, the Revolution, and with it, its particular discourse,
could only legitimate its own capacity to wield power, and distinguish
itself from the corrupt power of the Old Regime, by attacking power
itself.[14] To the degree that power in the Old Regime was ascribed to
women, that meant that the discourse of the Revolution was committed
to an anti-feminine rhetoric. It was a rhetoric with great investment in it
for the male politician, and analysis of it from this direction may explain
many of its salient features in a way not attempted before. In the analysis
of the old regime enormous power was ascribed to women – an ascription
which functioned to absolve men from responsibility both for the weakness of the monarchy and for its overthrow. Male politicians could find in
this analysis an escape from the guilt necessarily arising from their
participation in the destruction of an entire order of society and its
complex religious sanctions. What looked like a sacrilegious act had *in
fact* been a crusade for virtue. It is more relevant for our purposes,
however, to note how this analysis of the sexual corruption of the Old
Regime, and its legitimation of the Revolution, turn on a slide in meaning
between two definitions of 'virtue'. Women's personal virtue
(virtue = chastity) is equated with political virtue (virtue = putting state
above personal or sectional interests), like Brutus, who executed his sons
when they attempted to betray the Roman republic. The continuum
between the two senses carries a whole series of messages: that female
chastity is the prerequisite for political innovation undertaken in the
name of a universal will; that women are in any case threatening to the
Revolution, because any deviation from chastity = virtue involves the
collapse of political virtue, and because women can personalise politics
with their sexual favours, and factionalise it with competition for those
favours. 'Virtue' was in fact a two-edged word, which bisected the
apparently universalistic terminology of *le souvereign* into two distinct
political destinies, one male and the other female. All citizens were
part of *le souvereign*, but somehow one half of *le souvereign* could

only function at the price of the sexual containment of the other half.

It was through the word 'virtue', so crucial to the discourse of the Revolution, that power was taken from women both in the interior of that discourse, and as users of that discourse. It is also no accident that many of stock adjectives of the revolutionary discourse – 'chaste vertu', 'probité austère', 'vertu mâle et républicaine' – should enforce this impression of a discourse heavily weighted in gender terms. The accepted historiography of the Old Regime ascribed enormous power to women, power partly defined as sexual evil. The necessary conclusion was that political revolution could only take place if women were excluded from exercising power, and the niche formerly occupied by women's powerful vice was taken over by male virtue. As Olympe de Gouges remarked, 'women are now respected and excluded, under the old regime they were despised and powerful'.[15] All recent writing on women and the Revolution, which seems to emphasise women's *power*, however temporary, must explain why contemporary perceptions were so radically different.

And so it came about that the woman who refused to be respected but excluded was faced with a series of difficult choices, in the actual act of speaking in public as much as in the choice of words to speak. If she was not respected, there was no way of being heard; if heard, then the way was open for all sorts of attacks on a consequent loss of virtue – just the sort of attacks that were in fact made on the female activists of the political clubs and especially on the women's political club, the Société des républicaines révolutionnaires.[16] This explains some of the apparently very contorted attitudes taken up by women who wanted both participation *and* respect. One method was that provided by Mme Roland: to provide a forum for others, men, to speak in, whilst remaining silent, and hence respected, herself. Few more frustrating ways of becoming one of the best-known figures of the Revolution can be imagined:

> Je savais quel rôle convenait à mon sexe et je ne le quittai jamais. Les conférences se tenaient en ma présence sans que j'y prisse aucun part; placée hors du cercle et près d'une table, je travaillais des mains, ou faisais les lettres, tandis qu'on déliberait . . . je ne perdit pas un mot de ce qui se débitait et il m'arrivait de me mordre les lèvres pour ne pas dire le mien . . .
>
> Se taire quand on est seule n'est pas chose merveilleuse; mais garder constamment le silence au milieu des gens qui parlent des objets auxquels on s'intéresse, réprimer les saillies du sentiment qui vous oppriment lors d'une contradiction, arrêter les idées intermédiaires qui échappent aux raissonneurs, et faute desquelles ils concluent mal ou ne sont pas entendus, mesurer

> ainsi la logique de chacun en se commandant toujours soi-même, est un grand moyen d'acquérir de la pénétration, de la rectitude, de perfectionner son intelligence et d'augmenter la force de son âme.

Mme Roland's continual emphasis in her *mémoires* on her private, domestic, solitary life, even during Roland's two ministries, comes straight out of her acceptance of the idea that women can be valued only inasmuch as they wield corrupt power: 'on n'avait cherché à me voir que dans l'idée qu'il pouvait en être dans l'ancien régime, où l'on engageait les femmes à solliciter leurs maris'. When she was finally arrested and imprisoned in St Pélagie, she found with a degree of shock explicable only on these lines, that the authorities had taken little care to segregate her from the ladies of easy virtue (revealing phrase) also held within its walls: 'Voilà donc le séjour qui était réservé à la digne épouse d'un homme de bien. Si c'est là le prix de la vertu sur la terre, qu'on ne s'étonne donc plus de mon mépris pour la vie.' The long fight to possess both virtue and participation seemed to have passed so unsuccessfully that she was no differently viewed from the ladies of the town. It is against limitations like these, imposed by revolutionary discourse, that we have to redefine the *sort* of power Mme Roland in fact possessed.[17]

The conditions set for women's use of the revolutionary discourse by male politicians similarly contained enormous internal contradictions. It seemed that it was only within the sphere of sexual containment *par excellence*, the married home, that women could use the language of the revolution with the blessing of male political leaders. As a *section* leader from Orleans remarked in 1792: 'Les mères approndront à leurs enfants à parler de bonne heure le langage mâle de la liberté.'[18] All very well. But what to think of that language – and hence of the viability of the task of political education entrusted to women – when it was itself highly hostile to that guarantor of female respectability, the home? As remarked before, revolutionary discourse gloried in personified abstractions of virtue, most of them culled from the more austere, inflexible and unlovable figures of the history of the Roman republic. Brutus, a favourite reference figure to the men, was a source of especial difficulty to the women. Many women, in fact, found the entire Roman reference point difficult to sustain. A reading of private sources shows how many women, of all political views, and including many who consciously accepted their relegation to the domestic sphere, none the less reject Rome. Mme Jullien, wife of the significantly named Marc-Antoine Jullien, Jacobin deputy for the Drôme, went through a phase of very conscious rejection of the whole 'Roman fever', as she put it: 'Il faut redescendre au niveau commun, et penser que le mieux est l'ennemi du bien. Je me suis donc guérie de ma fièvre romaine, qui pourtant ne m'a jamais fait donner dans le républicainisme que par la crainte de la guerre civile.' Mme Roland's reactions were similar; and Mme Cavaignac, republican and mother of the future President, brought out the ambiguities better than anyone when considering the problem of teaching about republican virtue through the figure of Brutus:

> Il ne me paraît pas prouvé que Cataline lui-même fut le Cartouche qu'on nous a montré, et les injures de Cicéron, ce type de modérantisme, ne m'en donnait pas la certitude . . . Hélas, on ne se tromperait guère en ce monde, surtout dans ce bon temps de *chaste verité*, en tenant toujours pour prouvé le contraire de ce qui est officiellement établi . . . [for a brief period, however, even she was misled, and] . . . je tenais les deux Brutus en grande vénération: le premier qui a tué son fils, le second qui a tué son père.[19]

It was not simply that there was a 'separate sphere' for the exercise of female political virtue – it was that male personifications of virtue actually attacked and destroyed what they themselves defined as the physical location and necessary condition of female virtue, the home and family. For a woman to speak this indeed male language was in effect to endorse the destruction of her sphere, the home, should the higher male definition of virtue demand it. This would leave a woman, in the last analysis, with precisely nothing: neither a secure sphere of discourse for herself, nor an easy access to that of men.[20] Such an inconsistency could do nothing but undermine the authority of any woman who tried to use this revolutionary discourse, and it undermined it in ways never experienced by the male *sans-culottes*.

Authority in political discourse, in this time of complete conflation of the moral and the political, came from nothing so much as a perceived congruence between the moral discourse implicit in the words, and the capacity for moral personification which rested in the figure of the speaker. This was the source of Robespierre's power, as Furet has pointed out: that he fully personified the discourse he used.[21] He thus demonstrated the revolutionary discourse's capacity to legitimate not only a political order but also a *person*, by abolishing the incongruence between public and private roles. Women, on the other hand, were dubious about the enterprise of personification. Because their revolutionary respectability rested on their sexual containment within the male-dominated world of marriage and family they could never personify themselves as whole beings within that discourse. It is perhaps significant that the only group of women permitted to make a direct input into revolutionary discourse were actresses. Many a revolutionary public figure went to the great ladies of the Comédie Française for instruction on how to be, how to personify themselves.[22] But actresses were in any case not ordinary women: their profession turned them into embodiments of pure personification. Other, ordinary women, tended to view the enterprise with suspicion. Mme Cavaignac, for example, thought that her mother had too grand and simple a personality to *need* to be given a Roman name, such as Cornelia, mother of the Gracchi.[23] In refusing personification, women were also perhaps refusing to participate in the first political discourse of modern times to have that defining characteristic of modern 'totalitarian languages', in Jean Pierre Faye's phrase, which is the attack on the family.[24]

Here, the discourse of the Revolution is, of course, enormously different from that of the Old Regime, whose basic predicate was that of the intimate human body (the body politic), and the intimate family (the King as father of his people).[25] The discourse of the Old Regime is hesitant precisely in its relations with *le bien public*; that of the Revolution on the contrary is confident about the general will, but wishes to know nothing of the family in society, or the family *as* society.

We can thus also say that it may be no accident that a far more normal female response to the Revolution was not the contorted encounter with its discourse that we have so far been describing in the cases of women strongly tied to the new movement through family links and personal conviction; it was, far more, the rejection of the Revolution itself, and of the discourse that went with it. It has long been a commonplace of the history of the Revolution, from Michelet on, that counter-revolution was a movement in which women played an important, and enduring role, far more than they did in the Revolution itself. Recent research – as so often – has done nothing but confirm Michelet's perception.[26] Yet this is a fact that goes virtually unrecognised in the 'women's' history of the Revolution, which understandably enough prefers to focus on an image of woman as a political activist, and an activist on the correct, left-wing, progressive side. Yet it is now becoming clear that women's devotion to throne and altar during the Revolution were to set the stage for that decisive separation between men's politics and women's politics which occurred in the course of the following century, and led to the formation of radically different attitudes between the sexes on such crucial issues as the fate of the Church and of republicanism.[27]

It is also rarely, if ever, remarked that the Church had the supreme advantage, from a woman's point of view, of possessing the only other universalistic discourse on offer in the revolutionary period – and certainly the only other discourse with anything like the resonance of the discourse of the Revolution. It is this language which is overwhelmingly used by ordinary women who decide to protest against aspects of the

Revolution. It was the language of the Vendée. It is also used even within the highly politicised working class of Paris itself. The women, of whom little is heard in current feminist history, who did not endorse the *sans-culotte* demands of bread and Terror, overwhelmingly use the languages of the Gospel in their appeals for mercy.[28] Claude-Françoise Loissillier protested against the guillotine, for example, in the following way: 'C'est attaquer tout à la fois le Créateur et la créature: le Créateur, en détruisant son ouvrage; la créature, en la privant du bienfait de Dieu. Craignez surtout que cela n'attire sur vous et sur cette grande ville les grands fléaux de Dieu, en laissant faire cela plus longtemps.' Melanie Ernouf protested against the fall of the monarchy in very similar language: 'J'aime mon roi, je le regrette tous les jours et veux le suivre et me jetter dans les mains de ces vils assassins. Ils aiment les victimes: qu'ils s'abreuvent du sang pur des agneaux'. This discourse also competes with the 'revolutionary discourse' at the highest levels. It was long ago pointed out by Albert Mathiez, that many of the female prophets who emerge during the Revolution had contacts with male politicians which seem to have been more numerous and less obviously hostile than those which characterised the more 'feminist' women.[29]

So far, we have simply considered the many and considerable dis-advantages to the female speaker of the discourse of the Revolution. Yet in spite of this very negative analysis we are still faced with the problem that women did use this discourse repeatedly in their public statements, and that they used it in public contexts even in utterances made very much in the heat of the moment, as Soboul has pointed out.[30] Citizeness Auxerre, silk-weavers' leader, in the heat of the *prairial* days of 1795 burst out with, 'qu'ils étaient le souvereign, que les officiers municipaux et les autorités n'étaient que leur agents . . . et qu'il était bien étonnonant que le souvereign manquait de bois quand ses agents en étaient abondamment pourvus'. So we cannot, and do not, mean to establish the discourse of the Revolution simply as yet another historical obstacle for women in their efforts to gain political equality with men, having nothing to do with their real inner selves. Some reasons why women might *want* to use this discourse in public statements are obvious enough; their audiences, except in the very unusual case of the Société des femmes républicaines révolutionnaires, were generally of both sexes. It makes sense, further, for an excluded or peripheral group to use the discourse of dominant groups in demanding change, in order to gain the attention of such groups and to validate their own utterances. But there is another sense in which any universalistic language, whether it be the discourse of the Revolution, or of Christianity, has a positive function for women, as well as the very negative features we have so far concentrated upon. In one of the few studies in modern sociolinguistics to contribute much to the problems of women's historical encounters with public language, Robin Lakoff has pointed out that in 'ordinary life' women are continuously confronted with an impossible choice of language; if a woman

> refuses to 'talk like a lady', she is ridiculed and subjected to criticism as unfeminine; if she does learn, she is ridiculed as being unable to think clearly, unable to take part in a serious discussion: in some sense, as less than fully human. These two choices a woman has – to be less than a woman, or less than a person – are highly painful.[31]

There is no way out of this linguistic catch-22 (one which, as we have seen, trapped Mme Roland completely). But discourses which *appear* to be universalistic can be seen as a way of avoiding the problem for the female speaker, because they often offer an automatic authority and validation. There is also the point that the problem of 'lady-like language', arises and is enforced in very specific social situations; whereas the promise of the discourse of the Revolution, with its very rigidity, its set phraseology, its routinised allusions to the great personifications, is that it is relatively *impermeable* to the precise social and public setting in which it happens to be used. For the male speakers in the National Convention, for example, it was positively a disadvantage to be caught with the confines of the discourse when facing not only an audience of their peers, but also the less calculable reactions of the Parisian mob which packed the public galleries. But for women, it may well have seemed to work the other way, and the discourse's very rigidity may have offered them escape from the perennial moulding of the social situation which insisted on their feminity as the reason for denying them the right to speak with authority as public persons. The fact that all these hopes invested in the use of the revolutionary discourse by women were in the end disappointed, and that so many women came to reject the discourse itself, does not invalidate these points about the initial attractiveness of the language to the female speaker. This means that the relation of women to the revolutionary discourse is ambivalent and close, rather than one of complete rejection. In spite of its appearance, and in spite of the promises of the Revolution itself for universal citizenship, the discourse of the Revolution was far from being sex-neutral. But it was an instrument that women used in great numbers, whatever the misgivings and criticisms that many of them expressed, because of the way it seemed to promise authority to the otherwise compromised position of the female speaker in a public arena.

How has this necessarily brief survey helped us to understand more about the problems of women, and the nature of that discourse? To take the last point first: it is clear that certainly in the work of commentators such as Soboul, and less explicitly in that of non-Marxist historians such as Furet, linguistic analysis is dominated by class analysis. Revolutionary discourse is seen primarily as an exercise in mystification, a means whereby bourgeois politicians prevented the excluded social and economic groups from producing an autonomous discourse which would have given names to their specific discontents. The mystificatory use of language for the purposes of class warfare was not lost on contemporaries either. As the Abbé D'Olivier remarked, 'l'abstraction des droits égaux est une illusion redoubtable, et sans doute une supercherie inventée par les puissants et les riches'; the popular leader, Jacques Roux, took up the point two years later: ' "Liberty" is naught but an empty dream if one class of men can starve another with impunity. "Equality" is naught but an empty dream if the rich through their monopolies can exercise the power of life and death over others.'[32] So class in this view dominates language, and gives it its hidden relationships of power. This is a view with much truth to it. But once one asks the question of how the revolutionary discourse affected a gender rather than a social class, then whole new functions of this language are revealed. It becomes obvious that it is inadequate to analyse the discourse of the Revolution only as a more or less consciously utilised tool of class war; it is also, and just as much, a language fashioned for the war of the sexes.[33] In fact one could argue that the whole of the discourse, in its choice of adjectives, in the weight it puts on the gender-laden concept of *virtue*, in its whole implicit and explicit glorification of woman's sexual containment, in its identification of the female as all-powerful and all-corrupting, capable of changing the entire nature of political regimes by the use or possession of her body, is *even more* orientated to the mystification of women than it was towards the mystification of excluded social groups. Instead of the lynch-pin of the whole discourse being the word *virtue*, that word in fact stands revealed as the point of *maximum stress* within that discourse, and the point at which that discourse is most affected by the reverberations of its terminology in other, more 'normal' discourses. Women's position here challenged the gap between the reality of politics and the discourse of politics even more than did that of the socially and politically excluded as such, groups to whom the discourse automatically attached *virtue* from within the centre of the discourse. In the case of these excluded groups, the concept of virtue was of major importance in 'evacuating' (to use Barny's phrase) the discourse of a concrete political, factional reality; in the case of women, it was used not so much to evacuate political reality as to divide it and both to stigmatise and confine the female half of it. As long as women left unchallenged the equation of sexuality with political corruption, there was no way that they could arrogate to themselves and their cause the magic, validating power of an unproblematic use of the central concept of revolutionary discourse, that of virtue. This sentiment was even concurred in by the 'feminist' activist Olympe de Gouges:

> Women have done more harm than good. Constraint and dissimulation have been their lot. What force robbed them of, ruse returned to them; they had recourse to all the resources of their charms, and the most irreproachable person did not resist them. Poison and the sword were both subject to them . . . The French government especially, depended throughout the centuries on the nocturnal administration of women; the cabinet kept no secret from their indiscretion . . . anything which characterised the folly of men, profane and sacred, all have been subject to the cupidity and ambition of this sex . . .'

The revolutionary tribunal agreed, and sentenced exemplary numbers of prostitutes to death as a moral *and therefore political* menace:

> Le despotisme a toujours été l'ennemi des mœurs publics, que la prostitution était un des moyens qu'il employait pour affirmir son empire et perpétuer l'esclavage des citoyens [sic] par l'appat du libertinage et de la débauche; qu'on ne peut plus douter que les répaires de prostitution ne soient les asiles ordinaires des contre-révolutionnaires qui payent leurs infâmes plaisirs avec l'or de Pitt.[34]

It is thus obvious, to go to our original point, that one of the main explanations of why women, like the urban working class, found so little permanent gain from the revolutionary period may be linguistic. The series of deceptions and catch-22 positions in which the discourse of the Revolution ensnared them contributed enormously to their lack of long-term public authority. The failure of a 'women's movement' using a male-orientated political discourse was not only, however, completely foreseeable: it had the converse consequences, that those women who campaigned against the Revolution, using another universalistic discourse, far more adapted for women's needs as public persons, that provided by the Church, were those who were going to set the trend of women's political role, for all except a minority, for the next century in France. That role would be founded on a total separation of the political ideologies of men and of women, leaving men to reject the programmes and language of the Church and women to reject the programmes and language of secular republicanism.[35] Arguably, therefore, the discourse of the Revolution succeeded perfectly in carrying out its 'hidden agenda' of the exclusion of women from a public role, leaving for them recourse to the surviving universalistic language of the Church.

NOTES

1 Examples of this new emphasis might include François Furet, *Penser la révolution française* (Paris, 1978), translated as *Interpreting the French Revolution* (Cambridge, 1981): all citations will be made from this edition; Norman Hampson, *The French Revolution and Democracy* (Reading, 1983); Roger Barny, 'Les mots et les choses chez les hommes de la révolution française', *La Pensée* (1978), 96–115; Marc-Elie Blanchard, *St-Just et Cie – La Révolution et les mots* (Paris, 1980), reviewed by Serena Tuci-Torgussen, *Annales historiques de la Révolution française* 53 (1981), 332–4; Albert Soboul, 'Equality: on the power and danger of words', *Proceedings of the Consortium on Revolutionary Europe* 1 (1974), 13–21; Régine Robin, *Histoire et linguistique* (Paris, 1973). Also useful as a compendium of examples of the discourse is the older study by François Aulard, *L'éloquence parlementaire pendant la révolution française*, 3 vols. (Paris, 1886).
2 Furet, *Interpreting the French Revolution*, pp. 48–50.
3 E.g. as Robespierre wrote in his paper, *Le patriote français*, 2 September 1792, 'L'âme de la république, c'est la vertu, c'est-à-dire, l'amour de la patrie', quoted in Hampson, *French Revolution and Democracy*, p. 14; Furet, *French Revolution*, p. 59; Barny, 'Les mots et les choses', p. 99.
4 J. G. A. Pocock, 'The concept of language and the *métier d'historien*', E.U.I. Colloquium papers: *The Creation and Diffusion of political languages in early modern Europe*, Florence, 28–30 September 1983, p. 20. We follow here the distinction elaborated by Pocock between *langue* and *parole*, 'language' and 'discourse', the latter being 'a distinguishable language game' with 'its own vocabulary, rules, preconditions and implications' (pp. 3–4).
5 Barny, 'Les mots et les choses', pp. 109–110. The incapacity of the discourse of the Revolution to provide *legitimate* ways of discussing the interplay of sectional interests is discussed at length in Patrice Higonnet, *Class, Ideology and the Rights of Nobles during the French Revolution* (Oxford, 1981), *passim*.
6 The Revolution's use of the Brutus myth is discussed in R. L. Herbert, *David, Voltaire, 'Brutus' and the French Revolution: An Essay in Art and Politics* (London, 1972).
7 Furet, *Interpreting the French Revolution*, pp. 52–3, 128.
8 Examples of that tendency could include Mary Durham, 'Citizenesses of the Year II of the French Revolution', *Proceedings of the Consortium for the History of Revolutionary Europe* 1 (1972–4), 87–109; Darline Gay Levy, Harriet Branson Applewhite and Mary Durham Johnson, *Women in Revolutionary Paris 1789–1795: Selected Documents translated with Notes and Commentary* (Urbana, 1979); Olwyn Hufton, 'Women in Revolution, 1789–1796', in *French Society and the Revolution*, ed. Douglas Johnson (Cambridge, 1976), pp. 148–64. Non-feminist historians, and non-female ones, do no better: e.g. Albert Soboul, 'Sur l'activité militante des femmes dans les sections parisiennes en l'an II', *Bulletin d'histoire économique et sociale de la révolution française* 11 (1979), 15–26; L. Devance, 'Le féminisme pendant la révolution française', *Annales historiques de la révolution française* 49 (1977), 341–76. The older study by Baron Marc de Villiers, *Histoire des clubs des femmes et des légions d'amazones, 1793–1848–1871* (Paris, 1910), however, contains some perceptive remarks scattered *passim*.
9 Régine Robin, *Histoire et linguistique* (note 1).
10 Pocock, 'Concept of language', pp. 14–17; Furet, *French Revolution*, p. 50; Paul Fussell, *The Great War and Modern Memory* (New York and London, 1975).
11 John Gumperz, *Language and Social Identity* (New York and London, 1983); Robin Lakoff, *Language and Women's Place* (New York, 1975); Barrie Thorne and Nancy Henley, *Language and Sex: Difference and Dominance* (New York, 1975); Leonore Loeb Alder, Judith Orasanu and Miriam K. Slater, eds., *Language, Sex and Gender* (New York, 1979); *Women and Language in Literature and Society*, ed. Sally McConnell-Ginet, Ruth Borkes and Nelly Furman (New York and London, 1980); Howard Giles, W. Peter Robinson and Philip M. Smith, *Language: Social–psychological Perspectives* (New York and London, 1980); Barrie Thorne, Cheris Kramarae and Nancy Henley, *Language, Gender and Society* (New York, 1983); Cynthia L. Berryman and Virginia Eman, eds., *Communication, Language and Sex* (New York, 1980).

[12] N. Hampson, *French Revolution and Democracy*, pp. 14–16 and *passim*.

[13] I would like to thank Judith Sklar for her helpful discussion of this point. On Marie Antoinette, see Devance, 'Le féminisme' (note 8); the text of her interrogation by the Revolutionary Tribunal is given in H. Wallon, *Histoire du Tribunal Révolutionnaire de Paris*, 6 vols. (Paris, 1880–2), vol. 1, pp. 296–350.

[14] Furet, *French Revolution*, p. 66.

[15] Quoted in Applewhite, Levy *et al.*, *Women in Revolutionary Paris* (note 8), p. 93, from Olympe de Gouges, *Les droits de la femme* (Paris, 1791).

[16] Marc de Villiers, *Clubs des femmes*, p. 226, shows this line of attack on the 'club des citoyennes révolutionnaires' in 1794.

[17] Mme Roland, *Mémoires*, ed. Claude Perroud (Paris, 1905), pp. 63–4, 185, 201, 295–6.

[18] Camille Bloch, 'Les femmes d'Orléans pendant la Révolution', *La révolution française* 43 (1902), 46–67, pp. 61–2.

[19] Mme Jullien, *Journal d'une bourgeoise pendant la Révolution, 1791–1793*, ed. Edouard Lockroy (Paris, 1881), p. 31 (August 1791). For more discussion of Mme Jullien, see D. Blottière, 'Robespierre apprecié par une contemporaine: Mme Jullien de la Drôme', *Annales révolutionnaires* 4 (1911), 93–6. For Mme Roland, Claud Perroud, ed., *Lettres de Mme Roland*, 2 vols. (Paris, 1900–1), vol. 1, p. 107, and 'Je n'ai plus rien à envier aux antiques républiques' (letter of 5 January 1791); for Mme Cavaignac, *Les mémoires d'une inconnue (1780–1816)* (Paris, 1894), pp. 26–9. As much as Brutus was ritually invoked as the embodiment of republican virtue, so was Cataline invoked as the personification of the anti-republican plot.

[20] This dichotomy is also embodied in the art of the period; David's *Brutus* (Louvre), for example, rigidly separates on the canvas the tensely upright figure of Brutus from the swirling, fluid group of his wife and daughters bemoaning the execution of their son and brothers.

[21] Furet, *French Revolution*, pp. 56–7.

[22] For Hérault de Séchelles' pilgrimage to Mlle Clairon, see his (posthumous) account in the *Magasin Encyclopédique* I (1795), 396–416.

[23] *Mémoires d'une inconnue*, p. 29: 'le naturel et le simplicité de ses' manières [a] . . . empêche tout rapprochement entre elle et la matronne romaine'.

[24] J. P. Faye, 'Langues totalitaires', *Cahiers internationaux de sociologie*, 1964, pp. 36–41.

[25] Michael Walzer, *Regicide and Revolution: Speeches at the Trial of Louis XVI* (Cambridge, 1974), pp. 13–14.

[26] Roger Dupuy, 'Les femmes et la contre-révolution dans l'Ouest', *Bulletin d'histoire économique et sociale de la Révolution française* 11 (1979), 48–69.

[27] Bonnie G. Smith, *Ladies of the Leisure Class* (Princeton, 1981).

[28] Examples quoted in Henri Wallon, *Histoire du tribunal révolutionnaire de Paris*, vol. 3, pp. 382, 385, *floréal* 1793.

[29] A. Mathiez, 'Catherine Théot et la mysticisme chrétien révolutionnaire', *La révolution française* 40 (1901), 481–518.

[30] A. Soboul, 'L'activité militante', p. 26.

[31] Lakoff, *Language*, p. 6.

[32] Higonnet, *Nobles*, and Barny, 'Mots et choses, p. 114, from D'Oliviers's *Premier suite du vœu national* (Paris, 1790); Soboul, 'Equality', p. 17.

[33] See the perceptive comment by S. Alexander, 'Women, Class and Social Difference in the 1830s and 1840s', *History Workshop* 17 (1984), 125–49, especially pp. 134–5, on the relationship between male-led political Revolution, involving the strengthening of male ego as the Revolution succeeds, and the 'natural' converse process of the confinement of the female ego.

[34] Levy, Applewhite and Johnson, *Women*, p. 93, from Olympe de Gouges, *Les droits de la femme* (Paris, 1791); Wallon, *Tribunal*, vol. 2, p. 245.

[35] Bonnie G. Smith, *Ladies of the Leisure Class*, *passim* and conclusion.

7

WORDS AND INSTITUTIONS DURING THE FRENCH REVOLUTION: THE CASE OF 'REVOLUTIONARY' SCIENTIFIC AND TECHNICAL EDUCATION

Janis Langins

The adjective 'revolutionary' is a young word. It first appeared, not surprisingly, during the French Revolution. Like the Revolution itself, its meaning was protean and charged with passion, and its original usage was rather different from the one usually accepted today. This chapter contends that the ambiguity of this word helped to further the plans of some of the founding fathers of the Ecole Polytechnique – the model for the French system of higher scientific and technical education that emerged from the Revolution. By associating this newly founded school with 'revolutionary', a key word in the political jargon, its founders sought – and seem to have found – legitimacy for their institution at a particularly delicate political conjuncture. But the word also reflected the view that the institution was radically new and would contribute to the kinds of 'revolutions' in science that had appeared in scientific discourse shortly before the great political revolution of 1789. Accepting the view of François Furet, that the French Revolution ultimately affected political and historical consciousness to a significantly greater degree than administrative and economic structures, it will be suggested that an analogous conception could be proposed to interpret the development of institutions of scientific and technological education during the Revolution.[1] The new institutions inherited, if not everything, then at least quite a lot from the Old Regime; but what gave them new vigour and new scope was the idea of revolutionary change.

It can be argued that whereas the Revolution had little if any impact on the substance of scientific ideas,[2] it did make an enduring contribution to French science by the system of higher scientific and technical education that was set up from 1794 onwards.[3] This did much to increase the numbers, quality and homogeneity of the French scientific and engineering community and to further the already high prestige of the sciences in France. Although there were many different kinds of institutions dispensing scientific and technical education that had developed in the France of the Old Regime, especially during the eighteenth century, the Revolution noticeably accelerated the process of their growth and centralisation in Paris.[4]

Although education had attracted the attention of reformers in France before the Revolution[5] and had led to vigorous debates in the Convention during the Revolution,[6] the concrete legislative achievements of the French Revolution in the domain of education are almost exclusively confined to the period of the Thermidorean Convention – the time after the destruction of Robespierre in July 1794 to the beginning of the Directory Regime in October 1795. During this time there was a flurry of legislative activity that saw the foundation of the future Ecole Polytechnique (originally called the Ecole Centrale des Travaux Publics),[7] the ephemeral Ecole Normale of the Year III,[8] the medical schools,[9] the Ecoles Centrales (which lasted into the Consulate)[10] and the Conservatoire National des Arts et Métiers.[11] Part of this activity may have been due to 'moderates' in the Convention wishing to distance themselves from the dictatorship of the Robespierrist faction that many of them had tolerated and even supported during the Terror.[12] In fact, the rupture between the Thermidorean Convention and the Terror in political aims as well as educational policies is not nearly as great as most of the Thermidoreans would have liked to have people believe.[13] For example, the projects for the foundation of the Ecole Polytechnique and the Ecole Normale can be clearly traced back to the last months of the Terror.[14] This chapter will look at how language influenced the foundation of the Ecole Polytechnique, and try to describe the interaction between the political and linguistic context that facilitated the foundation of the school at that particular time.

Language was important during the French Revolution in two distinct yet related ways. On one hand, an influential body of opinion among the revolutionists believed that the triumph of the Revolution and the spread of enlightenment would be furthered by a conscious effort to impose a standard French on the territory of the Republic. The efforts to replace local dialects and foreign languages with French and the politics of language in general have been described elsewhere.[15] On the other hand, the language of politics is an equally important aspect of the Revolution and impinges directly on the subject of this chapter.

Words have always been important in politics, but during the French Revolution they often played a decisive part. Discussing the crucial role of Danton immediately before and after the violent overthrow of the monarchy in August 1792, Michelet wrote:

> Let no man say that the word is of little use in such moments. Word and action are together one. The powerful energetic affirmation that reassures hearts creates acts – that which is said is produced. Action is here the servant of the word, it follows

behind submissively, as on the first day of the world: *He said and the world was*.[16]

Aulard, who thought that revolutionary eloquence could be considered a distinct literary genre, was also aware of the political power of words perceived by Michelet, when he described the struggle in the Convention between the Girondins and Montagnards in 1792–3 as 'an oratorical duel between two parties animated by a mortal hatred for each other'.[17]

Philologists rather than historians were the first, however, to subject the language of the French Revolution to detailed analysis and look past the oratory that had attracted the attention of historians to study the actual composition of the language used in the Revolution.[18] For a long time the work of the traditional historian and the traditional philologist tended to remain isolated from one another. This isolation has been broken only fairly recently by the growth of modern linguistics after Saussure and the growing consciousness of the usefulness of the new methods for history.[19] An exhaustive and rigorous historico-linguistic analysis of even a single word can be extremely illuminating.[20] This chapter will also deal with a single word – the key word 'revolutionary' – but will content itself with a preliminary and partial lexicographic analysis that is necessary before the considerably more involved recourse to modern linguistic models can be usefully attempted.

Nowhere is it more true than in the political discourse of the French Revolution that words have a *sense* in which they are used that depends on the total context rather than a *meaning* that is fixed and universally valid. Attention will focus on the context of scientific and technical education in order to give one of the senses in which the word 'revolutionary' was used. Although the users of the word attempted to use it – fairly successfully – for their own purposes, it will be suggested that this word may have also affected the users themselves in their conception of the institution they were creating. One result was that the broad political context had some impact – through the medium of language – on the vision its founders had of the Ecole Polytechnique. This influenced the consciousness of the school's nature much more than it influenced the actual structure or course content of the school. Indeed, it will be argued that François Furet's general interpretation of the Revolution can be useful for understanding the development of scientific and technical education during this time as well.

Furet has proposed an interesting conceptual model of the Revolution that implicitly not only reaffirms the importance of words but puts them at the forefront of any analysis of the Revolution. Following Tocqueville[21] and to a lesser extent Alfred Cobban,[22] Furet rejects the dominant view that the Revolution was a total rupture between the 'Old' Regime and

'Modern' France. This view has arisen, he believes, because historians have taken the discourse about the Revolution by contemporary actors and spectators at face value and have consequently failed to escape the limits, presuppositions and conceptual framework of this discourse.[23] Instead, he perceives the Revolution as 'a perpetual outbidding of ideas over historical reality'.[24] There occurred a temporary invasion of reality by ideology, and words are the stuff of ideologies.

The reason for this was that Frenchmen of the Old Regime, in their vast majority excluded from meaningful political action, had channelled instead their political energies into the discussion of ideas. They did this without the sobering effect of contact with the reality of exercising power, and significantly men of letters and *philosophes* were their true political spokesmen.[25] When the Third Estate finally erupted into the political arena after 1789, its political behaviour continued to be characterised by the dominance of abstract ideas without empirical content inherited from the *cercles de pensée* before the Revolution.[26] Perhaps the dominant idea was the will of the people, and along with it came an antagonism to all power that was not a direct manifestation of this will. From this perspective, mere parliamentary legitimacy – based on a.wholly inadequate, and not direct, representative, democracy – was not sufficient for competitors for power. They therefore had to identify themselves with the popular will by *expressing* it in its own particular language. Hence, in the political clubs and assemblies, there arose veritable 'specialists' and 'experts' in this language because 'the semiotic circuit is the absolute master of politics'. 'The word replaces power as the sole guarantee that power belongs only to the people, that is to say, to no one. And contrary to power, which has the malady of secrecy, the word is public, [and] thus itself submitted to the control of the people.[27] This lasted until the destruction of Robespierre, and almost immediately after that ideology was tamed, manipulated, and became separate from power, rather than being coextensive with power.[28]

That the Revolution did have a specific language is evident to anyone with even a superficial acquaintance with its texts. The sacred virtue of equality is reflected in the use of the familiar *tu* and *citoyen*. Language is used to destroy the vestiges of the monarchical regime by renaming towns and institutions. The frequency of negative forms and terms connoting opposition, such as *sans-culottes, contre-révolution, anti-républicain* and *décatholiser* has attracted the attention of philologists,[29] and it mirrors a mentality that is novatory and at the same time always on guard against enemies and plots, real or imagined.[30]

Contemporaries, both friendly[31] and hostile[32] to the Revolution, had a distinct consciousness of the political aspects of language and its importance as a defining trait of the new society. The preface of the fifth edition of the dictionary of the French Academy, which included a supplement containing neologisms of the Revolutionary period, stated that the dictionary 'will be for all peoples and for all centuries the ineffaceable line that will trace and define in the same language, the limits of the Monarchical language and the Republican language'.[33]

Obviously, in the political discourse of the period, the words 'revolution' and 'revolutionary' had an important role. The noun 'revolution', in its political sense, is rather old and was used long before it was applied to the French Revolution, which in turn gave it wider currency and acceptance. I. B. Cohen has pointed out that there were two somewhat contradictory meanings of the word 'revolution' in the eighteenth century: a cyclical change (the older meaning) and 'a breach of continuity or a secular change of real magnitude'.[34] After 1789, the second meaning became dominant and eventually exclusive (outside the domain of physics and mechanics). Originally used in science – *On the Revolutions of the Heavenly Orbs* of 1543 by Copernicus immediately comes to mind – the word passed into social and political discourse as early as the sixteenth century but did not come into general use until after the Glorious Revolution of 1688. During the eighteenth century, this usage became well established and eventually returned to science to denote a major conceptual break with the past.

Rather oddly, however, the adjective 'revolutionary', which one might naturally consider a mere appendage of the noun, has its own distinct history. It seems only to have appeared in 1789, when it was first used by Mirabeau,[35] and after a period of somewhat wide and indiscriminate use during the Terror there followed a period of suppression and oblivion for several decades before its reappearance and normal usage towards the middle of the nineteenth century. The word had a somewhat fluid meaning. Originally it appears to have become common in legal and administrative contexts: thus there were 'revolutionary committees' and the notorious 'revolutionary tribunal'. Here the word indicated an emergency body set up during abnormal times of war and counter-revolution, where regular patterns of behaviour and due process were cut to a minimum and even ignored. It also implies a certain element of dynamism and power, in that these bodies were hierarchically pre-eminent relative to other branches of government or the administration and there was no appeal from their rulings. Thus, on 10 October 1793, the National Convention declared the government to be 'revolutionary until peace [had been signed]', by which it meant that the new republican constitution was suspended and the Convention assumed dictatorial power.[36]

In June 1793 Condorcet expressed misgivings about the dangerous vagueness of the word 'revolutionary' and wrote an entire article on the question.[37] He feared that its associations with liberation and progress could serve as a mask for repressive measures, which, although necessary in a time of crisis, might be abused and lead to permanent tyranny: 'Let us make *revolutionary* laws, but [only] to hasten the moment when we will cease to need to make them. Let us adopt *revolutionary* measures, not to prolong or to bloody the Revolution, but to complete it and precipitate its end.'[38] Ironically, Condorcet's article is dated 1 June 1793, the day before his Girondin friends were proscribed by the Convention under pressure from the Commune of Paris. His fears were only too justified and the word was quickly associated with the excesses of the Terror. It was a powerful weapon in the hands of the revolutionaries, who invoked it to justify drastic measures. They could do this because of the intrinsic malleability in the meaning of the word, a malleability which is apparent in Condorcet's own definition:

> From *revolution*, we have made revolutionary, and this word, in its general sense, expresses all that belongs to a *revolution*.
>
> But it has been made for our revolution, for that one which made in a few years one of the states most submissive for the longest time to despotism into the only republic where liberty has ever had as its basis an entire equality of rights. Thus, the word *revolutionary* only applies to those revolutions that have liberty as their object.
>
> One says that a man is revolutionary, that is, that he is attached to the principles of the revolution, that he acts for it, that he is disposed to sacrifice himself to sustain it.
>
> A revolutionary mentality is a mentality proper for producing [and] for directing a revolution made in favour of liberty.
>
> A revolutionary law is a law whose object is to maintain this revolution and to accelerate and regulate its progress.
>
> A revolutionary measure is one which can assure its success.[39]

This whole passage begs many questions. Since 'revolutionary' is a derivative of 'revolutions', but only of those 'which have liberty as their object', this leaves the reader unclear about what the precise aims or nature of 'revolutionary' activities are. 'Liberty' is a word as essential to the revolutionary idiom as 'the people' and the 'people's will', and it is also just as fuzzy conceptually. All in all, 'revolutionary' means seems to be as vague and as variable – anything that 'accelerates', 'regulates', 'assures success' – as the ends of revolutions whose object is 'liberty'. Depending on context, different meanings could be injected into what was a somewhat capacious and elastic word. Condorcet himself was a prisoner of this kind of discourse, whose danger he saw but could not prevent. If one accepts Furet's conception of the Revolution, one can see why its key words must necessarily have this characteristic. The changeable and vague will of the people being the ultimate source of legitimacy for political competitors jockeying for the ideological high ground, the rhetoric which reflected this will (expressed by public opinion) also fluctuated. A process of rhetorical outbidding (*surenchère*) occurs as those who reflected public opinion yesterday are left behind by those who both radicalise it and reflect it today. Thus, words are weapons in a power struggle where enemies change constantly, where rhetoric is hyperbole, and, correspondingly, action becomes extreme.

Saint-Just, in a famous speech on the occasion of the law of 26 Germinal Year II (15 April 1794), that banned nobles from Paris and fortress towns, illustrates the elasticity of words and at the same time his awareness of this elasticity and its dangers. After attacking the socially radical Hébertiste faction that had been recently destroyed, he deliberately assimilates them into the 'moderates' – enemies from a totally different political and social quarter. He goes on to claim that these 'moderates' have tried to use the word 'revolutionary' for their own malevolent ends: 'The moderates have abused the word revolutionary; they have sought to attach to it the idea of independence which they need to stifle the revolution with impunity. They were singularly harsh with the People, but were indulgent to the aristocracy.'[40] While on one hand Saint-Just attributes the excesses of the Revolution to its enemies hiding behind the cloak of the word 'revolutionary', he ends with a ringing declaration whose main implication is that there can be no limits to 'revolutionary' action: 'I finish with this invariable principle: The public authorities must religiously execute your decrees. That is the force and the sole rule of the administration of security of the Republic and the revolutionary government, which is nothing else than justice favourable to the People and terrible to its enemies.'[41]

Saint-Just, much like Condorcet, was trapped by the ambiguity of a word that he would not renounce because of its usefulness in the political struggle.[42] The word became one of the odious symbols of the Terror, and on 12 June 1795 the Convention decided 'to reform the language as well as the institutions created by our former tyrants [i.e. the vanquished Robespierrists]' in replacing the word 'revolutionary' in official designations.[43] (Thus, the *comités révolutionnaires* were ordered to become *comités de surveillance*.) When Fourcy, writing his history of the Ecole Polytechnique that was published in 1828, mentioned the 'revolutionary courses' that had launched the school, he felt obliged to enlighten his readers, in a footnote, on the meaning of this strange word 'revolutionary': 'This word had become the energetic symbol of *accelerated*, when acceleration was obtained at the expense of formality and the regularity of procedures. A revolutionary operation was not a good operation but it satisfied the needs of the moment.'[44] The 'cours révolutionnaires' Fourcy was talking about, which we may also translate, using Fourcy's own explanation, as 'crash courses', show that during the Terror the word 'revolutionary' had overflowed the bounds of purely political discourse and had become widespread in other domains. There were 'revolutionary processes of tanning' and there was 'revolutionary extraction of saltpetre and manufacture of gunpowder'. Even books were supposed to be sorted in a 'revolutionary' manner.[45] For the purposes of this chapter the most interesting phenomenon was the 'revolutionary courses' that first appeared in connexion with the 'revolutionary fabrication of saltpetre, gunpowder and cannon'. In addition to introducing new and accelerated methods of production developed by scientists like Berthollet, Pelletier and Fourcroy, the government had also decided on 2 February 1794 to set up special month-long courses where hundreds of students from all over France would be trained in the techniques of gunpowder and cannon manufacture.[46] On completion of the courses the students were supposed to return to their own localities and transmit their knowledge to others, and in this manner the entire country would quickly acquire a pool of skilled manpower.

The 'revolutionary' courses were intended to be short and elementary. They were to be sufficient in themselves without leading to any further course of study. The students – a fixed number from each of the administrative districts of France – were selected more for enthusiasm and loyalty to the Revolution than for intellectual or academic prowess. (The specification that 'at least one' student per district had to be literate gives some idea of the expected standards.) The teachers were the best scientists and technologists in the country who could be trusted by the revolutionary government. Among them were Périer, Monge, Fourcroy, Berthollet and Guyton. Thus, there would be an alliance of science and patriotism to perform hitherto unseen wonders of teaching.

Bertrand Barère, mouthpiece of the Committee of Public Safety, asserted that:

> The Old Regime would have required three years to open schools, train students, and organise courses in chemistry and armaments. The new regime has accelerated everything. It requires thirty days to teach picked citizens from the districts to refine saltpetre, to make gunpowder, to cast, mould, and bore cannon. It is thus that the influence of liberty renders all fruits precocious and all institutions easy . . . Pedantry will not instruct them. It is patriotism and science united together [which will attain] this prodigy of military and manufacturing instruction.[47]

Many people were impressed by the exercise. The wide publicity given to the courses, including a formal reception at the legislature for the students, during which they sang a special ode to saltpetre with music composed by Cherubini,[48] did much to popularise the concept of 'revolutionary' courses.[49] There appears to have been an enthusiastic attempt to imitate them in many and diverse fields by individual entrepreneurs. Some years later an unsympathetic observer recalled that:

> Those were the beautiful days of exaltation; everything was done *revolutionarily*; the streets were plastered with notices where one read: *revolutionary* course of mathematics, *revolutionary* course of physics, *revolutionary* course of chemistry, of anatomy, of botany, *revolutionary* education for the children of *sans-culottes*, etc., etc., etc. It was the fashion, the spirit of the times. One had to give a revolutionary course or be greatly suspected of ignorance, or even something worse![50]

Not just public opinion but the government, too, was impressed by the 'revolutionary' courses and saw them as a novel means of improving instructional efficiency. Even before the crash courses on gunpowder and cannon manufacture were ended the *Moniteur* printed the following item: 'This attempt at instruction for people sent from all districts and scattered at once over a large territory promises successes that would have remained unknown without this beautiful experiment. The revolutionary method will undoubtedly be employed by the government to multiply in a short time all kinds of instruction that public prosperity requires.'[51] Very rapidly these sentiments were translated into concrete action. Within months it was decided to set up schools using the new revolutionary methods to teach military science, agricultural techniques and pedagogy for elementary schoolteachers.[52] The first institution was the short-lived Ecole de Mars, the second was never founded and the third became the Ecole Normale of the Year III.[53]

Paul Dupuy, in his excellent centenary contribution to the history of the Ecole Normale, argued convincingly that this misunderstanding was the result of deliberate deception by the flighty intellectual Garat, who, from his post as chairman of the Commission of Public Instruction after Thermidor, successfully hoodwinked the Convention into accepting his fantastic ideas on education.[54] The Convention was easily fooled – or perhaps wanted to be fooled – because a few months before, during the Terror, the Committee of Public Safety had intended to implement a system of normal schools for rapid instruction in pedagogy for primary schoolteachers. With its more modest aims of disseminating basic literacy and republican morality, the original project was at least potentially feasible in revolutionary France. Furthermore, although even here there was no provision for teaching practical skills or the mechanical arts, the idea could certainly be perceived as useful by Jacobin legislators. It reminds one very much of crash programmes for promoting literacy in some Third World countries today. Garat hijacked this project and turned the original idea for normal schools into the grandiose Ecole Normale, that was to be, in Dupuy's words, 'a school for the high culture of science and philosophy'.[55]

It is clear that the Ecole Normale as it functioned in 1795 was quite different from the 'revolutionary' instruction in crash courses on gunpowder and cannon manufacture a year previously. Yet it is equally clear that these 'revolutionary' courses had originally provided the model for the school.[56]

The Ecole Centrale des Travaux Publics, as the Ecole Polytechnique was originally called, is another place where the rhetoric of 'revolutionary' courses was used to legitimise activities that had little to do with the first 'revolutionary' courses of February–March 1794. The chemist Fourcroy, who was also a deputy, had presented a law on opening the Ecole Centrale des Travaux Publics on 24 September 1794 – several months after a general law regarding public works had called for such a school.[57] After declaring that the aims of the new school were to provide badly needed engineers and to teach the sciences during a three-year course, he went on to say:

> If we were in ordinary circumstances, if the fatherland did not have such a pressing need for intelligent engineers, only the first third of students that the school of public works can receive would be admitted. The second third would be called up the following year and in three years the school would be full and conducted to the state of uniformity which it must achieve. But the needs of the Republic do not permit following such a slow course. A means of founding all at once all the departments of instruction in the school has had to be found. The revolutionary teaching, whose advantages are known to the Convention, has suggested to the Committee [of Public Safety] the means of attaining this aim. A sort of concentrated course lasting three months for each [subject] and given at the same time will include the totality of the teaching at the school and will provide complete although accelerated instruction, [which], at the end of this course, will permit dividing the students into three classes, each of which will immediately undertake the studies corresponding to each of the three years. [In this manner] . . . the school will be functioning in all its parts from its first institution.[58]

By mentioning extraordinary circumstances, the need for accelerated instruction, and the 'revolutionary teaching whose advantages are known to the Convention' Fourcroy made all the right noises needed to identify the new school with the 'revolutionary' method of instruction. Yet it is clear even from other parts of the same speech that there were some fundamental differences between the 'revolutionary' course at the Ecole Centrale des Travaux Publics and those on armaments manufacture. First, the students were more rigorously selected and were effectively required to have a relatively good preparatory education on admission to the school.[59] In fact, the knowledge of arithmetic and the elements of algebra and geometry they were required to have automatically ensured that they would come from a higher social and economic class than the workers who had paraded in the Convention seven months before. Secondly, the courses at the new school were not to be terminal courses. They were not meant to be complete in themselves but to serve as a beginning to a much longer course of instruction. Still, it might be argued that the 'revolutionary' courses at the Ecole Polytechnique that began on 21 December 1794 were exceptional in that they launched the whole institution in a much shorter time than the three years that would normally have been required.

However, the evidence shows that within two months of the opening of the 'revolutionary' courses their ostènsible purpose was quietly forgotten. It was decided that students graduating in what was supposed to be the final (third) year course of studies would remain at the school another year to do the second year curriculum. Furthermore, even the idea of using the courses as a means of classifying the students according to capacity was dropped without fanfare. Students were simply assigned to classes on the basis of their performance on their entrance examination.[60]

As this was happening the adjective 'revolutionary' was becoming unpopular and was soon to be banished from the official lexicon. Fourcroy, always the adroit politician, was quick to drop the word. In his speech to the Convention on setting up medical schools he still referred to the 'revolutionary movement, [which] directed by skilful legislators, knows how to draw from the very bosom of the ruins caused by its rapidity, the materials for the greatest and most solid edifices for public prosperity'.[61] But in the manuscript outline of his own course that was submitted to the council of the Ecole Centrale des Travaux Publics for approval less than two weeks later, he himself scratched out the word 'revolutionary' and replaced it with 'preliminary'.[62] By the time a syllabus of the courses was published at the beginning of February 1795, there was no trace of the adjective 'revolutionary'.[63] Indeed, in the middle of June 1795, Prieur de la Côte d'Or, one of the founders of the Ecole Polytechnique, was writing to a government committee that the new school was not 'one of those ephemeral productions one saw hatched by the enthusiasm of the moment and . . . it has not partaken of the impetuosity of the so-called *revolutionary* operations'.[64]

When Fourcroy had sung the praises of 'revolutionary' instruction back in September 1794, he had been finely tuned to a very complex and fragile political context.[65] Robespierre had been executed almost exactly two months earlier but the Jacobins were by no means destroyed. They were – or were thought to be – a political force to be reckoned with. Indeed, Fourcroy himself may still have been a member of the Jacobin Club,[66] and three days before he had begun to read his speech to the Convention on the organisation of the future Ecole Polytechnique, Marat's body had been voted to receive the honours of the Pantheon on 21 September 1794. But a power struggle in the legislature was just about to begin among the disparate elements of the coalition that had brought down Robespierre.

The political tide against the Jacobins had begun to gather momentum, for reasons that are rather complex. Moderates in the Convention were increasingly successful in associating the remnants of the radical Jacobins in the assemblies with the Terror – whose end had been greeted with a wave of enthusiasm by all classes of the population, for divers reasons. (The attack on 'vandalism' appears in this context to be an attack not only on the dead Robespierre but also on former allies, and now opponents, who were very much alive and could be linked to the 'tyrant'.) The internecine blood-letting of the Terror had left the radical and militant part of the populace without effective leadership. Thanks in large part to Robespierre's own activity, the Convention had managed to impose some degree of control over the municipal *sections* and the political clubs and was better able to resist their pressure. In the *sections* themselves, more moderate citizens, no longer cowed by the Terror, began to reassert their influence.[67]

The victors of this power struggle were the moderates, and in the period immediately after Fourcroy's speech Jacobin influence waned rapidly. In November 1794 the Convention closed the Jacobin Club. On 8 February 1795 – to use another neologism of the Revolution – Marat was 'depantheonised'. Less than a month later (2 March 1795), Barère, Collot d'Herbois and Billaud-Varenne, Robespierre's former associates on the Committee of Public Safety during the Terror, were indicted and arrested. After the failure of the street insurrections of Germinal and Prairial (April and May 1795), moderates were firmly in control of the Convention and the country. Concurrently, the idea of 'revolutionary' courses faded from the rhetoric of the administrators of the Ecole Polytechnique, and Prieur's denial of all connexion with 'revolutionary operations' marks the end of this fairly rapid evolution.

It may be significant that in the same brief to the government by Prieur where this apparent reneging occurs, the change of name from Ecole Centrale des Travaux Publics to Ecole *Polytechnique* is suggested publicly for the first time.[68] With its encyclopaedic connotations the new name conjured up the vision of an institution that was less immediately practical, concerned with a broader range of subject matter, and more committed to advanced teaching and even research. As Prieur put it:

> Not only will the *Ecole Centrale des Travaux Publics* train candidates for the different kinds of engineering positions, but from it will graduate architects, men capable of organizing great enterprises in manufacturing, either in the mechanical or the chemical arts, draftsmen of all kinds, even painters, [and] teachers of sciences as rare as they are precious. Finally, it is an inappreciable advantage just [to have] enlightened citizens who, following their dispositions and tastes, could enter the profession in which they think they would succeed best, especially when we need to repair all the disasters that the revolutionary crises brought with them.[69]

Although 'revolutionary' had now become a disreputable adjective (before it was to fall into temporary oblivion), Fourcroy's use of the word in his speech on the organisation of the Ecole Polytechnique shows that at that particular time, it had been a useful – perhaps indispensable – word that he had exploited with finesse. The question immediately arises about Fourcroy's sincerity in its use. In the final part of this chapter it will be suggested that the question is perhaps irrelevant, and that usage of the word must be viewed from a different perspective that is more useful in clarifying the attitudes of scientist–politicians to the revolutionary government of which they were a part. An examination of the chief founders of the Ecole Polytechnique[70] shows that almost all of them were intimately involved with the revolutionary government. Prieur de la Côte d'Or was actually the colleague of Robespierre on the Committee of Public Safety; Monge, Hassenfratz and Berthollet had been closely associated with the Committee's programme for military research and war production during the Terror, as had Guyton and Fourcroy, who were themselves deputies and members of the Committee after the Terror.[71]

Considering Fourcroy's legislative and administrative career one could be pardoned for classifying him as one of the *girouettes* (weathervanes) who had weathered the storms of the Revolution and had been all things to all masters.[72] The same man who on 9 December 1793 delivered an impassioned and dithyrambic plea for absolute free enterprise in education, as the best means of destroying 'fanaticism and doctoral superstition',[73] became, ten years later, Napoleon's Director of Public Instruction and the architect of his rigidly centralised Université Impériale. And during the Directory Regime it was Fourcroy who made a point of requesting the Council of the Ecole Polytechnique to change the title of its senior teaching staff from the more revolutionary and modest 'instituteur' to 'professeur'[74]. This shiftiness cannot have been motivated only by a desire for self-preservation and advancement. Fourcroy did exert himself to save colleagues during the Terror when it was undeniably risky to do so, and his alleged lack of action on behalf of Lavoisier after his arrest must be re-evaluated in the light of new evidence.[75] It now appears that Fourcroy did all he could to save him before his arrest, and only stopped doing so after Lavoisier's arrest when it was absolutely certain that he was doomed.[76] Fourcroy's behaviour becomes much more understandable if we remember that as a deputy of the Convention he was – to use a linguistic term – a member of a speech community very much in the public eye during the Revolution.

Fourcroy had entered the Convention by accident, when, as Marat's *suppléant* or replacement, he had automatically taken the place of the assassinated revolutionary martyr on 13 July 1793. During the summer of 1793, as the Terror established its grip on France, there were few choices regarding the kind of language that was to be used in the forum of the Convention – to ensure simple physical survival one either used the accepted code or stayed silent. There is some evidence that, initially, Fourcroy tried the latter alternative. On 8 December 1793, when he was the monthly president of the Jacobin Club, he was reproached by a member for not using his talents – presumably oratorical ones – in the Convention. The minutes of the club containing Fourcroy's reply are worth reproducing in full:

> FOURCROY: I will not enter into the details of the progress of my work since my childhood. I attest that I owe the facility of expressing myself as much to art as to nature. If this facility has been noticed in my medical lectures, I owe it to the profound study I have made of my profession for more than twenty years. After these twenty years of labour, I have succeeded, in teaching medicine, to feed my *sans-culotte* father and my *sans-culotte* sisters. I have spoken in the Convention at all times that I thought I could say something useful, but the study of the sciences and the arts has not permitted me to occupy myself to the same degree with politics and legislation. I have thought that the sage should not speak of things that he did not know perfectly but, on the contrary, should stick to his profession. As to the sort

of reproach a member has addressed to me, of devoting the major part of my time to the sciences, I declare that, on the contrary, I have always stayed at my post since I exercise a public function, that I have been seen at the Lycée des Arts only three times, and then only for the purpose of purging it (*sans-culottiser*).

Fourcroy is received in the midst of unanimous applause.[77]

Of the many points that could be retained in this interesting reply, the aspect most pertinent to this chapter is the evidence that Fourcroy's oratorical talents, even in an impromptu situation, were indeed considerable and that he had a deft command of the proper locutions to be used at the Jacobin Club and the Convention. His talents had already acquired him a great reputation as a lecturer before the Revolution,[78] and they undoubtedly helped him in the revolutionary assemblies.

Fourcroy's use of the obligatory political phrases does not imply his belonging to any particular faction, nor does it facilitate by itself the precise identification of any characteristic sub-variety of revolutionary ideology, because all factions in the Convention used the same code and the ideology behind the code was flexible and vague. There is a deadening uniformity in the stock denunciations of *aristocratie* and *fanatisme* coupled with the equally predictable eulogies of *sans-culottes* and the *Peuple* (usually *vertueux*), that at first sight seems to preclude fruitful analysis of revolutionary speech-making. Nevertheless, a more precise delineation of political positions or educational ideologies is possible by a more attentive reading of the text: reading between the lines and concentrating on apparently peripheral details will allow the reader to detect concrete differences between positions which seem rhetorically almost identical. Fourcroy's speech on the Ecole Centrale des Travaux Publics is a case in point. Along with the standard hyperbole of the exordium and the demand for good republican morality are requirements for a level of preliminary instruction that would automatically exclude any good *sans-culottes*, while the technical appendix attached to the speech,[79] which was not read to the Convention but merely distributed to the deputies, laid out clearly the organisation of a school whose material magnificence and numerous staff clearly implied the kind of 'privileged institution' that he himself had so ferociously attacked less than a year earlier.[80]

One sees in Fourcroy, then, another example of the 'bilingualism' that Furet detects in Mirabeau and Danton.[81] Mirabeau's secret correspondence with the Court contains proposals that are treasonable from a revolutionary's point of view when couched in the non-revolutionary language and standard discourse of Old Regime France; yet he makes those same proposals publicly in the assembly.[82] However, they are more discrete, less prominent, and his discourse is festooned with the essentially ritualistic code words that are weak on semantic content but strong on vague affirmations of ethical and political desirability and energetic affirmations of revolutionary faith.

That is not to say, of course, that code words like 'revolutionary' are without interest. It is one of those basic words which together form the general linguistic space that contains the more specific ideological terms making up the universe of discourse of the French Revolution.[83] Moreover, their usage and reception also provide a convenient litmus test of the political context, and the above discussion has attempted to provide an example of this.

But in addition to being an indicator the word does seem to have had a incantatory power of its own. In spite of an ideology of detachment from the hurly-burly of mundane life,[84] scientists were by no means immune either to feelings of terror during some stages of the Revolution or to the vague programmatical appeal of the word 'revolutionary'. Levin has given examples of the spreading use of the word 'revolution' in scientific discourse towards the end of the eighteenth century. Lavoisier, Fourcroy and Cabanis used the word in letters to colleagues, histories of their science or treatises, in a way that strongly suggests that the sociopolitical context formed new ways of perceiving the internal development of science itself by scientists.[85] While the precise mechanism of how this happened is complex and needs further study, it seems highly likely that for the case of words like 'revolution' and 'revolutionary' it did happen.

While the word 'revolutionary' could mean 'expeditious' and 'abnormal' on one hand, it could also mean – closer to its modern meaning – 'innovative' and 'creative' on the other. For the founders of the Ecole Polytechnique, their school was, in Fourcroy's words, 'without model in Europe' – a fundamentally new kind of institution that would radically affect the pace of scientific advance.[86] In that sense it was truly revolutionary. As a contemporary journalist, who later became a professor at the school, wrote:

> There is no doubt that after having received such lessons, the students of the *Ecole centrale* [*des travaux publics*] will perfect the arts whose processes they will have examined [and which] hitherto have been abandoned to chance and routine. One can presume that the teaching that they will receive, precious and unique on this earth, will develop among them geniuses who will push back the frontiers of science.[87]

In describing the motivations of the founders of the Ecole Normale, the physicist Biot wrote: 'It was desired that a vast column of light should emerge all at once from the midst of this devastated land and that it should rise so high that its immense brilliance could cover the whole of France and illuminate the future.'[88] Even though Biot felt no warmth towards the Revolution, the underlying imagery of this description – radical change, powerful effects and new beginnings – is similar to that of political revolutionaries whose perceptions of an 'Old' Regime and a 'liberating' Revolution have conditioned our thinking about the French Revolution to this day.

The word 'Polytechnique' may serve as a final example of new words conditioning new perceptions with a distinct programmatic effect, in a scientific institution that shows substantial continuity with the past. The word is a neologism of the French Revolution and appears in early 1795. It is almost certain that the man who coined the word was Prieur de la Côte d'Or, who publicly proposed it and later had it confirmed by law.[89] Prieur, whose important role in the Committee of Public Safety has already been mentioned, had a long-standing interest in questions of terminology and metrology. Although his own suggestions for units of length such as *décadore* and *longdix* have mercifully been forgotten, it was he who presented to the Convention the law of 18 Germinal Year III (7 April 1795) on the establishment of the metric system in France.[90] 'Polytechnique', then, is a new name, but its analogy with 'encyclopaedic' is as obvious to us as it was to contemporaries.[91] Indeed, the programmer and the organisation of the early Ecole Polytechnique could be fairly described as 'encyclopaedic' in its inspiration, pedagogy and technological ideas. Thus there is a real continuity with ideas (as well as institutions, like the military engineering school at Mézières) that extends over almost half a century.

Yet the new name is indeed a fitting symbol and reminder of a consciousness of novelty that may have been as important in the foundation and initial development of the school as the well-established structural continuity with the past. As Biot, who attended the school in the first year of its existence, wrote about its founders: '[they were] men used to general ideas whose thoughts had been further exalted and views enlarged by the Revolution'.[92] Perhaps the enthusiasm of professors and students for their school and for their attempts to impart a revolutionary *élan* to science and science teaching may have been magnified by both contemporary rhetoric and nostalgic hagiography, but it seems to have been present nevertheless.[93] Whether and how the self-consciousness of the school as a 'workshop of discovery'[94] affected the pace of scientific enquiry is a question that not only lies outside the scope of this chapter, but may be intrinsically too difficult to answer. It is remarkable, however, that the first years of the Ecole Polytechnique witnessed an efflorescence of scientific talent that has hardly ever been matched in a single institution in such a short time span and has assured its reputation to the present day.

The foregoing article has concentrated on a single important word in a much richer lexicon that forms the distinctive linguistic code used by politicians during the French Revolution. An analysis of the code as a whole requires a major long-term interdisciplinary study,[95] and even a look at a single aspect of a single word gives some idea of the scope of this problem. This chapter has presented such a preliminary analysis of this much more restricted subject and proposed an interpretation of the actions of a key figure like Fourcroy in the creation of a new institution of scientific and technological education like the Ecole Polytechnique. In spite of his posing as a 'sage [who] should not speak of things that he did not know perfectly but . . . should stick to his profession',[96] he was quite as adept as anyone else at using political jargon for his own ends. Indeed, a monitoring of his use of the word 'revolutionary' could serve as an excellent indication of the political temperature of the Terror.

A person like Fourcroy, who had a solid footing in both the scientific and political community of the time, used the word – sincerely or not – for his own purposes: as a guarantee of revolutionary legitimacy, a sign of voluntaristic enthusiasm, and an assurance of aims consonant with the popular will and the interests of the nation. It is not unreasonable to suppose, however, that the word also had some effect on its users. It illustrates a new kind of consciousness in the scientific community that things could be changed and changed radically – the same kind of consciousness that characterised the political situation, where a rhetoric of novelty and rejection of the old hid patterns of continuity that changed only very slowly. In scientific institutions the patterns of continuity were also accompanied by a rhetoric of novelty. The absorption of rhetoric and concepts from the general political culture was possible because, in Levin's words, 'cultural meanings can be transmitted and adopted more effectively if the culture-recipient [science] already possesses resources capable of being suitable matrices for these meanings. And in this case the effect was increased by the growing number of texts containing variants of the word combination "scientific revolution".'[97] It is not unreasonable to suggest that the related concept of 'revolutionary' benefited from the same situation.

For the founders of the Ecole Polytechnique, the word 'revolutionary' had provided first of all a certificate of legitimacy and an ostensible model, which was quietly changed to suit the purposes of the founders. More importantly perhaps, in a more elusive and less easily documented manner, it had helped to effect a metamorphosis of an existing configuration of institutions of scientific and technical education into a truly national institution linked to a self-styled revolutionary and democratic State. Words catalysed and moulded institutions whose vigour sprang as much from their perception of their own novelty as from their solid roots in the past.

NOTES

1 François Furet, *Penser la Révolution française* (Paris, 1978). All references to this work will be from the 'Collection Folio/Histoire' edition published by Gallimard.

2 For an overview of French science during this period by some of its more eminent contemporary practitioners, see the official reports addressed to Napoleon by the secretaries of the Institut: Georges Cuvier, *Rapport historique sur les progrès des sciences naturelles depuis 1789, et sur leur état actuel* . . . (Paris, 1810), and Jean-Baptiste-Joseph Delambre, *Rapport historique sur les progrès des sciences mathématiques depuis 1789 et sur leur état actual* . . . (Paris, 1810). The view that there was – and could be – no change in the substance of scientific ideas during the Revolution in spite of vague yearnings for a 'Jacobin science' is best presented by Charles C. Gillispie, 'The *Encyclopédie* and the Jacobin Philosophy of Science: A Study in Ideas and Consequences', in *Critical Problems in the History of Science*, ed. Marshall Clagett (Madison, 1962), pp. 255–89, and 'Science in the French Revolution', *Behavioural Science* 4 (1959), 67–101. This is not to say that the Revolution (and the political context in general) did not affect the pace of scientific change (see René Taton, 'L'Ecole Polytechnique et le renouveau de la géométrie analytique', in *Mélanges Alexandre Koyré* (Paris, 1964), vol. 1, pp. 552–64), the professionalisation and self-image of scientists (see Roger Hahn, *The Anatomy of a Scientific Institution: The Paris Academy of Science, 1666–1803* (Berkeley, 1971), and Dorinda Outram, 'The Ordeal of Vocation: The Paris Academy of Sciences and the Terror, 1793–95', *History of Science* 21 (1983), 251–73, and the important patronage networks that Outram has argued were more important than institutions in influencing the growth of scientific activity (see Maurice Crosland, *The Society of Arcueil: A View of French Science at the time of Napoleon I* (London, 1967), and D. Outram, 'Politics and Vocation: French Science, 1793–1830', *British Journal for the History of Science* 13 (1980), 27–43). For essay reviews of work on the history of French science, with many bibliographical references, see Maurice Crosland, 'The History of French Science: Recent Publications and Perspectives', *French Historical Studies* 8 (1973), 157–71 (intended for historians of France without particular knowledge of the history of French science), and Mary Jo Nye, 'Recent Sources and Problems in the History of French Science', *Historical Studies in the Physical Sciences* 13 (1983), 401–15.

3 Good introductions to this subject can be found in Nye, 'Recent Sources and Problems', and Antoine Léon in his works *Histoire de l'enseignement en France* (Paris, 1967), *Histoire de l'éducation technique* (Paris, 1961), and especially *La révolution française et l'éducation technique* (Paris, 1968). Valuable complementary information on French institutions of scientific education and research can be found in Crosland, *Arcueil*, and Hahn, *Anatomy*. A recent valuable overview of French education during the Revolution, with abundant citations from original documents and an important section on scientific and technical education in Chapters 7 and 8, is Dominique Julia, *Les Trois couleurs du tableau noir: La Révolution* (Paris, 1981). Less satisfactory is Joseph Fayet, *La Révolution française et la science* (Paris, 1960).

4 On institutions of scientific and technical education in the Old Regime, see Charles C. Gillispie, *Science and Polity in France at the End of the Old Regime* (Princeton, 1980), pp. 481–2 and 511–12, R. Taton, *Enseignement et diffusion des sciences en France au XVIIIe siècle* (Paris, 1964), and the somewhat dated but still useful F. B. Artz, *The Development of Technical Education in France 1500–1850* (Cambridge, Mass., 1966).

5 An overview of pedagogical thought that contains information on the eighteenth century

and is by no means dated is G. Compayré, *Histoire critique des doctrines de l'éducation en France depuis le seizième siècle*, 2 vols. (Paris, 1879). Also useful is F. Buisson, *Dictionnaire de pédagogie et instruction primaire* (Paris, 1887), while a book that looks less at public debates and more at concrete achievements is Roger Chartier, D. Julia and Marie-Madeleine Compère, *L'Education en France du XVIe au XVIIIe siècle* (Paris, 1976). See also *The Making of Frenchmen: Current Directions in the History of Education in France, 1679–1979*, ed. D. N. Baker and P. J. Harrigan (Waterloo, Ontario, Canada, 1980), and D. Julia, 'Les recherches sur l'histoire de l'éducation en France au siècle des Lumières', *Histoire de l'éducation* 1 (1978), 17–18, which has a useful bibliography.

[6] Still the best source of primary documents and preliminary analysis covering the period 15 October 1792 to 26 October 1795, in spite of occasional errors and a pro-Jacobin slant, is *Procès-Verbaux du Comité d'Instruction Publique de la Convention Nationale*, ed. J. Guillaume, 6 vols. (Paris, 1891–1907). On the activity of the Legislative Assembly in education, with a short preface on the Constituent Assembly, see *Procès-Verbaux du Comité d'Instruction Publique de l'Assemblée Législative*, ed. James Guillaume (Paris, 1889). See also D. Julia, *Les Trois couleurs*, and Robert J. Vignery, *The French Revolution and the Schools: Educational Policies of the Mountain 1792–94* (Madison, 1965).

[7] On the Ecole Polytechnique the best of the general histories remains A. Fourcy, *Histoire de l'Ecole Polytechnique* (Paris, 1828). It can be supplemented with Gaston Pinet, *Histoire de l'Ecole Polytechnique* (Paris, 1887), which must be used with caution for the earlier years of the school. See also J. Langins, 'The Ecole Polytechnique (1794–1804): From Encyclopaedic School to Military Institution' (University of Toronto Ph.D. thesis, 1979).

[8] Although the Ecole Normale Supérieure founded by Napoleon in 1808 considers itself a descendant of the Ecole Normale of the Year III founded by the Convention, these two institutions should not be confused. The best history of the Ecole Normale founded in 1795, to date, is by Paul Dupuy, 'L'Ecole Normale de l'An III', in *Le Centenaire de l'Ecole Normale 1795–1895* (Paris, 1895), pp. 21–209. See also Jean Dhombres, 'L'Enseignement des mathématiques par la "méthode révolutionnaire". Les leçons de Laplace à l'Ecole normale de l'an III', *Revue d'histoire des sciences* 33 (1980), 315–48. A seminar led by J. Dhombres at the Ecole Normale Supérieure plans to publish a critical and annotated edition of the courses taught at the Ecole Normale de l'An III for the bicentenary of the French Revolution.

[9] On the Écoles de Santé, see Auguste Corlieu, *Centenaire de la Faculté de Médecine de Paris (1794–1894)* (Paris, 1896).

[10] On the Ecoles Centrales, the somewhat outdated but still interesting article by L. Pearce Williams, 'Science, Education and the French Revolution', *Isis* 44 (1953), 311–30, should be supplemented by the work of R. R. Palmer, 'The Central Schools of the First French Republic: A Statistical Survey', in D. Baker, P. J. Harrigan, *The Making of Frenchmen*, D. Julia, *Les Trois couleurs*, Chapter 7, and Catherine Mérot, 'La Fréquentation et le recrutement des écoles centrales sous la Révolution' (thèse de l'Ecole des Chartes, Paris, 1985).

[11] Robert Fox, 'Education for a New Age: The Conservatoire des Arts et Métiers, 1815–30', in *Artisan to Graduate: Essays to commemorate the Foundation of the Manchester Mechanics' Institution*, ed. D. S. L. Cardwell, pp. 23–38.

[12] Hahn, *Anatomy*, pp. 290–4.

[13] According to Julia, *Les Trois couleurs*, pp. 14–15, there was a hard core of thirty members of the Committee of Public Instruction who served at least nine months. Of these, there were eight (including Fourcroy and Guyton) who served during the Terror and the Thermidorean period. Even the popular neologism 'vandalism', used to attack the vanquished Robespierrists after Thermidor, had been coined by Grégoire during the Terror (January 1794) and had been used by Jacobins to castigate counter-revolutionaries accused of wanting to 'proscribe educated people, banish genius and paralyse thought' (J. Guillaume, 'Grégoire et le vandalisme', *La Révolution française* 41 (1901), 155–80 and 242–69, pp. 172–3).

[14] Dupuy, 'L'Ecole Normale', pp. 40–1, and J. Langins, 'Sur la première organisation de

l'Ecole polytechnique: Texte de l'arrêté du 6 frimaire an III', *Revue d'histoire des sciences* 33 (1980), 289–313.

[15] J.-Y. Lartichaux, 'Linguistic Politics during the French Revolution', *Diogenes* 97 (1977), 65–84, Patrice Higonnet, 'The Politics of Linguistic Terrorism and Grammatical Hegemony during the French Revolution', *Social History* 5 (1980), 41–69, and M. de Certaux, D. Julia and J. Revel, *Une Politique de la langue – La Révolution française et les patois: L'enquête de Grégoire* (Paris, 1975).

[16] Jules Michelet, *Histoire de la Révolution française* (Paris, 1868, 1889), vol. 3, p. 307: 'Qu'on ne dise pas que la parole soit peu de chose en de tels moments. Parole et acte, c'est tout un. La puissante, l'énergique affirmation qui assure les cœurs, c'est une création d'actes; ce qu'elle dit, elle le produit. L'action est ici la servante de la parole; elle vient docilement derrière, comme au premier jour du monde: *Il dit, et le monde fut.*' (All translations are my own. Emphasis is by the author of quote except where the contrary is specified.)

[17] Alphonse Aulard, *L'Eloquence parlementaire pendant la Révolution française: Les Orateurs de la Législative et de la Convention*, 2 vols. (Paris, 1885–6), vol. 1, p. 37: 'un duel oratoire entre deux parties animés l'un contre l'autre d'une haine mortelle'.

[18] For example, Ferdinand Brunot, *Histoire de la langue française des origines à 1900*, 13 vols. (Paris, 1905–53), and Max Frey, *Les Transformations du vocabulaire français à l'époque de la Révolution (1789–1800)* (Paris, 1925).

[19] A.-J. Greimas, 'Histoire et linguistique', *Annales: Economies, Sociétés, Civilisations* 13 (1958), 110–14. For a book-length examination on the uses of linguistics for historians with detailed examples and warnings of pitfalls, see Régine Robin, *Histoire et linguistique* (Paris, 1973).

[20] F. Furet and A. Fontana, 'Histoire et linguistique', in *Livre et Société dans la France du 18e siècle*, 2 vols. (Paris/The Hague, 1965–70), vol. 2, pp. 95–228, deal with the words 'histoire' and 'méthode' in the titles of officially or semi-officially approved books in pre-revolutionary France. See also Annie Geffroy, 'Le "Peuple" selon Saint-Just', *Annales historiques de la Révolution française* 11 (1968), 138–44.

[21] A. Tocqueville, *L'Ancient régime et la Révolution* (Paris, 1856).

[22] A. Cobban, *The Myth of the French Revolution* (London, 1955). See the criticism of this work by G. Lefebvre, 'Le Myth de la Révolution française', *Annales historiques de la Révolution française* 28 (1956), 337–45. The debate on Cobban's thesis still attracts interest and Lefebvre's reply to Cobban was recently reprinted in the same journal where it originally appeared (*Ibid.*, 57 (1985), 1–7).

[23] Furet, *Penser*, pp. 35–6.

[24] *Ibid.*, p. 49: 'une perpétuelle surenchère de l'idée sur l'histoire réelle'.

[25] *Ibid.*, pp. 65–6.

[26] *Ibid.*, pp. 271–4. Furet bases much of his analysis here on the work of the relatively neglected French historian of Jacobinism, Augustin Cochin.

[27] *Ibid.*, pp. 83–6: '. . . le circuit sémiotique est le maître absolu de la politique' . . . 'La parole se substitue au pouvoir comme seule garantie que le pouvoir n'appartient qu'au peuple, c'est-à-dire à personne. Et contrairement au pouvoir, qui a la maladie du secret, la parole est publique, donc soumise elle-même au contrôle du peuple.'

[28] *Ibid.*, pp. 122–7.

[29] Frey, *Les Transformations*, p. 272.

[30] R. Cobb, 'Quelques aspects de la mentalité révolutionnaire (Avril 1793 – Thermidor An II)', *Revue d'histoire moderne et contemporaine* 6 (1959), 81–120.

[31] L.-S. Mercier, *Néologie, ou Vocabulaire des mots nouveaux, à renouveler, ou pris dans des acceptions nouvelles*, 2 vols. (Paris, 1801). According to Mario Mormille, *La 'Néologie' révolutionnaire de Louis-.Sébastien Mercier* (Rome, 1973), Mercier himself was a lexicographical revolutionary who represents the culmination and consolidation of an eighteenth-century literary movement away from the linguistic rigidity imposed by the Académie Française in the seventeenth century.

[32] J.-F. de La Harpe, *Du fanatisme dans la langue révolutionnaire* (Paris, 1796–7).

[33] *Dictionnaire de l'Académie françoise*, 5e éd., 2 vols. (Paris, 1798–9), p. x: '. . . sera pour tous les Peuples et pour tous les Siécles la ligne ineffaçable qui tracera et constatera dans

la même Langue, les limites de la Langue Monarchique et la Langue Républicaine'.

[34] I. B. Cohen, 'The Eighteenth-Century Origins of the Concept of Scientific Revolution', *Journal of the History of Ideas* 37 (1976), 257–88. See also F. Gilbert, 'Revolution', in *The Dictionary of the History of Ideas*, ed. P. Wiener (New York, 1973).

[35] E. Littré, *Dictionnaire de la langue française* (Paris, 1883), gives an example of the use of this word by Talleyrand that dates from after 1795. The earlier date and attribution to Mirabeau is given by James H. Billington, *Fire in the Minds of Men: Origins of the Revolutionary Faith* (New York, 1980), p. 516, n.26, who cites a thesis I have not been able to obtain by F. Seidler, 'Die Geschichte des Wortes Revolution. Ein Beitrag zur Revolutionsforschung' (Munich, 1955). Paul Robert, *Dictionnaire alphabétique et analogique de la langue française* (Paris, 1960–70), also gives the first date of use as 1789. If we accept this, then according to the *Oxford English Dictionary*, the term 'revolutionary' was used in English before it was used in French in a political sense by Gouverneur Morris in 1774. It does not seem, however, to have been well known or to have acquired wide usage, for the same source mentions Burke using it and regarding it as a characteristically French revolutionary neologism.

[36] See Brunot, *Histoire*, vol. 9(2), pp. 618ff. and 950 for a discussion of the uses of this word.

[37] M.-J.-A.-N.-C. de Condorcet, 'Sur le sens du mot révolutionnaire', in *Journal d'Instruction Sociale* (1 June 1793), reprinted in *Œuvres de Condorcet*, ed. A. Condorcet O'Connor and F. Arago, 12 vols. (Paris, 1847), vol. 12, pp. 615–24.

[38] *Ibid.*, p. 623: 'Faisons des lois *révolutionnaires*, mais pour en accélérer le moment où nous cesserons d'avoir besoin d'en faire. Adoptons des mesures *révolutionnaires*, non pour prolonger ou ensanglanter la révolution, mais pour la compléter et en précipiter le terme.'

[39] *Ibid.*, pp. 615–17:

> De *révolution*, nous avons fait révolutionnaire; et ce mot, dans son sens général, exprime tout ce qui appartient à une *révolution*.
>
> Mais on l'a créé pour celle qui, d'un des états soumis depuis plus longtemps au despotisme, a fait, en peu d'années, la seule république où la liberté ait jamais eu pour base une entière égalité des droits. Ainsi, le mot *révolutionnaire* ne s'applique qu'aux révolutions qui ont la liberté pour objet.
>
> On dit qu'un homme est révolutionnaire, c'est-à-dire, qu'il est attaché aux principes de la révolution, qu'il agit pour elle, qu'il est disposé à se sacrifier pour la soutenir.
>
> Un esprit révolutionnaire est un esprit propre à produire, à diriger une révolution faite en faveur de la liberté.
>
> Une loi révolutionnaire est une loi qui a pour objet de maintenir cette révolution, et d'en accélérer ou régler la marche.
>
> Une mesure révolutionnaire est celle qui peut en assurer le succès.

Condorcet's definition seems to have provided the basis for the definition given in the supplement of the fifth edition of the *Dictionnaire de l'Académie françoise* (note 33 above): 'Qui appartient à la Révolution, qui est conforme aux principes de la révolution, qui est propre à en accélérer les progrès, etc. *Mesures révolutionnaires. Gouvernement révolutionnaire.*'

[40] *Le Moniteur* of 27 Germinal Year II (16 April 1794): 'Les modérés ont abusé du mot révolutionnaire; ils ont cherché à lui attacher l'idée d'indépendance qui leur était nécessaire pour comprimer impunément la révolution. Ils avaient une dureté singulière envers le Peuple, mais ils étaient indulgens envers l'aristocratie.' 'Indépendance' in the sense used here could be translated as 'undisciplined' or 'maliciously anarchistic', as can be seen further on in the same speech where Saint-Just says 'Qu'on mette de la différence entre être libre et de se déclarer indépendant pour faire le mal.'

[41] *Ibid.*: 'Je termine par ce principe invariable; c'est que l'autorité publique doit religieusement exécuter vos décrets. Voilà la force et l'unique règle de la police générale de la République et du gouvernement révolutionnaire qui n'est autre chose que la justice favorable au Peuple et terrible à ses ennemis.'

[42] Saint-Just's conception of the word allowed even reactionaries to be revolutionaries: 'Et lui aussi [l'étranger] est révolutionnaire contre le peuple, contre la vertu républicaine. Il est révolutionnaire dans le crime. Pour vous, vous devez l'être dans le sens de la probité et du législateur'; *Rapport du 13 mars 1794*, cited by Robert, *Dictionnaire alphabétique*.

[43] Brunot, *Histoire*, pp. 656–7.

[44] Fourcy, *Histoire*, p. 25.

[45] Brunot, *Histoire*, p. 619.

[46] On these courses, see Camille Richard, *Le Comité de Salut Public et les fabrications de guerre sous la Terreur* (Paris, 1922), Chapter 13.

[47] *Le Moniteur* of 2 Ventôse Year III (20 February 1795), reporting on the session of the National Convention of 30 Pluviôse Year III (18 February 1794):

> L'ancien régime aurait demandé trois ans pour ouvrir des ecóles, pour former des élèves, pour faire des cours de chymie ou d'armurerie. Le nouveau régime a tout accéléré. Il demande trois décades pour apprendre aux citoyens dans les districts à raffiner les saltpêtres, à fabriquer la poudre, à mouler, fondre et forer les canons. C'est ainsi que l'influence de la liberté rend tous les fruits précoces et toutes les institutions faciles.
>
> Le pédantisme ne les instruira pas, c'est le patriotisme et la science qui se réunissent pour opérer ce prodige de l'instruction manufacturière et militaire.

[48] *Musique des fêtes et cérémonies de la Révolution française*, ed. Pierre Constant (Paris, 1899), pp. 448–51.

[49] The official ceremonies and celebrations to mark the end of the courses gave rise to one of the more memorable of the political festivals that were common during the French Revolution (Richard, *Le Comité*, pp. 476–82).

[50] Jean-François Barailon, *Opinion de J. F. Barailon (Député par le Département de la Creuse) sur l'Ecole Polytechnique, le rapport et le projet de résolution qui la concernent* (Paris, 1798), p. 18:

> On étoit alors dans les beaux jours de l'exaltation, tout se faisoit *révolutionnairement*; les rues étoient tapissées d'affiches où on lisoit: *Cours révolutionnaire de mathématiques*; *Cours* révolutionnaire *de physique*; *Cours* révolutionnaire *de chymie, d'anatomie, de botanique*; *Education* révolutionnaire *pour les enfants de sans-culottes*, &c., &c., &c. C'étoit la mode, c'étoit l'esprit du temps. Il falloit faire un cours révolutionnaire, ou être grandement suspect d'ignorance, même de quelque chose de pis!

[51] *Le Moniteur* of 11 Ventôse Year II (1 March 1794), quoting dispatch of previous day: 'Cet essai d'instructions donées à des envoyés de tous les districts, et repándues ainsi tout à coup sur une grande surface, promet des succès qui seraient restés inconnus, sans cette belle expérience. C'est une méthode révolutionnaire qui sera sans doute employé par le Gouvernement, pour multiplier en peu de tems les genres d'instruction que la prospérité publique exige.'

[52] Léon, *Révolution française et l'éducation technique*, pp. 154–7, and Antoine-François Fourcroy, *Rapport sur les mésures prises par le Comité de Salut Public pour l'établissement de l'école centrale des travaux publics, décrétée par la Convention Nationale, le 21 ventôse dernier*, . . . (Paris, 1794), p. 26, reprinted in J. Langins, *La République avait besoin de savants* (Paris, 1987).

[53] Arthur Chuquet, *L'Ecole de Mars (1794)* (Paris, 1899).

[54] Dupuy, *L'Ecole Normale*, pp. 45–51.

[55] *Ibid.*, p. 71.

[56] *Ibid.*, pp. 40–1.

[57] The Law of 21 Ventôse Year II (11 March 1794).

[58] Fourcroy, *Rapport*, pp. 19–20.

[59] *Ibid.*, p. 27.

[60] Letter from Guyton on behalf of the Council of the Ecole Centrale des Travaux Publics to the Commission des Travaux Publics dated 20 Ventôse Year III (10 March 1795) in MS 'Correspondance Administrative', Archives of the Ecole Polytechnique, Palaiseau.

[61] A.-F. Fourcroy, *Rapport et projet de décret sur l'établissement d'une Ecole centrale de Santé à Paris, fait à la Convention nationale, au nom des Comités de Salut public et d'Instruction publique . . . le 7 Frimaire de l'an 3 [27 November 1794] . . .* (Paris, 1794–5), p. 6.

[62] MS 'Cours ["révolutionnaire" deleted] préliminaire de physique particulière. 1ère partie. Substances salines', signed by Fourcroy and approved by Lagrange on 20 Frimaire year III [10 December 1794], Ancienne cote Art. 1, para. 1 sect. a, no. 60, Archives of the Ecole Polytechnique.

[63] *Programmes de l'Enseignement Polytechnique de l'Ecole Centrale des Travaux Publics* (Paris, 1795), reprinted in Langins, *Débuts*.

[64] Claude-Antoine Prieur, *Mémoire sur l'Ecole Centrale des Travaux Publics, Presenté à la Commission des Onze et aux Comités de Salut Public, d'Instruction Publique et des Travaux Publics* (Paris, 1795), p. 26: '. . . une de ces productions éphémères que l'on a vu éclore par l'enthousiasme du moment, et qu'elle n'ait pas participé à l'impétuosité des opérations dites *révolutionnaires* . . .'

[65] On the political situation in France after Robespierre's death, see François Furet and Denis Richet, *La Révolution française* (Paris, 1973), esp. Chapter 8. Still valuable for details is G. Lefebvre, *Les Thermidoriens* (Paris, 1937).

[66] Guillaume, *Procès-Verbaux*, vol. 4, p. 991, suggests that Fourcroy was a member of the Jacobin Club until at least the end of August 1794.

[67] On the revival of the influence of moderates outside the Convention, in the streets and municipal assemblies, see François Gendron, *La Jeunesse Doré* (Quebec, 1979), Chapter 1, and A. Soboul, *Les sans-culottes parisiens de l'an 2* (Paris, 1958), Pt. 3, Chapter 6.

[68] Prieur, *Mémoire*, p. 29.

[69] *Ibid.*, pp. 8–9.

[70] Langins, 'Ecole Polytechnique', Chapter 2.

[71] Hahn, *Anatomy*, pp. 257–63, Richard, *Le Comité*, Chapter 21, and J. Langins, 'Hydrogen Production for Ballooning during the French Revolution: An Early Example of Chemical Process Development', *Annals of Science* 40 (1983), 531–58.

[72] [Alexis Eymery], *Dictionnaire des girouettes . . .* (Paris, 1815).

[73] A.-F. Fourcroy, *Rapport et projet de décret sur l'enseignement libre des sciences et des arts* 19 frimaire an II (9 December 1793), reprinted in Guillaume, *Procès-Verbaux*, vol. 3, 97–105, pp. 100–1.

[74] MS 'Procès-Verbaux du Conseil d'Administration de l'Ecole Polytechnique', 18 Pluviôse Year V (6 February 1979), Archives of the Ecole Polytechnique.

[75] Outram, 'Ordeal', p. 268, indicates that Fourcroy saved his fellow scientists Darcet and Chaptal from imprisonment and intervened on behalf of Sage, Desault and Brogniart.

[76] Maurice Daumas, 'Justification de l'Attitude de Fourcroy pendant la Terreur', *Revue d'histoire des sciences* 11 (1958), 273–4, and R. Hahn, 'Fourcroy, advocate of Lavoisier?', *Archives internationales de l'histoire des sciences* 12 (1959), 285–8.

[77] *La Société des Jacobins*, ed. F.-A. Aulard, 6 vols. (Paris, 1889–97), vol. 5, p. 547:

> FOURCROY. – Je n'entrerai pas dans le détail de la continuité de mes travaux depuis mon enfance. J'atteste que je dois la facilité de m'exprimer autant à l'art qu'à la nature. Si cette facilité a été remarquée dans mes cours de médecine, je la dois à l'étude approfondie que j'ai faite de mon état pendant plus de vingt ans. Après ces vingt ans de travaux, je suis parvenu, en professant la médecine, à nourrir le sans-culotte mon père et les sans/culottes mes sœurs. J'ai parlé à la Convention toutes les fois que j'ai cru pouvoir y dire quelque chose d'utile; mais l'étude des sciences et des arts ne m'a pas permis de m'occuper également de politique et de législation; et j'ai cru que le sage ne devait point parler des choses qu'il ne connaissait pas parfaitement, mais au contraire se renfermer dans son état. Sur l'espèce de reproche que m'a fait un membre, de donner aux sciences la majeure partie de mon temps, je déclare qu'au contraire je suis resté toujours à mon poste depuis que j'exerce une fonction publique; qu'on ne m'a vu que trois fois au Lycée des Arts, et cela dans l'intention de le sans-culottiser.
>
> Fourcroy est reçu au milieu des applaudissements unanimes.

78 W. A. Smeaton, *Fourcroy: Chemist and Revolutionary* (Cambridge, 1962), p. 12. One of Fourcroy's students at the Ecole Polytechnique during the Empire who was not as impressed as others may have given him a back-handed compliment when he wrote that 'je n'ai jamais entendu dire moins de choses en mots plus pompeux' (Jean-Louis Rieu, *Mémoires de Jean-Louis Rieu*, in *Soldats suisses au service étranger* (Geneva, 1908–10), vol. 3, p. 116.

79 *Développemens sur l'enseignement adopté pour l'Ecole centrale des travaux publics* (Paris, 1794), reprinted in Langins, *République*.

80 Fourcroy, *Enseignement libre*, p. 100.

81 Furet, *Penser*, p. 99.

82 *Ibid.*, p. 86.

83 See M. Tournier, R. Arnault, L. Cavaciuti, A. Geffroy and F. Theuriot, 'Le Vocabulaire de la Révolution: Pour un inventaire systématique des textes', *Annales historiques de la Révolution française* 41 (1969), 109–24, and Geffroy, 'Le "Peuple"'. On a more popular level, see Michel Péronnet, *Les Mots clefs de la Révolution française* (Paris, 1983).

84 On the influence of the Terror on the formation of the self-image of the scientist as a detached seeker after truth, see Outram, 'Ordeal'. For a public manifestation of this self-image during the Terror, see Fourcroy's speech to the Jacobins, in note 77 above.

85 A. Levin, 'Venel, Lavoisier, Fourcroy, Cabanis and the Idea of Scientific Revolution: The French Political Context and the General Patterns of Conceptualization of Scientific Change', *History of Science* 23 (1984), 303–20.

86 Fourcroy, *Rapport*, p. 25.

87 H. Say, 'Instruction Publique. Ecole Centrale des Travaux Publics', *La Décade philosophique, littéraire et politique*, 10 Ventôse Year III (28 February 1795): 'Il n'est pas douteux que les élèves de l'Ecole centrale, après avoir reçu de pareilles leçons, ne perfectionnent beaucoup les arts dont ils examineront les procédés, abandonnés jusqu'a présent au hazard et la routine; et l'on doit présumer que l'enseignement, précieux et unique sur la terre, qu'ils vont recevoir, développera parmi eux des génies qui reculeront les bornes des sciences.'

88 J.-B. Biot, *Essai sur l'histoire générale des sciences pendant la Révolution française* (Paris, 1803), p. 63: 'On voulut qu'une vaste colonne de lumière sortit tout-à-coup du milieu de ce pays desolé, et s'élevât si haut, que son éclat immense put couvrir la France entière, et éclairer l'avenir.'

89 See note 68. It was Prieur who presented the law of 15 Fructidor Year III (1 September 1795) which officially changed the name of the school to 'Ecole Polytechnique'.

90 Georges Bouchard, *Un Organisateur de la victoire: Prieur de la Côte d'Or* (Paris, 1946), pp. 286–313.

91 J.-F. Barailon in a speech to the Conseil des Cinq-Cents on 10 Vendémiaire Year V (1 October 1796) quoted in the *Moniteur* of 15 Vendémiaire Year V (6 October 1796): '. . . l'école des travaux publics [sic], connue maintenant sous le nom *polytechnique*, sans doute à raison de la pluralité des sciences que l'on y enseigne. On aurait pu l'appeler *encyclopédique*, car on y demontre en ce moment jusqu'aux éléments d'anatomie et botanique'.

92 Biot, *Essai*, p. 59: '. . . des hommes habitués aux idées générales, et dont la révolution avait encore exalté les esprits et aggrandi les vues'.

93 Preface to the first issue of the *Journal de l'Ecole Polytechnique* 1 (1795): '. . . quel intéressant spectacle! qui ne se sentira heureux et ne se glorifiera pas d'avoir à contribuer à l'instruction, aux premiers essais, aux progrès, d'une jeunesse si chère à la République par l'espoir qu'elle lui donne!' See also F. Arago, 'Monge', in *Œuvres complètes* (Paris, 1854), vol. 2, pp. 484–506, and *Ecole Polytechnique: Livre du Centenaire 1794–1894*, 3 vols. (Paris, 1895), vol. 1, pp. xxxiii–xxxv.

94 *Développemens*, p. 21.

95 See note 77.

96 Tournier *et al.*, *Le Vocabulaire*. Most of the authors of this article calling for a systematic inventory of the text of the Revolution were members of the Groupe d'études sur le vocabulaire de la Révolution.

97 Levin, 'Venel, Lavoisier . . .', p. 308.

8

THE SOCIOLOGY OF A TEXT: ORAL CULTURE, LITERACY AND PRINT IN EARLY NEW ZEALAND

Don F. McKenzie

In New Zealand the twenty years or so immediately preceding 1840 span the movement from orality, through manuscript literacy, to the introduction of printing. In a minor way, therefore, they replicate in a specific and largely quantifiable context the Gutenberg revolution in fifteenth-century Europe. In that New Zealand context one significant document, the Treaty of Waitangi, witnesses to a quite remarkable moment in the contact between representatives of a literate European culture and those of a wholly oral indigenous one. It can be used as a test case for measuring the impact of literacy and the influence of print in the 1830s; and it offers a prime example of European assumptions about the comprehension, status and binding power of written statements and written consent on the one hand as against the flexible accommodations of oral consensus on the other. Its variant versions, its range of 'signatures' and the conflicting views of its meaning and status bring all those questions sharply into focus. Conversely, a fuller understanding of the conditions of orality and literacy at the time it was signed may help to define more accurately the ways in which the treaty might now be reconstructed, interpreted and applied.[1]

On 6 February 1840 forty-six Maori chiefs from the northern regions of New Zealand 'signed' a document written in Maori called '*Te Tiriti o Waitangi*', 'The Treaty of Waitangi'.[2] In doing so, according to the English versions of that document, they ceded to Her Majesty the Queen of England 'absolutely and without reservation all the rights and powers of Sovereignty' which they themselves individually exercised over their respective territories. That act of assent became the substantive ground of British sovereignty over New Zealand.[3] Beneath a statue of Queen Victoria in the city of Wellington, the European literacy myth implicit in that event of 1840 is complacently enshrined in the image of a Maori chief – as I say – 'signing' the treaty with quill pen (Plate 2). The reality, as the printer William Colenso knew, and as we shall see as we meditate the sociology of that text, was different.

Twenty-five years earlier, the indigenous New Zealanders had been completely illiterate. They were a neolithic race with a wholly oral culture

Plate 2   From a bas-relief on a statue of Queen Victoria, Cambridge Terrace, Wellington, erected to mark the Queen's jubilee in 1887. Hobson is seated; Henry Williams (with glasses) stands to his right; the Maori chief is anonymous. All plates reproduced by kind permission of the Alexander Turnbull Library, Wellington, New Zealand.

and their own body of myths. Not one of their myths, however, was so absurd as the European myth of the technologies of literacy and print as agents of change and the missionaries' conviction that what took Europe over two millennia to accomplish could be achieved – *had* been achieved – in New Zealand in a mere twenty-five years: the reduction of speech to alphabetic forms, an ability to read and write them, a readiness to shift from memory to written record, to accept a signature as a sign of full comprehension and legal commitment, to surrender the relativities of time, place and person in an oral culture to the presumed fixities of the written or printed word.[4] When Samuel Marsden bought 200 acres of land at Rangihoua in 1814 for the first mission station, he drew up a deed of conveyance and solemnly had the Maori chief 'sign' it by drawing on it a copy of his *moko* or facial tattoo pattern. The price was twelve axes, itself a potent symbol of the shift from a neolithic culture to the iron age, the de-afforestation of New Zealand and the pastoral economy to come. But the subtler, much more elusive and indeterminate technology was literacy.

Consider its stages. In 1815 Thomas Kendall, the first resident missionary, faced the problem of re-enacting one of the most momentous transitions in human history, the reduction of speech to its record in alphabetic form. Put like that, it sounds portentous, as in a literal sense it was. But just imagine the problems of trying to capture strange sounds alphabetically, the miracle that underlies all our books. When one early traveller recorded what he thought he heard as the Maori word for a paradise duck, he wrote *pooadugghiedugghie* (for *putangitangi*) and for the fantail *diggowaghwagh* (for *piwakawaka*), neither of which forms translates visually the aural beauty of the originals. The place-name *Hokianga* was rendered *Showkianga, Sukyanna, Jokeeangar, Chokahanga.* Another village, *Kerikeri*, was heard and rendered as *Kiddeekiddee, Muketu* as *Muckeytoo.* Those spellings are not only aurally inefficient, but to a differently accultured English eye they may appear crude and culturally primitive, thus reinforcing other such attitudes.[5]

The absence of a philology (let alone a grammar and syntax for a non-European language) made a rational orthography hard to devise. Yet until there was an orthography, the teaching of reading and writing was obviously impossible, and printing, of course, depended upon a standard set of letter forms. Kendall's first rough list of 1815 was revised and sent off to Samuel Lee, Professor of Arabic at Cambridge. Kendall and two Maori chiefs, Hongi and Waikato, joined him there in 1820, and together they produced *A Grammar and Vocabulary of the Language of New Zealand.* It was printed later that year by R. Watts, printer to the Church Missionary Society in London. Kendall, unlike Marsden, was determined that Maori should not be anglicised; *c, q* and *x* were dropped for a start, but the *Grammar* at that stage still included letters for non-Maori sounds thought necessary for foreign words – *f*, hard *g*, *j*, *v*, *z* – and so it still ran to five vowels, eighteen consonants and one digraph *ng* (as in Ngaio Marsh). It included sample sentences such as 'the performance of the white man is good, the performance of the white man is exceeding good', but linguistically at least the performance of the white man still left room for improvement. Should stress marks be included, how should long vowels be distinguished (by macron or doubling?),[6] were all remaining letters really needed (since greater simplicity would enhance its efficacy)?

In the next ten years – by 1830 – the alphabet was in fact reduced to five vowels and nine consonants, with only two forms remaining unsettled, *h* and *w*. There were attempts to indicate a palatal *h* by adding an apostrophe (as in *H'ongi*) and the unvoiced *w* (pronounced rather like *f*), again by an apostrophe or by the combination *wh*. Colenso, as printer, argued for the doubling of long vowels (to avoid special sorts), the simple *h* (to avoid the troublesome Greek-style apostrophe), and a digammic *v* for *wh* (to avoid setting two letters where one would do) although *wh* was confirmed in 1842.[7] By then the foreign consonants plus *b*, *d*, *l*, *s* and *y* had been dropped and foreign words were rendered in Maori forms: so 'missionary' became *mihanere*, 'governor' *kawana*; I leave you to guess *komite*. Those decisions about letter forms were typographically efficient but culturally explosive, for by giving English words a Maori semblance they disguised their quite different conceptual import. But, clearly, the first great book printed in New Zealand, Colenso's Maori New Testament of 1837, is inconceivable without this prior shift from acoustics to optics, the visualisation of sound in a simplified and standardised alphabet, and the human motivations at work in bringing it about. Today the Maori language is written with the five vowels, and ten consonants *h*, *k*, *m*, *n*, *p*, *r*, *t*, *w*, *ng*, *wh*.

The pre-print years of its evolution (1815–30) were also those in which the missionaries made a tentative start to teach reading and writing. The decision to teach those skills in the vernacular had long since been settled elsewhere; in Bengal, for example, it generated a remarkable renaissance in the indigenous culture.[8] It also seemed an efficient policy. English was difficult to master and would have split the population; a universal conversion of parent and child, of old and young, was only conceivable if they were bound together by a common speech within which the new learning could pass quickly, unimpeded by language barriers. More than that, the missionaries were all too well aware that English would give the Maori access to the worst aspects of European experience. By containing them culturally within their own language, they hoped to keep them innocent of imported evils. By restricting them further to the reading of biblical texts and vocabulary, they limited the Maori to knowledge of an ancient middle-eastern culture; at the same time the missionaries enhanced their familiar pastoral role by making the Maori dependent on them morally and politically as interpretive guides to Pakeha [European] realities. Missionary expectations of a firmly directed Maori literacy policy are betrayed in comments by Williams and Puckey. In 1833 William Williams wrote that 'A reading population, whose only book is the Word of God, cannot fail to make a great moral change in the face of the country, as soon as that Word begins to take effect.'[9] And in 1842, when he should have known better, William Puckey rejoiced that the Maori 'having no other books to read but Scripture and productions from Scripture, their pursuits must all be of a sacred nature'.[10] Such a vision implied that priority should be given to the translation of the Scriptures into Maori. This ideological bias was reinforced by doctrinal strife in 1839–40, just when the policy should have been relaxed but when the Church Missionary Society faced competition from Bishop Pompallier's Catholic mission and press.[11] To study Colenso's printed output is simply to look at the expression of those policies.

Later in the century that emphasis on biblical texts was to have a profound effect on Maori consciousness, providing a new source of imagery in song and story and sharpening the expression of economic and political pressures on Government. But no such consequence was in the minds of the missionaries in the 1830s when the stress they placed on the scriptures in Maori implied ideals whose naivety is now patent. It is also present in the programme to teach reading and writing in the mission schools. The enthusiastic reports back to London of the remarkable desire of the Maori to learn to read, the further stimulation of that interest through native teachers, the intense and apparently insatiable demand so created for books, formed the cumulative pressure to supply the one instrument thought essential to give instant and local effect to universal literacy as the principal means to personal salvation. I mean, of course, printing.

But what was the reality? Kendall set up the first school with thirty-three pupils in 1816, but it was not until the early 1830s that numbers were at all significant. There is almost complete agreement in the reports, not only that the schools were effective but that the Maori achieved literacy with the greatest of ease. Of another school it was said in 1829: 'Not six years ago they commenced the very rudiments of learning: now, many of them can read and write their own language, with propriety, and are complete masters of the First Rules of Arithmetic.'[12] A visitor to one mission in 1833 noted:

> I was not prepared to find, among a people who had previously no written language, so many who had benefitted from the

> instruction given in our Mission Schools . . . [In the Boys'
> School] I observed all ranks and ages, Chiefs and subjects, old
> and young, bound and free, receiving and communicating
> instruction, with a degree of decorum and regularity which
> would have reflected credit on a school of the same kind in
> England. Catechisms, reading, spelling, writing on slates from
> dictation, and cyphering, formed the employment of the upper
> classes, while the lowest were engaged in learning the alphabet
> and forming letters . . . [In the Girls' School] The senior classes
> read remarkably well, and write equally from dictation on slates
> . . . Men of hostile tribes, even, now lay aside their antipathies,
> and unite for instruction, disregarding the person of a teacher,
> even if a slave, and valuing instruction even from a child.[13]

The highly literate rhetoric of that description is itself revealing: the
writer, a Captain Jacob, transforms the school's routines into a vision of
the society he wishes to see evolving, one indeed better than his own. Of
the mission station at Waimate he remarked:

> The writing of the senior classes was really better than that of
> most school-boys in England; and what struck me much, it was
> remarkably free from orthographical mistakes; which can only
> be accounted for from the simplicity of their language, each
> letter of which admits but one simple sound. Here also I
> observed Chiefs and subjects, freemen and slaves, all
> incorporated into classes.[14]

Hobbs, writing in January 1833, noted:

> For this long time past it has become fashionable for the young
> people to try to learn to read . . . Such is the wish of many of the
> Natives to learn to read, that on several occasions they have
> brought pigs, which would weigh from fifty to an hundred
> pounds, and offered them as payment for a book, consisting of
> sacred portions of the Scriptures, and the Liturgy of the Church
> of England.[15]

The impression is also given by the missionary reports that once the
rudiments were known, many a Maori pupil would go off and teach
others:

> In every village there are several of the Natives who can read and
> write: and a School is established among them by the Natives
> themselves, where a number are taught to read and write; and
> old and young are taught their Catechism. Their desire for books
> is very great.[16]

. . . many of the Natives, who are living at a distance, manifest a great desire for instruction; and with very little assistance from us, they are learning to read and write; and their efforts have so far been crowned with success that they know some of the letters of the alphabet and can write them.[17]

. . . there are many villages where Schools are conducted entirely by the Natives, and some of them making considerable proficiency in reading and writing. The day is not far distant, when the people generally will be able to read for themselves, in their own tongue, the wonderful works of God.[18]

But such reports are essentially anecdotal, and less informative as objective accounts than they are as expressions, at worst, of wishful thinking or, at best, of a readiness to define literacy, and therefore later the effective impact of printed texts, at a level far below that demanded by the social changes to which the Maori were being exposed.[19] It is as if the very notion of literacy itself compelled a heightened language of self-approval and infinite promise. Victims of their own myths, the missionaries found what they wanted to find, and reported what they knew their London committee wished to hear. Marsden, Williams, Hadfield and Pompallier were intelligent men, but what could they have understood by the words 'reading' and 'writing' for them to say:

The natives were carrying in their hands, the Litany, and the greater part of the Church Service, with their Hymns, written in their own language. The Church Service, as far as it has been translated, they can both read and write with greatest ease.[20]

I was much pleased to find, that wherever I went I found some who could read and write. The Church Service had been translated into the Native language, with the Catechism, Hymns, and some other useful pieces. They are all fond of reading; and there are many who have never had an opportunity of attending the schools who, nevertheless, can read. They teach one another in all parts of the country.[21]

What 'teaching one another' might have meant is suggested by Henry Williams:

One young man began to ask the meaning of letters. I wrote them down for him, and in half an hour he knew them all, and was teaching several outside. Numbers of others came until I had no paper left of any description on which to write a copy. At length they brought small pieces, to have the letters written for them, and about 200, old and young, were soon employed teaching and learning the letters with the greatest possible interest. [Next morning] the boys brought their papers for me to hear them their letters and asked what they were to learn next.[22]

Vast numbers learn to read and write who do not attend school, by possessing themselves of a book or part of a book, and spelling it over until they are fully acquainted with every word in it.[23]

They easily learn to read and write without the necessity of constant teaching. It is only necessary to give them a few leaflets of easy reading, and to write some characters on bits of slate to enable them to read and write their own language within three months.[24]

By comparison, R. K. Webb, in *The British Working-Class Reader*, says that at the Borough Road School, London, in the early nineteenth century, it took twelve months to teach a child to read, and between three and four years to write well and calculate.[25] A more realistic account of the nature of Maori literacy is that given by Fairburn in 1838:

There is scarcely a petty tribe now to be met with, where there are not some who can write and read. I mention this more particularly, as it must sound strange to an English ear to be told that we have met with many of the self-taught Natives who could write on a slate or paper so as to make their wants known, while they could not read a single line from the book. Their habits of idleness . . . are in some respects favourable to their learning to read. Since they have got books among them, they make use of them, I have not the smallest doubt, in the way of amusement, in teaching other; it seems to have superseded their once favourite game of Draughts.[26]

That at least suggests the minimal competence achieved by many so-called 'readers'.

If we reflect that the teaching of elementary reading is primarily oral/aural, not visual, because it involves the pronouncing and repetition of letters, syllables and words (a practice reinforced where there are few books, fewer texts and group teaching), we can appreciate how oral repetition from memory might masquerade as reading; and the Maori – used to an oral tradition – had a most retentive memory.[27] The interconnexion is evident in Kemp's report of 1832: 'For want of more Translations of the Scriptures, the Natives are almost at a stand: some have committed to memory all that has been printed: I hope this will soon be remedied by more being printed.'[28] Or Williams in 1832: 'We feel the want of books for the Natives very greatly: what they at present possess,

they, generally, know by heart.'[29] Other specific reports have their
general interest:

> The Natives manifest a strong desire to learn to read the
> Scriptures . . . Wherever I go amongst the Natives, I hear
> portions of the Catechism repeated. One Native, who, though he
> cannot read, has learned a considerable part of the Catechisms,
> puts the Questions to those around him; and then he and the
> others repeat the answers.[30]

> [I] visited a tribe in which the only teaching was done by a Maori
> who had learned to read at Paihia and, returning to his village,
> read the Scriptures to his countrymen. Before this time they were
> in the habit of meeting, and repeating from memory, the Con-
> fession and Lord's Prayer, not any one being able to read.[31]

> My attention was called . . . to a blind man reading the Scriptures
> . . . He came to me some time since, and requested that I would
> let him have a complete book. I asked of what use a book would
> be to him, as he was blind. He replied that it would be of great
> use; for though he could not see, he could hear; and by posses-
> sing one he could let others read to him, until he should see it
> with his heart . . . I [later] saw the poor fellow lying on the
> ground with his book open before him, as though he was
> pondering over its contents, repeating aloud verse by verse.[32]

'Poor fellow'? The memorised text, of course, makes one a living library
in a way the read book cannot. Repetition of the catechism – known by
heart, not read by *eye* – was after all the higher proof of conversion.
Simply to illustrate the illusory nature of the presumed shift from orality
to literacy, I quote Sir Apirana Ngata, writing on 'The Maori and Printed
Matter' as late as 1940:

> The people preferred to hear the matter, whether written or
> printed, read to them. Not only did this relieve the labour of
> spelling out words, syllable by syllable, but it was closer than
> mute transference through the eye to what they had been
> accustomed to: it was nearer the old-time narrative of adept
> raconteurs, or of poetical and priestly reciters. More than that,
> the genius of the race preferred education through the ear,
> conveyed by artists in intonation and gesticulation . . . The
> printed matter indeed achieved a limited popularity, but for
> every one who owned a copy of the Scriptures and Church
> Liturgy or Rawiri, there were in my boyhood days still fifty or
> more content to listen to and memorize the words which were

read out of the printed books by the ministers, teachers, or lay-readers.[33]

If reading, the passively receptive and more easily acquired art, could be so easily evaded, what of writing? This was the active counterpart of reading, a personally *expressive* skill, but one much harder to acquire. It was inhibited by the primitive nature, cost and scarcity of quills, ink and paper. A slate may prove that one can write, but not that one can write to any purpose. Just as the oral element in reading persisted to limit the full and easy visual perception of texts, so too a reliance on writing and a readiness to use it could only grow slowly from a long acquaintance with documents.[34] Oral witness held its primacy over written evidence for centuries in Europe; to have expected a non-literate people to reverse that disposition within a decade was unrealistic, and to presume that it has yet happened would be a mistake.[35]

The main use of literacy to the Maori was not reading books for their ideas, much less for the access they gave to divine truths, but letter writing. For them, the really miraculous point about writing was its portability; by annihilating distance, a letter allowed the person who wrote it to be in two places at once, his body in one, his thoughts in another. It was the spatial extension of writing, not its temporal permanence, that became politically potent in gathering the tribes and planning a war a decade and more later.[36] Historical time, defined by dated and legally binding documents, represented a much more profound challenge to an oral culture used to reshaping its past traditions to accord with present needs. It is a challenge that is still resisted.

On a journey in 1833 Williams received several letters which had been sent on to him and his Maori attendants and he records the reaction of other Maori who had not seen letters before:

> This was an interesting particular for the people of the place, as they were thus enabled to see the nature and value of written characters, by the testimony of these their countrymen. Our boys seemed to look for, and read over *their* letters, with as much pleasure as we did *ours*, to the delight of all around; they repeated them aloud, to the admiration of their auditors, who were struck with wonder at hearing, as they described it, 'a book speak': for though they expect that a European can perform an extraordinary thing, yet they cannot understand how it is that a New Zealand youth can possess the same power.[37]

In the early 1830s we see the hesitant beginnings of letter writing in written requests for baptism, proving (as William Yate put it) that 'the heart of the sanguinary and untutored New Zealander is at the heart of the civilized and polished Englishman'.[38] The originals, of course, were in Maori.

> I, Pahau, am now writing a Letter to you. Perhaps you will not be pleased with it, and send it back; and then, perhaps, my heart will be sad, and I shall cry. Now, then, I am going to write to you. Read it first, from the top to the bottom, on this side and on that side, before you say 'Nonsense,' and throw it away from you and tear it to pieces. Now, Mr Yate, listen to what I am going to say upon this paper. I have been thinking and thinking about what I am going to write; and now I am thinking you will shut your ears, and will not listen to me. This is what I am going to write: – Remember, that if you say 'Nonsense,' it was you who said we were to put down our wishes in a book.[39]

Another letter begins, in a vein reminiscent of Caxton: 'My ink is not good, my paper dirty, and I am altogether ashamed.'[40] Yet another, from husband and wife: 'There are many mistakes in our two's Letter: and Mary says, "Do not send it: wait and talk when he comes to Kerikeri".'[41]

Those translations are insensitive (Yate's use of 'our two's' for the dual pronoun in Maori reflects upon him, not the writer), but there is no mistaking the diffidence, the insecure handling of this tool, the anxieties attending exposure by this medium. These were not untutored New Zealanders. They were the literate elite in Maori, not draught-players turned scribblers but those trained to readiness for baptism. The effective use of letters for political purposes was many years away. Nor did printing of itself become a re-expressive tool for the Maori until the late 1850s.[42] When it did so – in Maori newspapers – the essential motives, the effective contextual forces, were economic, political and military, not religious. *He wahine, he whenua, e ngaro ai te tangata* – by women, and by land, men perish. The forcing issue for the Maori, then as now, was land. Only when literacy began to serve that supreme social interest could it be significantly achieved. Its roots in the texts of an alien religion were inevitably shallow, despite the technology of printing.

But for the missionaries, printing was the great hope. 'We feel very much the want of a Printing Press, to work off some copies of portions of Scripture, which could be read by several natives now with us,' Davis had written to the Church Missionary Society in 1827.[43] In 1828 Williams wrote: 'We want a printer, and a printer we must have.'[44] The plea to the Church Missionary Society was twice repeated in 1829. When the long-sought-after press did arrive, it was an anti-climax, proving that technology in itself is nothing without a human mind and dedicated skill to make it work in a context where it matters. In 1830, William Yate brought a small press from Sydney, and fifteen-year-old James Smith to help him. Neither Yate nor Smith had any professional competence.

In his journal for September 1830 Yate noted that, in printing off a few hymns in the native language, 'we succeeded beyond our most sanguine expectations'. These were the first items ever printed in New Zealand. 'We thank you for the Press,' he wrote back to London, 'and have no doubt but that, with the blessing of God, it will be an instrument of great good in this Land. You will perceive by a copy of a Hymn forwarded by this conveyance, that we shall be able, in a short time, to manage it.'[45] Others took his tone. Kemp reported that 'The Schools will receive great benefit from the Press, for we shall be able to get portions of the Scriptures printed, as they are wanted.'[46] No copy of their Hymns is known to survive but Yate and Smith also printed a small catechism in Maori, both extant copies of which testify to the printers' gross incompetence in planing the type, locking the forme and making ready. Writing of a new translation a year later, Yate faced facts: 'We shall not . . . be able to print it here.'[47]

Henry Williams, two years after that first experiment, told his masters:

> You have sent us out a Printing Press of a certain description and a specimen of its production has been sent to you, accompanied with many expressions of delight – but these were first feelings excited by the novelty of the work: there stands the poor thing enshrined in cobwebs as an exciter for further expectations and desires. It has been examined by a printer of some experience who said he would not possess it as a gift . . . Had we something respectable, our work would be more so than it is at present.[48]

As the Maori proverb says (one later recorded by Colenso), 'even a little axe, well used, brings plenty of food'. But with Yate as food gatherer, the missionaries starved. Defeated in his own efforts, Yate returned to Sydney the following year to supervise the printing of what, when it arrived, he described as 'the most valuable cargo that ever reached the shores of new Zealand' – 1,800 copies of a book containing eight chapters of Genesis and almost half the New Testament.[49] On receiving these books in 1833, Williams wrote home: 'I hope our good friends in London will see in time the necessity of allowing a press and a printer. The book contains 250 pages and abounds in typographical errors, not less . . . than two to a page. It must not be offered without correction. So much for colonial work.'[50] In 1836 Colenso was even less complimentary about this early Australian export to New Zealand; 'poor things, they reflect no credit on the printer, less on the binder, and still less on the editor – it has been computed that there are not less than 1000 errors in the work'.[51] Yate's ignominious effort in 1830 deprived William Colenso of the honour of being literally New Zealand's first printer, a New Zealand Caxton, as Coupland Harding was later to call him.

William Colenso, a cousin of the bishop of that name, was born in Penzance in 1811 and on 3 September 1826 was bound for six years to a local printer, John Thomas.[52] While still in his time he read his first paper to the Penzance Natural History and Antiquarian Society (on Phoenician trade with west Cornwall) and compiled a history of Penzance, *The Ancient and Modern History of the Mounts*, which was printed and published by Thomas in 1831. In October 1833 he moved to London and found work with Richard Watts and Son, Crown Court, Temple Bar, printers to the Church Missionary Society and the British and Foreign Bible Society.[53] Some anonymous articles he wrote for the religious serial *The Pilot* came for printing to Watts, who recognised Colenso's handwriting. This led to an introduction to Dandeson Coates, lay secretary to the Society, just as the New Zealand missionaries were again supplicating for a press. Commissioned as printer by the Society and preparing to leave for New Zealand in 1834, Colenso wrote in his diary: 'In addition to Satan's temptations at having no interest in Jesus, he assails me with "You are going abroad, and are unfit for the work".' In fact there was none fitter. Colenso arrived at Paihia in the north of New Zealand on 30 December 1834. The next day, he records, 'Numbers of Natives came to see me – and when they found I was a Printer were quite enraptured – crying out *Pukapuka*.' Saturday, 3 January 1835 was, as he wrote to Coates,

> A memorable epoch in the annals of New Zealand – I succeeded in getting the Printing Press landed. I was obliged to unpack it on board, but, I am happy to say, it is all safe on shore. Could you, my dear Sir, but have witnessed the Natives when it was landed, they danced, shouted, and capered about in the water, giving vent to the wildest effusions of joy. Enquiring the use of this, and the place of that, with all the eagerness for which uncivilized nature is celebrated. Certes, they had never seen such a thing before! I trust soon to be able to get it to work. May the father of Mercies . . . grant me strength and ability to work it for His Glory! May it be instrumental, under His blessing, in bringing thousands to the Cross of our Immanuel! – and of sending away that Sombre pall of darkness and gloom, which 'the Prince of the power of the Air' has so long successfully wrapped around the inhabitants of these islands.[54]

In fact, getting the Stanhope ashore had been far from easy, and lest the parcels of type be seized for making musket balls they could not be unpacked until safely landed. Most revealing, however, for what it implies about the symbolic power of 'the press' as distinct from the realities of using one, is Colenso's list of necessary articles which he found to be absolutely wanting:

> For the information of Printers I will just set down a few of them; though I almost fear my relation will scarcely be believed. There was no wooden furniture of any kind, nor quoins . . . no galleys, no cases, no leads of any size, no brass rule, no composing-sticks, (save a private one of my own that I had bought two years before in London, a most fortunate circumstance!) no inking table, no potash, no lye-brushes, no mallet and shooter, no roller-irons and stock, though there was a massy cast-iron roller mould, and . . . no imposing-stone nor page-cord; and, worst of all, actually *no printing paper!!*[55]

So ignorant and incompetent were Colenso's mentors about the art by which they set so much store. Colenso found a local joiner who made him a few galleys, a small inking table, some furniture and quoins, although he complained that these last 'were wretched things (partly owing to the want of proper and seasoned wood,)' and gave him 'an enormous amount of labour, vexation and trouble'. The joiner also made him

> two or three pairs of type-cases for the printing office after a plan of my own. For as the Maori language contained only 13 letters (half the number in the English alphabet), I contrived my cases so, as to have both Roman and Italic characters in the *one* pair of cases; not distributing the remaining 13 letters (consonants) used in the compositing of English, such not being wanted . . . Such an arrangement proved to be a very good one while my compositing was confined to the Maori language only; but when I had any English copy to compose it was altogether the reverse! then I had to pick out the discarded English consonants as required from their lots put up in paper parcels. Fortunately this occurred but rarely; except at the time of the Treaty of Waitangi (1840), when I had necessarily much printing work to do for the Government of the Colony; and having no extra cases, was obliged to place the letters required in little lots on tables, and on the floor![56]

With the press in place and type disposed, it was agreed that as all parties, European and Maori, wished to see something printed, the missionaries should supply some writing paper, that the first sheet from the press should be in Maori from the New Testament, and that it should be small. The Epistles to the Ephesians and Philippians was chosen. Colenso set it up, and on 17 February 1835 pulled proofs of what he then thought was the first book printed in New Zealand, 'the printing office being filled with spectators to witness the performance'. On 21 February, twenty-five corrected copies were printed and stitched and cut round for the Missionaries; their wives kindly furnishing a few sheets of pink blotting-paper from their desks wherewith to form coloured paper covers for these tracts; which, of course, had first to be pasted on to stronger paper. This little book was in post 8vo., Long-Primer type, and consisted of 16 pages in double columns. For leads I was driven to the miserable substitute of pasting paper together, and drying and cutting it up! . . . And not being able to manufacture a roller, I was obliged to do my best with a small makeshift 'ball' of my own contriving.[57]

Knowing nothing of Yate's earlier efforts, Colenso wrote home to Coates:

This 'first fruits' of the New Zealand Press, which the Lord hath pleased to allow me to begin and complete, is very much liked by the Natives. – May it, being the 'Word of God', be the means of making thousands 'wise unto Salvation' – and the preface, as it were, to a more glorious diffusion of Gospel light over these benighted lands.[58]

On 19 May he printed what was in fact the first English book, eight pages octavo, a report of the New Zealand Temperance Society. Given the later history of New Zealand's licensing laws, it was indeed a prophetic start.

Earlier that year, on 23 March, having heard that supplies of paper and more equipment for him had reached Sydney, he began setting his one great work, the complete Maori New Testament. It was a demy-octavo, set in small Pica, and running to 356 pages. He pulled the first sheets of a run of 5,000 copies on 23 June 1836. The Maori pressmen he later employed and paid 3s. a week were soon disenchanted by 'the many disagreeables inseparable from this new and wonderful art of printing', as Colenso put it, but on two subsequent occasions he was able to secure the help of some American sailors who had trained as pressmen before going to sea. Of the second pair he wrote:

The wages I paid these two men were, at first, the same as to the two former pressmen, 5/- per day; but after a short time, at their own request, their pay was altered to 25 cents, or 1/- each per 'token,' (10 quires = $\frac{1}{2}$-ream,) besides which, as they could not be always at press-work, they were paid 12 cents, or 6d per hour for other work connected with the Printing-office and Binding-room, and Warehouse, – as, in drying, and pressing, and folding the sheets, &c.; but would never do anything in the way of distributing type, and even if a letter should be drawn out, or be broken in their working-off the forms, (which sometimes though rarely did happen,) they would not, or more properly could not well, replace it; and spoiled paper (if any) they had to pay for, – which, however, did not amount to much. Upham worked alone at Press for a period of six months, after his companion left, (always a disagreeable and slow process for *one* person,) and, of course, from that time he was paid 2/- per 'token.' He was a very good and trusty pressman, and kept the 'colour' well up, and his rollers, &c., in nice working order.[59]

Colenso records that when the book was finished, in December 1837, 'the demand for copies became great beyond expression, from all parts of New Zealand', and finding it impossible to bind them fast enough he sent off lots of 500 at a time to Sydney to have them done (poorly done, as he later complained). Since the Maori were said to value more highly any article they paid for than one given to them free, the books were sold at 4*s*. each. As evidence of interest and demand, Colenso makes the incidentally valuable point (distinguishing reading from writing) that 'as not many of the principal Maori Chiefs or their sons could then write, many of them travelled on foot and barefooted to Paihia, from very great distances, to obtain a copy'. William Jowett, responding as clerical secretary of the Church Missionary Society to Colenso's expressed wish for ordination, advised him to turn his thoughts

> to the peculiarly useful (and therefore honourable) department which you *do* occupy. The sight of that New Testament in the Native language, which you have been privileged to carry through the Press, is such a sight as fills my heart with indescribable joy. Think now to what great ends it is capable of becoming instrumental . . . it will, moreover, help the fixing of the language; and school-books, and many other books, will grow out of it. No doubt the spirit of GOD will use this sword.[60]

There is one excellent point in Jowett's response to which I shall return, but here I just wish to note again the ecstatic tone which belies both the actual achievement and the future promise of literacy.

How many Maori could read before Colenso arrived? In 1833 Yate had estimated that some 500 in the north could do so. In 1834, Edward Markham ventured 'not less than ten Thousand people that can Read, write and do sums in the Northern end of the Island'.[61] Refining such impressionism by apparently objective fact, one historian turns to the presumed demand for and effects of printing: between January 1835 and January 1840 Colenso printed 3,500,000 pages of religious material, and in 1840 he produced over 2,000,000 more – figures as ignorantly impressionistic (though true) as Yate's and Markham's.[62] Added to the further information that Colenso's New Testament was reprinted in London in 1841, 1843 and 1845 (each time in 20,000 copies), it reinforces the missionary notion of widespread literacy and the immense impact of print. On those figures, by 1845 there was at least one Maori New Testament for every two Maori people in New Zealand. Colenso felt confident to write in his journal in 1840:

> Here I may be permitted to remark the Press has been an inst[rument] of very great good in this land . . . Howr. partial it may be supposed I am in my opinion, I believe (and that belief too is deduced from what I have seen and heard on the spot) that the press has been more effective (under God) as an instr[ument] of good among this people during the last 5 yrs. than the whole body of miss[ionaries] put together.

As Colenso's day- and waste-books, paper-book and ledger all survive, we can detail everything he printed for the years 1836–43. In terms of *histoire-du-livre* econometrics we can say exactly what his output was; but instead of using figures like three and a half million and two million *pages*, a printer or bibliographer would use a quite different measure. The basic unit of printing is not the page but the sheet, and in the five years from January 1835 until January 1840 Colenso's output amounted to only sixteen items and required type to be set for only 34.15 sheets. The New Testament alone accounted for 22.5 of those 34.15 sheets and for 122,500 of the grand total of 145,775 perfected sheets which came off his press and made up the various copies of those sixteen items. A single octavo book of 224 pages printed in 5,000 copies will run up a total of 1,120,000 pages. It sounds impressive but in printing terms it is only 5,000 copies of each of fourteen sheets. In 1840, Colenso printed eleven items, involving 18,875 sheets and 89,313 perfected sheets. One book, the Psalms, accounted for a third of the setting and two-thirds of the presswork. Colenso's output as printer, and therefore the effects of his work, were not at all on the scale suggested by 'millions of pages' and by the self-congratulatory tone of missionary reports and his own letters.

If this technical view of Colenso's output checks us slightly, what other evidence is there of reception? It is well known that people in an oral society, seeing books for the first time, often treat them as ritual objects: 'Many people who know not a letter wish to possess themselves of a copy of the translated Scriptures because they consider it possesses a peculiar virtue of protecting them from the power of evil spirits.'[63]

At an early church service, 'Many of [the Maori] thought it highly proper that they should be armed with books. It might be an old ship's almanac, or a cast-away novel, or even a few stitched leaves of old newspapers.'[64]

The book was given a totemic power of warding off not only evil spirits: in 1836 it was said that a Maori fighting party had refused to storm a *pa* (a fortified village) because of a printed Bible inside it and contented themselves with a blockade.[65] In 1839 Taylor recorded seeing Maori with mission books (or at least odd leaves from them) rolled up and thrust through holes in the lobes of their ears.[66] Books were also useful for making roll-your-own cartridges. One book so used was Milner's *Church History*, thus giving a slightly different sense to the phrase 'the church militant'.[67] Colenso picked up such a cartridge in which the paper came from II Samuel and bore the words from Chapter 19, v. 34: 'How long have I to live?'[68] Markham said his servants melted down his pewter spoons in 1834 to make musket balls of them, 'and the first Volume of my Voltaires, "Louis 14. et 15." torn up and made Cartridges of them'.[69]

As the number of New Testaments disseminated was reaching saturation point (one to every two Maori) in the early 1840s – just when the impact of printing should have been at its height – we find Selwyn noting 'A general complaint in all parts of the country, that the schools are not so well attended as heretofore'. He remarked 'a growing indifference to religion, and a neglect of the opportunities for instruction'.[70] Another missionary comments that 'We have gained a very large portion of this people but we have no hold on their children.'[71] By 1844, Hadfield could say at last that 'It appears every year more evident that our present system of conveying instruction to these people is wholly inadequate to their present wants; they have been brought to a certain point, and we have no means of bringing them beyond that.'[72]

What we have here is not only disillusionment about the actual extent to which literacy of the most elementary kind had been achieved, but a clear example of the way in which even the most sophisticated technology (print) will fail to serve an irrelevant ideology (an alien religion).[73] The missionaries and their great instrument of truth had failed lamentably to equip the Maori to negotiate their rights with the Pakeha in the one area that really mattered to them – land. Nor was it merely a failure in creating literacy in Maori. In 1844 almost no Maori spoke (let alone read) English. In that year a settler said he had met only two who did so.[74] Selwyn recognised the need to break away from the old policy and in 1843 produced the first primer to help the Maori read English. Colenso followed up in 1872 on a Government commission with *Willie's first English Book*, 'Written for young Maoris who can read their own Maori Tongue and who wish to learn to read the English Language'. For all his piety, Colenso saw also the need for another innovation: 'in order to the greater and more general use of the work, all words and sentences of a strictly religious nature have been purposely omitted'.

Historians have too readily and optimistically affirmed extensive·and high levels of Maori literacy in the early years of settlement, and the role of printing in establishing it. Protestant missionary faith in the power of the written word, and modern assumptions about the impact of the press in propagating it, are not self-evidently valid, and they all too easily distort our understanding of the different and competitively powerful realities of societies whose cultures are still primarily oral. Yet, as Jowett told Colenso when congratulating him on completion of the Maori New Testament, printing had helped to fix the Maori language – albeit in one dialect and with some dangerous neologisms. Colenso himself was later to make the point that the oral memory, as a faculty, too easily absorbed and perpetuated the new and corrupt words born of settlement and trade, taking up the simpler and degenerate forms used by the settlers.[75] Had it not been for the missionaries and Colenso's printing, the language as it was at an early stage of European contact might well have been irretrievably lost.

I wish now to focus on one test of the missionaries' efforts to teach literacy in the 1830s, one test of Colenso's effect after five years' printing, one example of a 'text' which offers textual and contextual problems. I return to the Treaty of Waitangi. (The name, by the way, means 'the waters of lamentation'.) *An Authentic and Genuine History of the Signing of the Treaty of Waitangi* was written at the time by Colenso although it was not printed until 1890.

On the morning of 30 January 1840 Colenso printed in Maori 100 copies of a circular letter inviting Maori chiefs in the northern area to meet at Waitangi on 5 February. An English draft of the treaty (a composite version by three men, Hobson, Freeman and Busby) had been cobbled together by the 3rd and was given to Henry Williams on the 4th to translate into Maori. The first English draft has not survived.[76] Williams's translation was discussed with the chiefs on Wednesday, 5 February; alterations were made and the revised Maori version copied on to parchment that night by Richard Taylor. The original copy of that revised Maori version has not survived. The fair copy of it, made by Taylor on Wednesday night, was presented to the chiefs next day, 6 February, for their signatures. It is this document in Maori, a revised version of a translation into Maori made from a composite English draft no longer extant, which is in the most literal sense the Treaty of Waitangi. But its textual complexities do not end there.

Hobson also sent abroad, either to Sydney or to London, five English versions of the treaty. There are minor differences in three of them, but the other two bear a different date, differ from the others in the wording of their preamble, and differ critically from each other in the second article. According to Ruth Ross, the extant Maori version, the actual treaty as signed by the chiefs on 6 February, is not a translation of any one of these five English versions, nor is any of the English ones a translation from the Maori. They must therefore descend, with greater or less accuracy and no authority, from the first full English draft, now lost, and made before the Maori translation in its first and revised forms. One English version sent to the Secretary of State was endorsed by Williams, who said it was 'as Literal a translation of the Treaty of Waitangi as the Idiom of the Language will admit of'. This cannot have been true, but a comparable disregard for strict textual accuracy in our own day has led to the inclusion of one of the unauthoritative English versions as a Schedule to the Waitangi Day Act (1960).[77] Other complications of textual authority derive from the fact that names were added to the treaty over the next seven months, thirty-nine such names being found on an English copy which the signatories, being illiterate, could not have read even if they had known the language.

That last example puts at its most extreme my argument about the non-literate state of the nation in 1840 after ten years of intensive teaching and five years of proselytic printing. But even if we confine ourselves to the Maori text, how literate were the signatories? As Cressy has said, 'only one type of literacy is directly measurable – the ability or inability to write a signature', and because the evidence of signatures or marks is, in Schofield's words, 'universal, standard and direct', it has come to displace the merely anecdotal, subjective, inescapably impressionistic evidence found in missionary reports and hitherto accepted by historians.[78] Applying this test to the Treaty of Waitangi, what do we find? The number of signatories is in fact uncertain; estimates vary from 512 to 541, and, in the manner common to many societies with mass illiteracy, many of the names given were written out by the government clerk on behalf of the chief concerned. On my count the highest possible number of personal signatures, as distinct from crosses, *moko*-patterns or apparently quite meaningless marks, is seventy-two.[79] In almost every case the signatures are so painfully and crudely written as to show clearly that they have not been penned by signatories practised in writing and therefore fluent in the art. We are forced to conclude, given these numbers, that the Maori in the commemorative plaque is unlikely to have been able to read what he was signing in even the most literal way. Even if he could do that, the odds are loaded against his knowing how to write his own name. Even if he could do that, the evidence suggests that he wrote painfully and with only the most elementary competence. The presumed widespread, high-level literacy of the Maori in the 1830s is a chimera, a fantasy creation of the European mind. Even at Waitangi the settlement was premised on the assumption that it was, for the Maori, an oral–aural occasion.

Consider the way in which the treaty was presented to them: it was read out to them by Henry Williams. That is, it was received by them as an oral statement, not as a document drawn up in consultation with them, pondered privately over several days or weeks and offered finally as a public communiqué of agreements reached by the parties concerned. Without begging any questions about Pakeha intent to deceive, even the Maori language itself was used against the Maori. First, much of the detail of the English draft was presumed by Williams to be inexpressible in Maori translation. Second, the forms of Maori used to communicate Pakeha intentions were, as Ruth Ross has said, not indigenous Maori but Protestant Pakeha Missionary Maori, learnt from the distinctive dialect of the northern Ngapuhi tribe. Not only the concepts, but many of the words, for all their Maori form, were English.

This is not to say that the Maori present were unaware of such things, but only that their mode of dealing with them was oral. It is a mode which has its own dignities, but it has left virtually no matching record to complement the Pakeha one. Those present were free to speak on Wednesday, 5 February, but not thereafter. Hobson had intended to allow them the whole of Thursday to talk among themselves and gave notice that the meeting would be reassembled on Friday for the signing. The plan was changed and somewhat to Hobson's surprise the meeting resumed on Thursday, 6 February. Hobson was content to receive any signatures on that day from those willing to sign and anxious to leave; but he would not allow any discussion, 'this not being a regular public meeting'. This meant the effective proscription of any further oral argument by those who might have wished to discuss the matter further, and of any at all by those chiefs who only arrived at Waitangi on the Thursday. Although Hobson assumed that a public meeting would still be held on the Friday, the parchment copy of the treaty in Maori was read out as a finished document on the Thursday (its completion on the Wednesday night presupposed that Maori modification would go no further). Those present on Thursday were called upon to sign, and the business of Waitangi was fully despatched that same day.

On the Wednesday Hobson had explained, with Williams translating, that if the chiefs did sign the Queen would protect them. In an important sense this was true: many Maori wanted the British to establish some legal authority over their own unruly European settlers and traders and incidentally by their authority to inhibit intertribal strife. Busby, in a half-truth, said the Governor had not come to take away their land but to secure them in the possession of what they held. But Te Kemara called his bluff and asked for the return to him of the very land on which they were standing. Rewa, eloquent but sad, added, 'I have no lands now – only a name, only a name!' Kawiti rejected Hobson's plan: 'We are free.'

Hakiro supported him: 'We are not thy people. We are free.' Tareha: 'No, we only are the chiefs, the rulers. We will not be ruled over. What, thou a foreigner up, and I down! Thou high, and I, Tareha, the great chief of the Ngapuhi tribes, low! No, never, never.' With a flair for the dramatic, he held a canoe paddle high in the air to deride Hobson's intolerable ambition. Tareha, says Colenso, was also clothed in a filthy piece of coarse old floor matting simply to ridicule Hobson's supposition that New Zealanders needed the extraneous aid of clothing, &c, from foreign nations.[80] At the end of that day – the only one of public debate – Maori opinion was clearly opposed to the surrender of sovereignty and therefore of the absolute control of their own lands.

The next day, Thursday, 6 February (now celebrated as a public holiday), some 300–400 Maori were, in Colenso's words, 'scattered in small parties according to their tribes, talking about the treaty, but evidently not understanding it'. Nevertheless, Hobson now wanted to make an end. Colenso's printed report runs:

> The Native chiefs were called on in a body to come forward and sign the document. Not one, however, made any move nor seemed desirous of doing so till Mr. Busby, hitting on an expedient, proposed calling them singly by their names as they stood in *his* (private) list, in which list the name of Hoani Heke (known, too, to be the most favourable towards the treaty) happened to be the first – at least, of those who were this day present. On his being called by name to come and sign, he advanced to the table on which the treaty lay. At this moment I, addressing myself to the Governor, said, –
>
> 'Will your Excellency allow me to make a remark or two before that chief signs the treaty?'
>
> The Governor: 'Certainly, sir.'
>
> Mr. Colenso: 'May I ask your Excellency whether it is your opinion that these Natives understand the articles of the treaty which they are now called upon to sign? I this morning' –
>
> The Governor: 'If the Native chiefs do not know the contents of this treaty it is no fault of mine. I wish them fully to understand it . . . They have heard the treaty read by Mr. Williams.'
>
> Mr. Colenso: 'True, your Excellency; but the Natives are quite children in their ideas. It is no easy matter, I well know, to get them to understand – fully to comprehend a document of this kind; still, I think they ought to know somewhat of it to constitute its legality . . . I have spoken to some chiefs concerning it, who had no idea whatever as to the purport of the treaty.'
>
> Mr. Busby here said, 'The best answer that could be given to

that observation would be found in the speech made yesterday by the very chief about to sign, Hoani Heke, who said, "The Native mind could not comprehend these things: they must trust to the advice of their missionaries".'

Mr. Colenso: 'Yes; and that is the very thing to which I was going to allude. The missionaries should do so; but at the same time the missionaries should explain the thing in all its bearings to the Natives, so that it should be their very own act and deed. Then, in case of a reaction taking place, the Natives could not turn round on the missionary and say, "You advised me to sign that paper, but never told me what were the contents thereof" [a comment implying Maori inability to read it].'

The Governor: 'I am in hopes that no such reaction will take place.'

So Colenso gave up, having expressed his conscientious feeling, and discharged what he felt strongly to be his duty. Then forty-six chiefs, anxious to get home, played this new game and put their marks on the parchment they could not read. They included chiefs who had declaimed *against* signing; but (as Colenso records of one of them) 'Marupu, having made his mark (as he could neither read nor write) shook hands heartily with the Governor' and left.

In one sense, of course, Maori illiteracy was not in itself the critical problem: an oral contract before witnesses could be given legal standing and marks are legally acceptable as signatures. The reality, however, is that all who draft documents secure an initiative, determine the concepts and choose the linguistic terms by which to reveal or conceal them. A collective oral response is rarely unanimous about details of wording; it tends to assume continuing discussion and modification; and, lacking a documentary form, it is weaker in its power to bind when a group disperses. The illiterate's inability to respond in kind is, after all, critical.

For the Maori present, the very form of public discourse and decision-making was *oral* and confirmed in the consensus not in the document. It is inconceivable that Williams's explanations to them in Maori were wholly one-way, that there was no response and no demand for reverse mediation. In signing the treaty, many chiefs would have made complementary oral conditions which were more important than (and certainly in their own way modified) the words on the page. For the illiterate, the document and its implications were meaningless; for the barely literate, the ability to sign one's name was a trap. At the end of the first day, as Hobson went to his boat, an elderly chief rushed in front of him and looked staringly and scrutinisingly, says Colenso, into the Governor's face. Having surveyed it, he exclaimed in a shrill, loud and mournful voice, *'Auee! he koroheke! Ekore e roa kua mate.'* Colenso was reluctant to translate but on being pressed did so: 'He says, "Alas! an old man. *He will soon be dead!*" ' – and he was, but the document lives on.

At this point we may return to textual criticism. The circumstances described above do not mean that the treaty is a fraud and the documents useless. It means that they are only partial witnesses to the occasion. Reconstructing a more authentic version of the understandings reached between Maori and Pakeha in 1840 is a demanding task, but not one unusually so to those who edit texts or construct statutes.

One of the most important elements in any such textual reconstruction is recognition of the Declaration of Independence (Plate 3) as a complementary document, first subscribed on 28 October 1835 by thirty-four chiefs of whom only four signed their own names. In the next four years a further eighteen chiefs subscribed, of whom only three signed (again with difficulty) their own names. It was these chiefs who constituted the invitation list for the meeting at Waitangi on 5 and 6 February 1840; it was these chiefs who were on Busby's private list and whom he called upon to sign 'singly by their names as they were written in the List of the Confederated Chiefs'. (I quote Colenso's manuscript draft of his account: the printed version refers simply to Busby's '(private) list'.) Because the last signature to the Declaration had been subscribed as late as 22 July 1839, it is clear that this Declaration continued to be a living affirmation of Maori sovereignty. Its second article specifically refers to *Ko te Kingitanga ko te mana* . . . . 'All sovereign power and authority' was said 'to reside entirely and exclusively in the hereditary chiefs and heads of tribes in their collective capacity'. The third article provided for annual meetings at Waitangi, and it was these chiefs who were the main guests there on 5 and 6 February 1840. As Claudia Orange has shown, Maori understanding of the treaty was undoubtedly formed by their sense that the independence (*rangatiratanga*) and the sovereignty (*mana*) they had affirmed in 1835 and reaffirmed by further subscriptions as late as 1839, was not nullified by the treaty. British Colonial Office attitudes may have changed in the meantime, but for the Maori one document did not supersede the other: they lived together, one complementing the other.

It is in this context now that we must ask what it was that the Chiefs of the Confederation are presumed to have surrendered at Waitangi in agreeing to the first article of the treaty. In all the English versions of the treaty the chiefs 'cede to Her Majesty the Queen of England, absolutely and without reservation, all the rights and powers of Sovereignty'. The question here is what the English meant and the Maori understood by the word 'Sovereignty'. Did it mean that the chiefs gave up to the Crown their personal power and supreme status within their own tribes, or was it only something more mundanely administrative, like 'governorship'? In

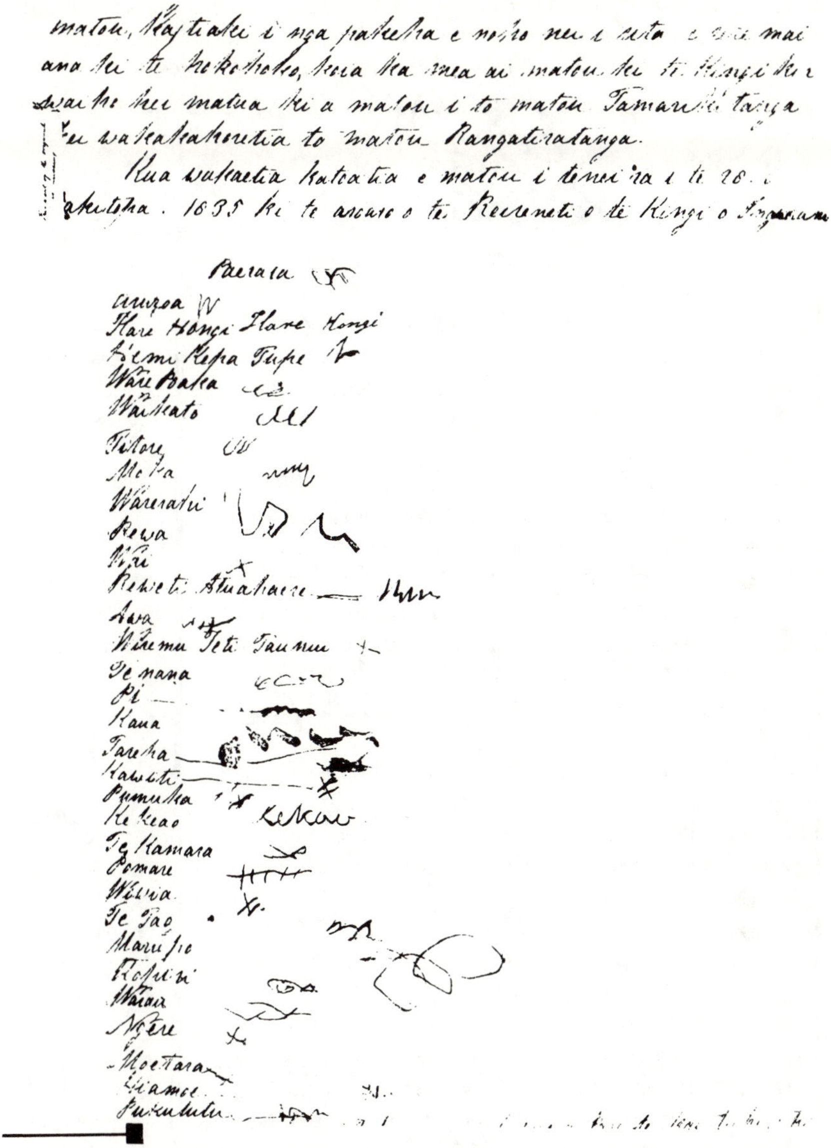

matou, kaitiaki i nga pakeha e noho nei i uta e rere mai ana ki te hokohoko, koia ka mea ai matou ki te Kingi kia waiho hei matua ki a matou i to matou Tamarikitanga kei wakakahoretia to matou Rangatiratanga.

Kua wakaaetia katoatia e matou i tenei ra i te 28 o Oketopa 1835 ki te aroaro o te Reireneti o te Kingi o Ingarani

Hare Hongi
Waikato
Titore
Moka
Warerahi
Rewa
Reweti Atuahaere
Wiremu Tete Taunui
Pi
Kauwiti
Pumuka
Kekeao
Te Kamara
Pomare
Te Tao
Marupo
Moetara

Plate 3 From the verso of the Declaration of Independence subscribed by thirty-four hereditary chiefs or heads of tribes at a meeting convened at Waitangi on 28 October 1835.

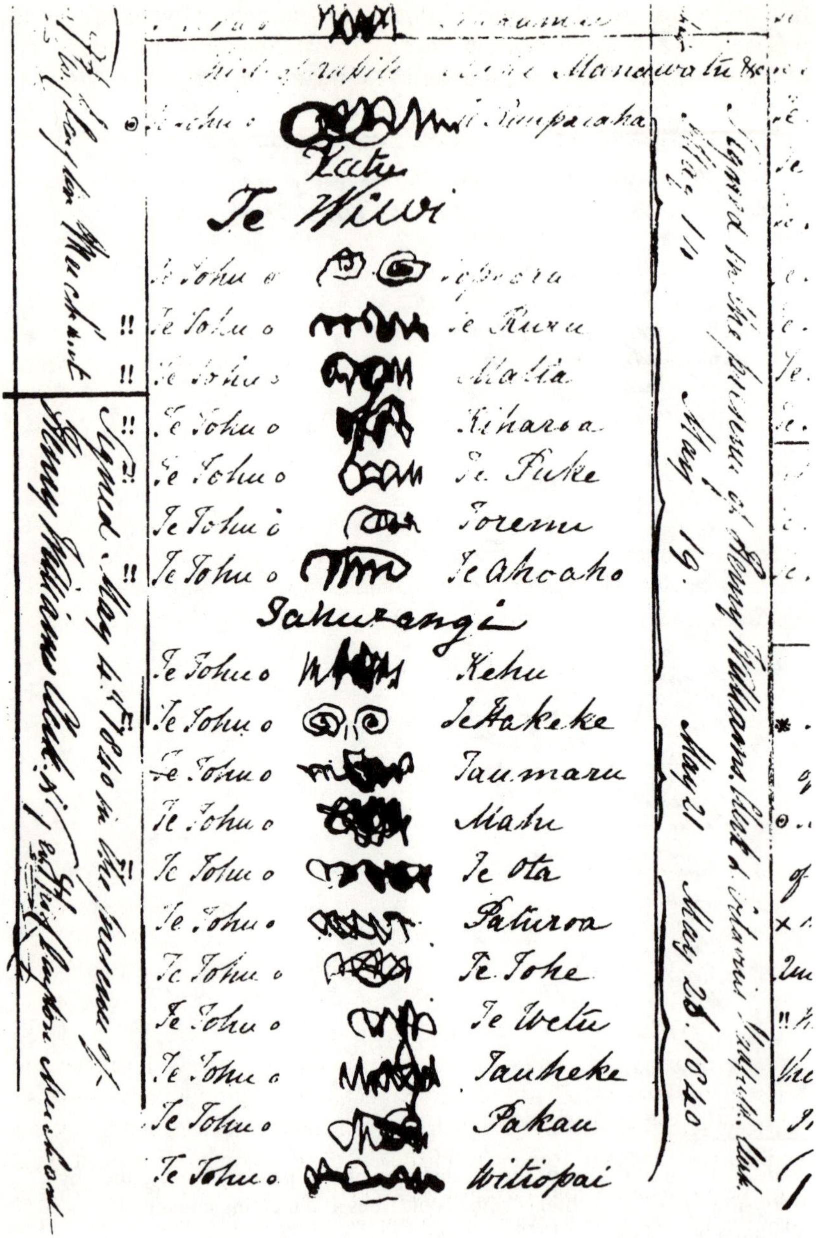

Plate 4　From a sheet supplementary to the Treaty of Waitangi listing those chiefs of the Otaki, Kapiti and Manawatu districts who assented to its terms.

fact the word used by Henry Williams to translate 'Sovereignty' was precisely that: *kawanatanga*, not even a translation but a transliteration of 'Governor' (*kawana*) with a suffix to make it abstract. Such was his translation for the order of morning service: 'that all our doings may be ordered by thy governance'. What he significantly omitted in translating 'Sovereignty' (which the Maori were being asked to surrender) was the genuine Maori word *mana*, meaning personal prestige and the power that flowed from it, or even the word *rangatiratanga*, meaning chieftainship, the very words used in 1835 to 1839 to affirm Maori sovereignty over New Zealand. He had used both words in translating Corinthians Chapter 15, v. 24 with its references to the 'kingdom of God' and 'all authority and power'. By choosing not to use either *mana* or *rangatiratanga* to indicate what the Maori would exchange for 'all the Rights and Privileges of British subjects', Williams muted the sense, plain in English, of the treaty as a document of political appropriation.[81] The status of their assent is already questionable enough, but (since he could not read) had any Maori heard that he was giving up his *mana* or *rangatiratanga* he could never have agreed to the treaty's terms. Williams's Maori version of Hobson's composite English one set the trap which King Lear fell into when (in a version published in 1608) he said to Albany and Cornwall:

> I doe inuest you iontly in my powre,
> Preheminence, and all the large effects
> That troope with Maiestie . . .
>   onely we still retaine
> The name and all the addicions to a King

where 'addicions' implies *mana*, the attributes of ultimate personal prestige and sovereignty as distinct from merely delegated authority.

Other textual problems are created by the versions. In the second article the word *rangatiratanga* does appear in a context which (in Maori) seeks to assure the chiefs of the *rangatiratanga* or 'full possession of their lands, their homes and all their possessions'. Four of the five English versions, however, spell out that provision to read 'full, exclusive and undisturbed possession of their Lands and Estates, Forests, Fisheries and other properties which they may collectively or individually possess'. Although technically the English version has no textual authority, its explicit references to forests and fisheries have become a matter of great import, and Maori today have found good reason to plead the intention of the English versions against the sparer wording of the Maori one.[82] On the other hand, the Maori word for what is guaranteed by the Crown (*taonga*, or precious possessions) is almost infinitely extendable and may include any or every element of Maori culture, including the language itself. Even more significantly, indeed tragically, the English versions of the second article also require the chiefs to 'yield to Her Majesty the exclusive right of Pre-emption over such lands as the proprietors thereof may be disposed to alienate, at such prices as may be agreed upon'. Williams's Maori version omitted to spell out and thereby legitimate under the treaty the Crown's *pre-emptive* right to purchase Maori land. As a consequence, the English versions have been taken to bestow legality on the actions of successive Governments, while the Maori version seems morally to justify the deep sense of grievance still widely suffered over Maori land issues.[83] Once more, Colenso, writing to the Church Missionary Society, did not 'for a moment' suppose that the chiefs were aware that 'by signing the Treaty they had restrained themselves from selling their land to whomsoever they will', and cited one Maori who, although he had signed the treaty, had since offered land for sale privately. On being told that he could not do that, he replied: 'What? Do you think I won't do what I like with my own?'[84]

From a European point of view, one conditioned to accept and apply document-based historical evidence as 'literally' true or false, the English versions of the treaty have proved a potent political weapon in legitimating government of the Maori, even though standards of textual and historical truth also derived from European traditions oblige us to acknowledge the Maori version as the only authoritative document, that which states the terms and bears the written marks of assent. From a Maori point of view, the truth is not so confined, and signatures bear no absolute authority. For the Maori, as I have already indicated, the 'text' was the consensus arrived at through discussion, something much more comprehensive and open than the base document or any one of its extant versions. Williams later defended himself, saying that he had explained the text *orally*; but only the documents survive, and successive Governments have chosen the English ones to act on when these best served their ends. At a later treaty meeting, Mohi Tawhai said that 'the sayings of the Pakeha float light, like the wood of the *whau* tree, and always remain to be seen, but the sayings of the Maori sink to the bottom like stone'.[85] Manuscript and print, the tools of the Pakeha, persist, but words which are spoken fade as they fall.

Print is still too recent for the Maori. Oral traditions live on in a distrust of the literal document, and in a refusal by many young Maori to accept political decisions based on it. Pakeha and Maori versions of the past continue to collide. During a Russian scare in the 1880s the Government of the day pre-empted the purchase of Maori land at Bastion Point, a fine site overlooking Auckland harbour. When a more recent Government proposed to resell it for luxury housing, it was occupied for several months by Maori protesters. In my mind's eye, I can still read the vivid television news pictures of police and military vehicles as they moved in on 25 May 1978 to evict the squatters. At such moments literacy defines itself for many as a concordat of sword and pen, of politics and script – to the dismay and frustration of those whose modes are oral. Pakeha continue to assume 'sovereignty' where radical Maori persist in believing that nothing so sacred as *mana* has ever been ceded under the treaty, that Maori sovereignty was, and is, intact.[86]

In the reports Colenso has left us, he shows his perception of the complex relationships of oral witness, text, print and political and economic power. For us, the texts in context quickly deconstruct and lose their 'literal' authority – no book was ever bound by its covers. The book, in all its forms, enters history only as an evidence of human behaviour, and it remains-active only in the service of human needs.

But must the story end there, in a conflict of irreconcilable versions? In terms of a sociology of the text, it is impossible to regard the Maori version as complete, although it carries the highest authority, nor the English ones as authoritative, although they are far more explicit. Like many dramatic texts, each has been born, here maimed and deformed, of the pressures of context. In the rarefied world of textual scholarship, it would be commendably scholarly to deny any possibility of conflation, any notion that 'the text' of the Treaty of Waitangi is anything other than its distinct historical versions. To conflate the versions would be to create a text that never was. The distinguished textual scholar Sir Walter Greg had little patience with such timidity: many editors, he wrote, 'produce, not editions of their author's works at all, but only editions of particular authorities for those works'.[87] The principle of reconstructing an ideal text from all the versions is vitally operative in legal opinion on the interpretation of treaties as documents which must be interpreted in the spirit in which they are drawn. In New Zealand, under the Treaty of Waitangi Act, an advisory tribunal was set up and directed by Government 'to determine the meaning and effect of the Treaty as embodied in the two [*sic*] texts' and 'to decide issues raised by differences between them'. It was essentially an editorial direction which recognised the social inutility of a clutter of versions as distinct from the social value of a harmonised text.

The Waitangi Tribunal, however, affirmed an even higher principle: 'A Maori approach to the Treaty would imply that its *wairua* or spirit is something more than a literal construction of the actual words used can provide. The spirit of the Treaty transcends the sum total of its component written words and puts narrow or literal interpretations out of place.'[88] That spirit is only recoverable if texts are regarded not simply as verbal constructs but as social products. Crucial to that development is Pakeha recognition of their own myth of literacy and recognition of the status of oral culture and spoken consensus. For many Maori, the spirit of the treaty is best served by the Maori text, in which *kawanatanga* means what it says (governorship, not sovereignty), in which the *taonga* guaranteed by the Crown include all that is materially and spiritually precious, in which Maori and Pakeha share the Queen's protection as equal partners. So understood, the treaty in Maori is a sacred covenant, one which is *tapu*, and with a *mana* which places it above the law, whereas the English version distorts its effect and remains caught in the mesh of documentary history and juridical process. As the Maori always knew, there is a real world beyond the niceties of the literal text and in that world there is *in fact* a providential version now editing itself into the status of a social and political document of power and purpose. The physical versions and their fortuitous forms are not the only testimonies to intent: implicit in the accidents of history is an ideal text which history has begun to discover, a reconciliation of readings which is also a meeting of minds. The concept of an ideal text as a cultural and political imperative is not imposed on history but derives from it and from an understanding of the social dynamics of textual criticism.

Colenso died in 1899 at the ripe old age of eighty-eight, thirty-six hours after penning his last letter to Coupland Harding, and left to Harding £200 for his son, William Colenso Harding, and all his printing materials, including 'my sole composing-stick – with which I did so much work both in England and in New Zealand'. Harding was a worthy recipient and was later to note: 'It was in this stick that the Maori New Testament of 1837 was set, and also the Treaty of Waitangi – Truly, a venerable relic.'[89]

NOTES

[1] This chapter is based on an address delivered to The Bibliographical Society, London, on 15 February 1983, and subsequently published in *The Library*, 6th ser., 6 (1984), 333–65.
[2] I have consulted the treaty documents as reproduced in *Facsimiles of the Declaration of Independence and the Treaty of Waitangi*, ed. H. H. Turton (Wellington, 1877; reprinted 1960).
[3] I am most grateful to Paul McHugh for his legally informed endorsement of my claim that Maori assent to the treaty became the substantive ground of British sovereignty over New Zealand. There is, however, a body of opinion which regards the treaty as having had no effect and British sovereignty as arising rather from the occupation and settlements of lands inhabited by uncivilised native peoples.
[4] The phrases 'European myth of . . . literacy and print as agents of change' and 'from memory to written record' allude to Harvey Graff's *The Literary Myth: Literacy and Social Structure in the Nineteenth-Century City* (New York, 1979), to Elizabeth L. Eisenstein's *The Printing Press as an Agent of Change: Communications and Cultural Transformations in Early Modern Europe*, 2 vols. (Cambridge, 1979), and to M. T. Clanchy's *From Memory to Written Record: England 1066–1307* (London, 1979).
[5] William Colenso, *Fifty years ago in New Zealand. A Commemoration; a Jubilee Paper; a Retrospect: a Plain and True Story* (Napier, 1888), p. 27. Edward Markham, writing in 1834, took a different view, criticising what he saw as an over-simplified orthography because it obscured regional and dialect differences, 'Thus making the Language poorer instead of enriching it': *New Zealand or Reminiscences of it*, ed. E. H. McCormick (Wellington, 1963), p. 62. The circumstances surrounding the reduction of spoken

languages to their first alphabetic or syllabic forms seem to have received little attention. Judith Binney, *The Legacy of Guilt* (Auckland, 1968), pp. 177–85, discusses Kendall's work in the Maori language; see also Johannes Andersen, 'The Maori Alphabet', in *A History of Printing in New Zealand 1830–1940*, ed. R. A. McKay (Wellington, 1940), pp. 57–74. Joyce Banks, of the National Library of Canada, is currently working on the Cree syllabary (which is still in use). Tamsin Donaldson, 'Hearing the First Australians', in *Seeing the First Australians*, ed. Ian Donaldson and Tamsin Donaldson (Sydney, 1984), looks at the motives underlying nineteenth-century attempts at writing down two Australian languages, Ngiyampaa and Wiradjuri, and at the effects of European assumptions on the forms these writings took.

6   The length of vowels is an important discriminator of meanings in Maori: kākā is a parrot; kăkă a garment, fibre or stalk; kăkā is red-hot; kākā a bittern or, as adjective, poisoned-by-the-tutu. Practice in indicating long vowels still varies.

7   *Fifty years ago*, pp. 24–7, 47–9.

8   See David Kopf, *British Orientalism and the Bengal Renaissance: The Dynamics of Indian Modernization 1773–1833* (Berkeley and Los Angeles, 1969). A distinction must be drawn, of course, between reviving in print an already literate culture, as in Bengal, and capturing the current forms of an oral culture in all its diversity and levels of textual authority: see Bruce Biggs, 'The Translation and Publishing of Maori Material in the Auckland Public Library', *Journal of the Polynesian Society* 61 (1952), 177–91.

9   Letter of 1 October 1833, *Missionary Register* (November 1834), p. 513. William Brown, *New Zealand and its Aborigines* (London, 1845), p. 101, had been told 'the natives would only learn every species of vice through the medium of the English language'.

10 Letter of 6 June 1842, cited by C. J. Parr, 'A Missionary Library, Printed Attempts to instruct the Maori, 1815–1845', *Journal of the Polynesian Society* 70 (1961), 429–50, p. 445.

11 Woon to the Wesleyan Mission Society, 24 November 1838: 'The press will be a mighty engine in exposing the errors of [the Papists'] system', *Wesleyan Mission Notices*, new series, 9 (1839), p. 142. Henry Williams, 2 December 1840: '[we need] a vigorous effort at this time to meet the present demand for books before the Papists come forward with their trash', cited by Parr, 'A Missionary Library', p. 447. The Roman Catholic mission arrived in 1838, its main press (a Gaveau) on 15 June 1841.

12 G. Clarke, *Missionary Register* (December 1829), p. 372.

13 William Jacob, 13 March 1833, *Missionary Register* (January 1834), p. 60.

14 *Ibid.*, p. 61.

15 *Missionary Register* (February 1834), p. 119.

16 G. Clarke, 4 June 1833, *Missionary Register* (December 1833), p. 550.

17 William Puckey, 6 January 1835, *Missionary Register* (July 1836), p. 155.

18 G. Clarke, 12 February 1833, *Missionary Register* (October 1833), p. 468.

19 The most useful accounts of literacy among Maori in the early period are C. J. Parr, 'A Missionary Library', *loc. cit.*, and 'Maori Literacy 1843–1867', *Journal of the Polynesian Society* 72 (1963), 211–34; and Michael D. Jackson, 'Literacy, Communications and Social Change', in *Conflict and Compromise: Essays on the Maori since Colonization*, ed. I. H. Kawharu (Wellington, 1975), pp. 27–54. Related studies are G. S. Parsonson, 'The Literate Revolution in Polynesia', *Journal of Pacific History* 11 (1967), 39–57, and Gérald Duverdier, 'La pénétration du livre dans une société de culture orale: le cas de Tahiti', *Revue Française d'Histoire du Livre*, n.s., 1 (1972), 27–51. Parr's thoroughness in noting so many primary references to Maori reading and writing in the 1830s and 1840s has greatly eased my own search, and I have found Jackson's admirable discussion most pertinent to my own because it is specifically concerned to examine Maori social change from the useful vantage point of literacy (p. 28). Michael Jackson also directed me to Manfred Stanley's 'Technicism, Liberalism, and Development: A Study in Irony as Social Theory', in *Social Development: Critical Perspectives* (New York, 1972), 274–325, a suggestive discussion of the philosophical implications of technology for social structure and (if proleptically and only implicitly) *histoire du livre*.

Nevertheless, I argue that early missionaries and recent historians have alike misread the evidence for Maori literacy. If it ceases to be true of the 1840s, the conventional view of the rapid attainment of literacy by the Maori in the 1830s must be wrong: a literacy with any potency for social change is not skin-deep. Having accepted the missionaries' euphoric accounts of the 1830s, Parr asks of the 1840s: 'What happened? Where were the self-appointed teachers, the hundred mile journeys to obtain books and instruction, the eager learners of letters, the crowded day schools of only a dozen years before?' (Maori Literacy', p. 221). Although few Maori are today, in the simplest functional sense, illiterate, the written and printed word is not the mode which they habitually use. The question is therefore an even more fundamental one than whether or not the Maori failed to become fully literate in the 1830s, or why the missionaries failed to teach them full literacy. It is, rather, why has the Maori 'failed' to become literate at all? Or, to shift the burden of guilt, what is it about literacy and books that makes these technologies so inadequate to cope with the complex realities of a highly civilised social experience which the Maori know but which the literate mind too readily and reductively perhaps tries to capture in the book?

[20] Marsden, 14 March 1830, *Missionary Register* (January 1831), p. 58.

[21] Marsden, February 1837, *Missionary Register* (April 1838), p. 137.

[22] *The Life of Henry Williams*, ed. H. Carleton (Wellington, 1948), p. 137.

[23] Hadfield, 22 July 1840, cited by Parr, 'A Missionary Library', p. 438.

[24] J. F. B. Pompallier, *Early History of the Catholic Church in Oceana* (Auckland, 1888), p. 47.

[25] (London, 1955), p. 17. Illiteracy was probably high among British working-class settlers. My own paternal grandfather was illiterate, signing both his marriage certificate and his will with a cross; and my paternal grandmother, like many a Maori chief and medieval king, 'wrote' her letters by dictation.

[26] 30 April 1836, *Missionary Register* (July 1839), p. 348.

[27] See Duverdier, 'La Pénétration', 41–42, and William Ellis, *Polynesian Researches, during a Residence of nearly eight years in the Society and Sandwich Islands*, 2 vols. (London, 1829), vol. 1, pp. 492–3, vol. 2, p. 20. Duverdier draws most of his material from Ellis.

[28] 3 January 1832, *Missionary Register* (September 1832), p. 406.

[29] 6 July 1832, *ibid.* (May 1833), p. 243.

[30] C. Baker, 26 December 1831, *ibid.* (September 1832), p. 407.

[31] Fairburn, 30 April 1838, *ibid.* (July 1839), p. 348.

[32] Henry Williams, 29 August 1834, *ibid.* (November 1835), p. 258.

[33] In McKay, *A History of Printing in New Zealand*, pp. 48–9.

[34] This point is well made by Clanchy, in *From Memory to Written Record*.

[35] Among those who currently affirm Maori rights and protect Maori *mana*, those more conciliatory towards European attitudes stress the complimentary ease and speed with which Maori are said to have become literate, those less conciliatory and more radical the supreme importance of the oral tradition and virtual irrelevance of the European 'book'. In practice, the oral mode rules. By compelling those who speak eloquently to substitute a mode in which they are less fluent, literacy can function insidiously as a culturally *regressive* force. Such at least is how many Maori experience it.
   As Jane McRae reminds me, there are few Maori writers and very few who write in Maori, but the tradition of oral composition and exposition continues; it is the only tradition with 'literary' structures or styles, and the 'sound' text is usually all there is to be read. Even within University Departments of Maori Studies, the book is suspect. Manuscripts and printed texts in libraries, publications by Europeans on Maoridom, are seldom consulted; oral etiquette, debate and transfer of knowledge on the *marae* or meeting ground are what matter. Such conditions encourage the spontaneous, orally improvised, dramatic recreation of shared stories or themes and an *evolutionary* concept of texts; the fixed text, catching in print an arbitrary moment in the continuum of social exchange, demands a different sense of history and its own literal re-play. See Michael King, 'Some Maori Attitudes to Documents', *Tihi Mauri Ora: Aspects of Maoritanga*, ed. Michael King (Auckland, 1978), pp. 9–18.

[36] Jackson, 'Literacy, Communications, and Social Change', p. 38; see also A. Buzacott, *Mission Life in the Islands of the Pacific* (London, 1866), pp. 66–7.

[37] *Missionary Register* (September 1834), pp. 418–19.

[38] *Ibid.* (April 1832), p. 192.

[39] *Ibid.*, Letter 6.

[40] *Ibid.*, Letter 7.

[41] *Ibid.* (October 1834), p. 460. See also *Letters to the Rev. William Yate from Natives of New Zealand converted to Christianity* (London, 1836).

[42] See W. J. Cameron, 'A Printing Press for the Maori People', *Journal of the Polynesian Society* 67 (1958), 204–10; and Johannes Andersen, 'Maori Printers and Translators', in McKay, *A History of Printing in New Zealand*, pp. 33–47. An official Government newspaper, *Te Karere o Nui Tireni*, later *Te Karere Maori*, had been printed in Maori from 1842 to 1846 and doubtless established an early role for this medium.

[43] Cited by Parr, 'A Missionary Library', p. 432.

[44] *Ibid.*

[45] July and September 1830, *Missionary Register* (January 1831), p. 67.

[46] *Ibid.*

[47] 28 April 1831, *ibid.* (March 1832), p. 150.

[48] 6 July 1832, Letters of Henry Williams, vol. 2 (1830–8), typescript in the Auckland Institute and Museum.

[49] *An Account of New Zealand* (London, 1835), p. 232.

[50] *Life of Henry Williams*, p. 185.

[51] Letter to Dandeson Coates, 9 January 1836.

[52] A.. Bagnall and G. S. Petersen, *William Colenso; Printer, Missionary, Botanist, Explorer, Politician; his Life and Journeys* (Wellington, 1948), is the standard life. Colenso's journals and his correspondence with the Church Missionary Society are in the Hocken Library, Dunedin; his day- and waste-books, paper-book and printing-house ledger are in the Alexander Turnbull Library, Wellington; his correspondence with Coupland Harding is in the Mitchell Library, Sydney; his personal memorandum book, kept while he worked for Watts and travelled to New Zealand, and his will are in the Hawkes Bay Museum and Art Gallery. An edition of his printing-house records and a thorough study of his work as a printer remain to be done. R. Coupland Harding has written three brief accounts: 'New Zealand's First Printer', *The Inland Printer* 7 (1889–90), 504–6; 'Relics of the first New Zealand Press', *Transactions and Proceedings of the New Zealand Institute* 32 (1900), 400–4; 'William Colenso: some Personal Reminiscences', *The Press* (Christchurch), 27 February 1899. Harding also printed several of Colenso's papers, including *Fifty years ago in New Zealand*. See also H. Hill, 'The Early Days of Printing in New Zealand: a Chapter of Interesting History', *Transactions and Proceedings of the New Zealand Institute* 33 (1901), 407–26; and Johannes Andersen, 'Early Printing in New Zealand', in McKay, *A History of Printing in New Zealand*, pp. 1–31. The fate of Colenso's Stanhope press is unknown; his Columbian is probably that now in the Dominion Museum, Wellington; his table model foolscap Albion (Hopkinson and Cope No. 1964, dated 1845) is in the Hawkes Bay Museum and Art Gallery.

[53] Colenso's memorandum book for this time details his wages and the way in which they were made up for composing, correction, altering heads, share of 'fat', or reduced by candle fine and error in casting (the last cost him 16*s*. 4*d*.), along with other sharply observed features of an early nineteenth-century printing house.

[54] Colenso Papers, Hocken Library.

[55] *Fifty years ago*, p. 6. Writing to Coupland Harding on 31 December 1890, Colenso recalled Williams's first encounter with practical printing: 'Mr. W., evidently, had never seen Type-setting before: he was often in the Pg. Office, & well do I remember his Exclamation of pleasing surprize on seeing a line spaced out in cpg. stick – "he had often wondered how it was done to have all the lines of equal length".'

[56] *Fifty years ago*, p. 7.

[57] *Ibid.*, p. 9.

[58] 16 March 1835, Colenso Papers, Hocken Library; also *Missionary Register* (July 1836), p. 164.

[59] *Fifty years ago*, p. 19.

[60] 17 December 1838, reprinted in *Fifty years ago*, pp. 21–2.

[61] For Yate, see Eric Ramsden, *Marsden and the Missions* (Sydney, 1936), p. 28; for Markham, *New Zealand or Recollections of it*, p. 55. Sensing that the figure he had heard might be optimistic, Markham qualified it in a note: 'For fear of exageration [*sic*] say 8000.'

[62] Harrison M. Wright, *New Zealand, 1769–1840: Early Years of Western Contact* (Cambridge, Mass., 1959), p. 53. Wright's figures are calculated from the tables (titles, formats, edition quantities) supplied by Colenso in *The Missionary Register* (1840), p. 512, and (1841), p. 519. To keep the comparative base I have used the same source, but a more exact calculation would have to include a few jobbing items excluded from Colenso's reports but included in his ledger.

[63] Richard Davis, 10 November 1832, cited by Wright, p. 176.

[64] G. Clarke, *Early Life in New Zealand* (Hobart, 1903), p. 31.

[65] Whiteley, 22 December 1836, cited by Parr, 'A Missionary Library', p. 445.

[66] 28 April 1839, *ibid*.

[67] *Life of Henry Williams*, p. 60.

[68] *Fifty years ago*, p. 42.

[69] *New Zealand or Recollections of it*, p. 32.

[70] 15 June 1843, cited by Parr, 'Maori Literacy', p. 212.

[71] Thomas Chapman, 28 March 1846, *ibid*., p. 213.

[72] Cited by Parr, 'A Missionary Library', p. 446.

[73] As Stanley writes, 'Physical machinery [sc. books?] cannot "make" men do anything. People act or fail to act on the basis of their interpretations of the world around them, interpretations embodied in language, institutions, and social organization. The physical world created by human innovative effort reflects – in the forms of material objects – human assumptions, values, desires, and aspirations' ('Technicism, Liberalism, and Development', p. 279). The first part is true of Maori resistance to literacy, the second of the missionaries in the value they imparted and imputed to the book. Paradoxically the Maori is very sensitive to (because suspicious of) the very form of a book, and gives an expressive intention to features which a European takes for granted as mere 'accidentals' and has virtually ceased to see. For example, in a review of Michael King's *Maori – a Photographic and Social History* (Auckland, 1983), Keri Kaa questions the very depiction of corpses: 'The pictures of the tupapaku (corpses) I found most disturbing . . . My initial reaction was to ask: Whose Nanny is that? Whose Mother is that? Do their mokopuna [children] mind about their taonga [precious heirlooms] being displayed for all the world to see?' And again, 'There is a strange combination of pictures on page 35. At the top of the page is a picture of a tangi [funeral], underneath it one of a woman cooking. Anyone who understands the concepts of tapu and noa [lifting of tapu] would appreciate that the two should never be mixed by being placed together *on a page*' (my italics). *The New Zealand Listener*, 24 September 1983, p. 99.

[74] Brown, *New Zealand and its Aborigines*, p. 99. Augustus Earle, *Narrative of a Residence in New Zealand*, ed. E. H. McCormick (Oxford, 1966), pp. 133–4, wrote: 'I cannot forbear censuring the missionaries, inasmuch as they prevent the natives, by every means in their power, from acquiring the English language.' See also J. S. Polack, *Manners and Customs of the New Zealanders*, 2 vols. (London, 1840), vol. 2, p. 147: '[The Maori] take much delight in speaking the English language, and had the Missionaries chosen to have taught the children this tongue, what an immense store of able works could at once have been put into the hands of the native youth, instead of a few imperfect translations on one subject, that may teach mechanical devotion, but can never mentally illuminate the native mind.'

[75] 'On Nomenclature', in *Three Literary Papers* (Napier, 1883), p. 9. In this paper Colenso also discusses the orthography of place names on maps and in school geographies, raising many of the issues recently dramatised by Brian Friel in his play *Translations* (1981). See also H. W. Williams, 'Reaction of the Maori to the Impact of Civilization', *Journal of the Polynesian Society* 44 (1935), 216–43, esp. pp. 234–5.

[76] Some drafts survive: one by Hobson of the preamble; one in the hand of Freeman, Hobson's secretary, of the three articles and another version of the preamble; a fair

copy of a draft by James Busby. But they do not themselves constitute the English text given to Williams to translate. Although Colenso provides an unrivalled account of the treaty occasion, by far the most perceptive analysis of the texts and their implications is that of R. M. Ross, 'Te Tiriti o Waitangi: Texts and Translations', *New Zealand Journal of History* 6 (1972), 129–67. The account I give of the relationship of the texts is based wholly on Ross.

[77] To add insult to injury, the Maori text printed as the first schedule to the Act contains, in the second article, numerous misprints.

[78] It is also the most reductive form of 'literacy' test. See David Cressy, *Literacy and the Social Order: Reading and Writing in Tudor England* (Cambridge, 1980), p. 53; and R. S. Schofield, 'The Measurement of Literacy in Pre-Industrial England', in *Literacy in Traditional Societies*, ed. Jack Goody (Cambridge, 1968), p. 319. Although signatures are the only absolute test of minimal literacy, many who signed with a mark may have been able to read but not write: see below, note 79.

[79] See Fig. 4 for a sample. The treaty is supplemented and ultimately constituted by a collection of sheets subscribed in different parts of the country between 6 February and 3 September 1840. In later times some Maori who could in fact write their own names are said to have used their *moko* to give documents a more sacred sign of approval, but in the 1840 treaty genuine *moko* appear to be rare. The seventy-two signatures suggest a maximum literacy level of about 12% or 13%, or, to use the international convention of stating illiteracy levels, an illiteracy level of between 87% and 88%. Margaret Spufford, *Small Books and Pleasant Histories* (London, 1981), p. 21, offers a convenient comparison. In East Anglia in the seventeenth century '11 per cent of women, 15 per cent of labourers, and 21 per cent of husbandmen could sign their own names, against 56 per cent of tradesmen and craftsmen, and 65 per cent of yeomen'. In a survey taken in the larger Wellington area in 1848, the European population was given as 4,824. Of those, 2,530 or some 52% (1,583 male, 947 female) were said to be able to read and write, and 924 (470 male, 454 female) to be able to read only. A general summary of the Maori population taken in the Wellington area in 1850 records (under 'Moral Condition') a total of 4,711, of whom 1,148 or some 24% were said to be able to read and write, and 414 to be able to read only. See *Statistics of New Munster, New Zealand, from 1841 to 1848* (Wellington, 1849), Table 30; and *New Zealand: Further Papers Relative to the Affairs of New Zealand. Papers by Command [1420]* (London, 1851), p. 245.

[80] Graphic as it is, Colenso's account of the Maori speeches understandably does scant justice to the originals. As he wrote much later, 'Some of the New Zealanders were truly natural orators, and consequently possessed in their large assemblies great power and influence. This was mainly owing to their tenacious memories, to their proper selection from their copious and expressive language; skilfully choosing the very word, sentence, theme, or natural image best fitted to make an impression on the lively impulsive minds of their countrymen . . . the orator's knowledge of their traditions and myths, songs, proverbs and fables was ever to him an inexhaustible mine of wealth . . . All the people well knew the power of persuasion – particularly of that done in the open air – before the multitude' (*The New Zealand Exhibition* (Wellington, 1865); section on 'Ethnology: On the Maori Races of New Zealand', pp. 70–1). What Hobson was up against may be judged from his letter of 17 February 1840, reporting the Hokianga meeting at which he had sought further subscriptions to the treaty: 'The New Zealanders are passionately fond of declamation, and they possess considerable ingenuity in exciting the passions of the people. On this occasion all their best orators were against me, and every argument they could devise was used to defeat my object' (Facsimiles, p. [x]). Maori orators, it should be noted, often enjoyed playing devil's advocate. Colenso vividly recounts the anger of Te Kemara ('eyes rolling . . . extravagant gestures and grimace'), but adds: 'And yet it was all mere show – not really intended; as was not long after fully shown, when they gave their evidence as to the fair sale, &c., of their lands before the Land Commissioners, I myself acting as interpreter.'

All quotations here and below relating to the discussion and signing of the treaty on 5 and 6 February are taken from Colenso's own eye- and ear-witness report, *The Authen-*

tic and Genuine History of the Signing of the Treaty of Waitangi (Wellington, 1890), principally pp. 32–3. Written immediately after the events described, it was read and its accuracy confirmed by James Busby, who was also present.

[81] I do not impute to Williams any intention to deceive the Maori by his choice of terms. Attempts to establish a legal basis for the control of British subjects in New Zealand by extra-territorial jurisdiction had proved unsuccessful. Furthermore, unless Britain formally secured sovereignty, neither Britain nor the Maori could establish an exclusive claim to the islands as against claims that might be made by other European powers. (The Declaration of Independence of 1835 was a device to establish the chiefs' collective territorial rights and forestall an imminent French claim.) In furthering both concerns, however dubious the exact legal status of the treaty, the British Government was anxious to secure Maori assent and genuinely hopeful that British sovereignty would not disrupt Maori life. Nevertheless, cultural and linguistic suppositions on both sides, compounded by European assumptions about literacy and the status of documents, frustrated that hope, and later (if then still unforeseen) patterns of immigration destroyed it. Williams certainly shows himself, at that critical time, to have been less sensitive than Colenso to Maori modes of understanding.

A succinct and balanced account of many of the issues pertinent to the treaty and British annexation of New Zealand will be found in Mary Boyd's 'Cardinal Principles of British Policy in New Zealand', in *The Treaty of Waitangi: Its Origins and Significance* (Wellington, 1972), pp. 3–15. W. A. McKean discusses aspects of international law as they affect the status and interpretation of the treaty (*ibid.*, pp. 35–48) but does not substantiate his claim that there is no substance in the argument that the chiefs were misled or failed to understand the purport in English of what they were signing (pp. 45–6, notes 91 and 92). The best account of the evolution of Colonial Office attitudes to British sovereignty and Maori interests is Peter Adams, *Fatal Necessity: British Intervention in New Zealand 1830–1847* (Auckland, 1977). An interesting account of later Maori interpretations of the treaty is Claudia Orange, 'The Covenant of Kohimarama. A Ratification of the Treaty of Waitangi', *The New Zealand Journal of History* 14 (1980), 61–80. The minutes of the Kohimarama Conference of July 1860 reveal confusion or ignorance about the meaning of the treaty. One Ngatiawa chief said, 'It is true I received one blanket. I did not understand what was meant by it; it was given to me without any explanation by Mr Williams and Reihana.' Paora Tuhaere dismissed the treaty as 'Ngapuhi's affair', and the Ngapuhi chiefs there present did reveal greater understanding and acceptance of it as a covenant unifying Pakeha and Maori. Tuhaere also remarked: 'The treaty is right, but it came in the time of ignorance and was not understood,' adding that those Maori who signed but were not present at Waitangi had least understanding of it. The Conference skirted the delicate issue of sovereignty to stress rather the Queen's role as protector, allowing the Maori to believe that they retained sovereignty or *mana* over the land and political equality with the Governor under the Queen's protection and hence direct access to her.

[82] Fishing rights have again become a matter of contention in this century, most recently in 1983 when the then Government proposed to direct into the sea effluent from a synthetic petrol plant at Motunui. The subsequent *Report, findings and recommendations of the Waitangi Tribunal on an application . . . on behalf of the Te Atiawa Tribe in relation to fishing grounds in the Waitara district* (Wellington, 1983) includes a valuable résumé of many textual issues raised by the present paper.

[83] Sir Apirana Ngata's literal translation from the Maori of the second article reads: 'The Queen of England confirms and guarantees to the Chiefs and Tribes and to all the people of New Zealand the full possession of their lands, their homes and all their possessions, but the chiefs assembled and all other chiefs yield to the Queen the right to alienate such lands which the owners desire to dispose of at a price agreed upon between the owners and person or persons appointed by the Queen to purchase on her behalf' (*The Treaty of Waitangi: An Explanation* (Christchurch, 1950), p. 7).

[84] Letter begun 24 January 1840, cited by Bagnall and Petersen, *William Colenso*, pp. 93–4. Again I acknowledge the kind help of Paul McHugh. The Crown's pre-emptive right to extinguish the native title had been long practised in colonising overseas territories,

and was most vigorously affirmed in the Royal Proclamation of 1763 which was seen as protecting North American Indian lands from unscrupulous appropriation. The English land law assumption that all rights to land derive from a grant by the Crown clearly did not apply to new territories, where the aboriginal title rested at law, not upon a grant from the Crown, but (exceptionally) upon the Crown's recognition of aboriginal rights. To the British mind, however, it was unthinkable that aboriginal and heathen notions of title should control the form of land transfers to British settlers, and so the pre-emptive right was adopted as a way of converting Crown-recognised title into Crown-derived title. From the British point of view, it was undoubtedly seen as preventing the chaos which must have followed from the operation of a mixed system, and at the same time (if fairly administered) as protecting the Maori from land-jobbers. One has to concede that neither Hobson nor Williams could have communicated the full import of 'pre-emptive' to those who were asked to assent to the treaty, but by so simplifying the issue in his translation of the second article into Maori, Williams again showed less readiness than did Colenso to penetrate 'the Native mind' and 'explain the thing in all its bearings . . . so that it should be their very own act and deed'. One might be accused of arguing from hindsight were it not for Colenso's contemporary insight.

85 Cited by Ross, *op. cit.*, p. 152, from British Parliamentary Papers, 1845, xxxiii, 108, p. 10. Despite the transience of the spoken word, there is a wealth of Maori speech in manuscripts still to be studied. Some are *tapu* and cannot be consulted, but the written transcripts of evidence delivered in Maori land courts are a rich source of information about language and forms of oral witness to land rights as declaimed in court. Elsdon Best records that when he was secretary to the Land Commission, an old man recited 406 songs for him from memory, a genealogy which took three days to recite and included over 1,400 persons in proper sequence, and much other evidence on the occupation of certain lands: *The Maori School of Learning: Its Objects, Methods and Ceremonies* (Wellington, 1923), p. 5. See also Jane McRae, 'Maori Manuscripts in Public Collections', *New Zealand Libraries* 44 (1983), 8–11.

86 See, for example, Donna Awatere, *Maori Sovereignty* (Auckland, 1984), and Bruce Jesson, 'Reviewing the Sovereignty Debate', *The Republican* 48 (1983), 3–17, 19–20.

87 'The Rationale of Copy-Text', in *Collected Papers*, ed. J. C. Maxwell (Oxford, 1966), p. 384.

88 *Report*, 52–63; the immediate quotation is on p. 55. *A Bill of Rights for New Zealand. A White Paper* (Wellington, 1985), p. 37, proposes 'that the Treaty of Waitangi is to be regarded as always speaking and shall be applied to circumstances as they arise so that effect may be given to its spirit and true intent'. Nevertheless, Pakeha intentions to give legal effect to the treaty in a Bill of Rights, however strongly entrenched, would destroy its *tapu* state and make it vulnerable to legislative change: its *mana* would then be lost. As indicated in note 35 above, an oral culture will generate, not a fixed text, but a variety of versions which have their local and topical value in giving life to the *wairua* of the 'text' which comprehends and transcends them all. Treaties are likely to become a more frequently used resource, not only for ethnohistorical studies, but for concepts of text in complex political, linguistic and cultural contexts, for their mixed modes of oral and written discourse, for their synchronic and diachronic dimensions, for their continuing human implications (they are not exactly dramatic fictions), and for the forcing circumstances which compel the law to offer what are essentially editorial judgments. David R. Miller of the Newberry Library tells me that the microfilming of 9,552 Iroquois treaty documents has been completed. An associated study has just been published: *The History and Culture of Iroquois Diplomacy: an Interdisciplinary Guide to the Treaties of the Six Nations and League* (Syracuse, 1985). The value of treaties as texts for analysis of diplomacy as a matter of cultural as well as political contact is well demonstrated in Dorothy V. Jones's *Licence for Empire: Colonisation by Treaty* (Chicago, 1983). A. S. Keller, O. J. Lissitzyn and F. J. Mann, *Creation of Rights of Sovereignty through Symbolic Acts, 1400–1800* (New York, 1938), remains a convenient historical summary of European attitudes and practice.

89 Letter to G. Robertson, 1 March 1899: Mitchell MS AC 83/4.

9

THE HISTORIAN AND THE *QUESTIONE DELLA LINGUA*

Jonathan Steinberg

In 1861 not more than 2 to 3% of the Italian population would have understood Italian.[1] The overwhelming majority of the population were illiterate and spoke what were various regional languages or dialects, some of them only distantly related in form, grammar, accent and vocabulary to standard Italian. It was not then uncommon nor is it now for standard Italian speakers to be unable to understand certain dialects. The struggle to impose standard Italian on a more or less unwilling population formed a part of the struggle to unify the peninsula after centuries of division. The *questione della lingua* or the 'language question' came to stand as a short-hand for the whole complex of issues about language, politics and power.

Language and nationality seem to us so naturally to go together that it is hard to recall how recently they fused. Frederick the Great spoke French and thought that a perfectly normal thing for a German prince to do. It seems odd to us, for we think of the French as the people who speak French, but even that is not self-evident, as Eugen Weber has shown. In 1863, 8,381 out of 37,510 French communes spoke no French and roughly 10% of all French schoolchildren under the Third Republic between the ages of seven and thirteen came to school speaking only *patois*.[2]

Patois, Mundart, dialetto are some of the terms used to describe the speech of ordinary people. 'Quand il s'agit de la terre,' wrote Emmanuel Labet in 1912, 'on pense en patois.'[3] Peasants spoke *patois* and gave to their tools, their contracts, their weights and measures, customs, practices and feasts a rich local vocabulary, often without equivalent in the high speech, or more accurately, the written speech.

There was, then, an impenetrable 'dark wood of dialect', as Tullio De Mauro has called it, which separated not only higher and lower culture at the time but the linguistic and political realities from those who tried to study them. What, after all, is dialect? The famous American dialectologist Raven I. McDavid, Jr, summed up the difficulties: 'Is dialect a form of speech sharply contrasting with standard language? Is each local dialect assumed to be pure and uniform? Is the standard language itself considered as a dialect? Does the standard language itself have regional varieties? The answer depends on the cultural situation but in part on the investigator.'[4] As the Toronto sociolinguist Gianrenzo Clivio explained, 'from a strictly linguistic point of view . . . a language is a dialect that has an army and a navy and an air force; that is the only difference really from a linguistic point of view'.[5] In other words, the State defines or fails to define the line between language and dialect. To McDavid's personal and cultural criteria, Clivio adds the political and administrative.

Eastern Europe provides fine examples of the interaction of linguistics and politics. In his *Studi di lingvistica generala* published in Bucharest in 1955, Professor A. Graur, a leading Romanian student of linguistics, observed carefully that the study of the dialect spoken in the Moldavian SSR on the other side of the Russo–Romanian frontier had 'not only a theoretical interest but . . . also serious political implications'.[6] Indeed it had, for if Moldavian were not officially a separate language, then it must be a dialect of Romanian; if the Moldavians spoke a regional form of Romanian, then they belonged to the Romanian people and the Russians were occupying territory whose inhabitants belonged to Romania, not Russia. It was not surprising that Professor Graur concluded that 'in the Moldavian Soviet Socialist Republic the official language is a romance idiom called the Moldavian language . . . The language is very close to Romanian so there is no difficulty in mutual understanding. However since there is a different orientation, one must speak of different languages.'[7] The 'different orientation' was Stalinist not linguistic, but the point made by Clivio still holds. A language or a dialect is not a given, not easily distinguished from other languages, from its own variants or from dialects, and it is not enough, as McDavid puts it, 'to go out to some reasonably isolated place and listen to the quaint sayings of the natives'.[8] I have no idea if Moldavian *is* Romanian or not; indeed on a certain level the question may be meaningless. I do know that language questions cannot be answered any more easily than any other historical question and no answer without an economic, social and political dimension can be adequate.

The odd thing about the *questione della lingua* is how rarely historians ask it. As recently as 1968 a leading historian of French education published a study of its evolution from 1800 to his own day without mentioning the existence of *patois*.[9] In effect, he left out the single most obvious fact confronting the typical schoolmaster in the French countryside for most of the period covered – that his pupils spoke either no or very halting French. The myth of the one, indivisible French State obscured the realities from the observers who bothered to look. In other respects those who saw turned away in disgust. To the nineteenth-century French or Italian observer dialect was the language of 'savages'. Peasants were often thought of as ignorant brutes whose tongue was simply bad speech, an attitude not unknown today in inner city schools in the English-speaking world.

The eighteenth century, on the other hand, had a much livelier appreciation of the language question, in this as in other respects closer to us than to the culture of the following period. Some of this preoccupation with language undoubtedly reflected the emergence of secular states after the decline of religious warfare and some of it the Enlightenment's interest in rationality and uniformity. In Germany the philosopher Christian Thomasius tried to lecture in German at Leipzig as early as 1687 but the ensuing row drove him out. The new University of Halle founded in 1694 was the first institution of higher learning in the German lands which permitted instructors to lecture in German, and by 1711 the majority of lectures were 'in der Teutschen Sprache'.[10] Leibniz devoted two works to the improvement of the language, but it was Johann Christoph Gottsched in his *Deutsche Sprachkunst* of 1748 who settled the controversy over which German was the proper model. For Gottsched, 'das mittelländische oder übersächsische', the so-called *Meissnisch* or Saxon variant, was the best high German *Mundart*.[11]

About a generation later, enlightened Italian writers attacked the same problem. Melchiorre Cesarotti saw the establishment of rules for standard language as a means to 'toglier la lingua al despotismo dell'autorità e ai capricci della moda e dell'uso per metterla sotto il governo legittimo della ragione'.[12] Usage and irregularity were for Cesarotti simply not rational; standardisation would eliminate them. The philosopher Antonio Genovesi decided to offer lectures at the University of Naples in Italian for the first time in 1765, nearly eighty years after Thomasius had been so daring at Leipzig. It is far from clear why there should have been such a delay but it may have to do with the dominance of the Roman Catholic Church, the prestige of Latin in its original cultural environment and its linguistic closeness to Italian. Genovesi's reasons for wanting to lecture in Italian reveal a vague national feeling, or, perhaps, more precisely a reaction to the dominance of French culture which also moved German intellectuals at the same time:

> Ho impreso a scrivere in nostra lingua un corso di filosofia, per quei giovanetti che son curiosi di sapere se le scienze potessero così parlare italiano, come una volta parlarono greco e poi latino. Il motivo che mi muove è una massima, che può stare che sia falsa, ma l'ho nondimeno per vera, cioè che ogni nazione, che non ha molti libri di scienze e di arti nella sua lingua, è barbara.[13]
>
> (I have undertaken to write a course of philosophy in our language for those young people who are curious to know if the sciences could speak Italian as they once spoke Greek and then

Latin. The motive which moves me is a maxim, which may turn out to be false, but which nevertheless I hold to be true, that is, that any nation which has not got many works of science and art in its own tongue is barbarous.)

It was in the 1760s and 1770s that the grounds for using the standard language began to shift. In 1765 and 1766 a group of young Milanese intellectuals published a journal entitled *Il Caffè*. *Il Caffè* was an imaginary coffee house whose proprietor and customers engaged in lively conversation on the model of Addison and Steele. In an early issue the proprietor tried to find out the identity of one of his guests. The visitor said that, no, he was not Milanese, nor from any other north Italian city. Finally, exasperated, the proprietor demanded to know who on earth he was, to which the stranger answered, 'Sono italiano' – 'I am Italian', an answer which startled the proprietor and his guests. The national feeling expressed in *Il Caffè* has overtones of early Romanticism as well. Along with the attack on regional identities and narrowness so well expressed in the Italian phrase *campanilismo*, i.e. the world view which extends as far as the sound of bells from the local church tower (*campanile*), the young intellectuals who wrote *Il Caffè*, all then in their mid-twenties, attacked the formalities and rigidity of the conception of language adopted by purists. The Academia della Crusca, a distinguished Florentine academy, attempted to regulate the usage of literary Italian. If Italian were to become again a living vehicle of national sentiment, it would have to break the academic framework. In this spirit Alessandro Verri made his famous 'renunciation before a notary on the part of the authors of this paper of the vocabulary of the Academia della Crusca', which appeared in an early number of *Il Caffè*. As he put it: 'se le cognizioni umane dovessero stare ne' limiti strettissimi che gli assegnano i grammatici, sapremmo bensì che carozza va scritta con due erre ma andremo tutti a piedi'.[14] This plea for natural expression can be found in Goethe's account of his youth in Strassburg towards the end of the same decade. Young men began to wear their hair unpowdered and to feel German, not cosmopolitan. It was in 1770 that Goethe had the '*Offenbarung*' (revelation) which he describes in *Dichtung und Wahrheit*. Sketching the west portal of the Münster in Strassburg, he suddenly saw that the faces carved on the arches were like those of the passers-by on the streets, that the building was not 'gothic', i.e. barbarous, as his French masters had taught him, but a German building, an expression of what he was to call '*Deutsche Baukunst*' (German architecture).[15]

All over Europe in the late 1760s and early 1770s the attack on the formality of high speech spread. Language had to be made more natural, less rational, rigid and dry. In this subtle change of sentiment, no work was more important than a little essay written by Johann Gottfried Herder in 1769. The Prussian Academy of Sciences had advertised a prize essay competition on the question of whether language was divinely or humanly inspired. Herder won the competition, and the little work entitled 'Abhandlung über den Ursprung der Sprache' appeared in Berlin, published by Christian Friedrich Voss, in 1770. Herder answered the question set by the Prussian Academy with a firm no. Language was not divinely inspired nor an expression of the laws of general nature but a social product, mutable and irregular, which reflected the progress of human society from lower to higher forms of awareness. Language grew, Herder argued, by the complexity and change of social relations. He saw too the reciprocal quality of all language: 'das erste Merkmal, das ich erfasse, ist Merkwort für mich und Mitteilungswort für andere' (the first sign which I grasp is a symbol for me but a means of communication for the other person). Grammar was not immutable but subject to social change and evolution: 'Deklinationen und Konjugationen sind nichts anders als Verkürzungen und Bestimmungen des Gebrauchs der Nominum und Verborum nach Zahl, Zeit und Art der Person. Je roher also eine Sprache desto unregelmässiger ist sie in diesen Bestimmungen und zeigt bei jedem Schritt den Gang der menschlichen Vernunft' (Declensions and conjugations are nothing more than abbreviations and determinations of the use of nouns and verbs by number, tense and type of person. The cruder the language the more irregular it is in such determinations and the more it shows in every forward step the course of human reason).[16]

Here was a new conception of language, one which rejected general nature in favour of specific natures. The universal laws of reason must now give place to the historic expressions of individual peoples. But what was a people? Herder saw it as a social hierarchy growing from small restricted codes to the general or national '*Sprache*'. But what if they manifestly did not speak it as was the case in every economically backward state in Europe? The *Volk* spoke dialect of one kind or another (Herder called it *Mundart*) and in general could neither read or write. The *questione della lingua* became less and less a matter of disputes within the same social group and began to involve horizontal relationships as well. Manzoni's bold decision to write a novel in Italian, taken in the 1820s, implied that there was now or would soon be an Italian society in which all classes might participate.

The making of a unified Italian State demanded a unified national language. The realities in Italy were very different. As De Mauro has shown, only a fraction of the population would have recognised Italian if they had heard it. Indeed the Visconti Venosta brothers, when they spoke Italian on the streets of Naples in 1861, were assumed to be

Englishmen. The Neapolitans had never heard Italian spoken. Italian had frozen into a language very like Latin, useful for lyric poetry and high culture but unavailable to a society both illiterate and economically backward.[17] As Rosario Romeo has shown in his magisterial study, in 1860 the island of Sicily had 358 communes. Of these only 268 had any schools at all and those that existed were wretched, incompetent places.[18]

Even in civilised Piedmont, the language problem was difficult, as the English economist Nassau Senior found out on his journey in 1850. The Marchesa Arconati explained:

> Even in Piedmont, difference of language is our great difficulty. Our three native languages are French, Piedmontese and Genoese. Of these French alone is generally intelligible. A speech in Genoese or Piedmontese would be unintelligible to two thirds of the assembly. Except the Savoyards, who sometimes use French, the Deputies all speak in Italian; but this is to them a dead language in which they have never been accustomed to converse. They scarcely ever therefore can use it with spirit or even with fluency. Cavour is naturally a good speaker, but in Italian he is embarrassed. You see that he is translating; so is Azeglio; so are they all, except a few lawyers who have been accustomed to address the tribunals in Italian.[19]

But what was Italian? In Florence Nassau Senior had a chat with the editor of a liberal paper, *La Costituzione*, who pointed out the problem:

> It does not consist merely in the prevalence of dialects, at least as far as we're concerned, for what was formerly called the Tuscan dialect is now recognised as the Italian language. But there are two Italian languages, the old, or written one, and the modern, or spoken one. In French or in English a man writes as he speaks, but if I were to speak the language of Machiavelli it would be ridiculous; if I were to write as I speak it would sound intolerably vulgar. Even to a Tuscan, therefore, written Italian is a dead language.[20]

In the mid-nineteenth century the *questione della lingua* in Italy meant the resuscitation of a rarefied high speech and its imposition on the masses. Throughout the nineteenth century grammarians, lexicographers, schoolteachers and administrators struggled to unify, purify and diffuse the national language.

An interesting parallel is the case of Slovakia. There the poet Ludovit Stur, in his *The Slovak Tongue or the Necessity of Writing in this Tongue* of 1846, proposed to raise the educated speech of persons of central Slovakia to the status of a national language. No one dialect served as the base but a composite of several.[21] Slovakia provides a useful contrast to Italy because there was no great Slovak literary tradition on which to draw and hence both the artificiality of linguistic nationalism and the interplay of language with other factors is more obvious than in the Italian case. Stur's Slovak was essentially a modern Protestant form of old Czech, the legacy of Jan Hus. It was not at first accepted by Catholics, for whom the old Czech did not belong to their religious heritage. Moreover, unlike previous attempts to create literary codes, Stur abandoned the earlier identification of Slovakia with a larger non-linguistic *natio ungarica*, as in effect the Magyars themselves had done by abolishing Latin as the official language of the Kingdom in 1844.

Finally, Stur's choice of an artificially homogenised central Slovakian variant forced those Slovaks who had learned to write Czech or those Czechs who regarded the Czechs and Slovaks as one people to make hard choices. In effect choice of language determined identity, not the other way round. As in the Moldavian case cited earlier, the pen can be as mighty as the sword in establishing political communities, especially if the pen is used by a fanatical nationalist.

The nineteenth-century nationalist shared with eighteenth-century writers a common attitude to the speech of ordinary people. Where for the enlightened grammarian of the eighteenth century, dialect was not wrong, merely an impediment to the pleasing uniformity which reason dictated, the existence of dialects in the nineteenth century threatened the fabric of the State. The *questione della lingua* became a matter of imposing uniformity of speech in order to make what had been a patchwork of peoples into a national community. The problem is very well known today outside Europe.

Since the end of the Second World War dialect in Europe has made a curious recovery. It is no longer the case that dialect is unequivocally the speech of the ignorant. In Piedmont in the past twenty years it has become fashionable again in all social circles to speak Piedmontese, not Italian. German Switzerland has begun to abandon standard German in situations where ten years ago the use of dialect would have been unthinkable. Gianrenzo Clivio persuaded me to try an experiment when I made a documentary for the BBC on language and dialect in Italy.

I recorded two conversations. In the first I asked three Piedmontese speakers, two businessmen and an academic, to talk in Piedmontese about a subject of their choice. Within seconds they had launched into an unconstrained conversation about theatre in Turin. Later, in Salerno, I recorded a conversation by a group of young university graduates and professional people connected with a theatre company devoted to performing and singing popular dialect art. The latter group were quite unable to speak dialect in the presence of the microphone. Amidst much embarrassed laughter and hesitation they slipped into Italian. 'We are,' one of them explained to me sheepishly, 'a subject people.' For the southerners dialect still stood for the low culture; the microphone for the high. In its presence they had to speak Italian, the language of authority and of the social mobility which they themselves embodied.

Just as distinctions between languages have profound political implications and are themselves frequently the result of political or economic changes, so the relationship between high speech and low speech or between language and dialect reflects the social relations among the speakers. In Turin persons of all classes speak Piedmontese easily and naturally. They move from Italian to Piedmontese without difficulty or embarrassment. In effect, they are bi-lingual. In Salerno language and dialect have distinct social connotations in which language is high and dialect low. Dialect may not be used in all situations. The young Salerno intellectuals are what sociolinguists call di-glossic, in this respect like Swiss German speakers who reserve certain activities for *Hochdeutsch* and others for *Mundart*. In contrast to southern Italy no social taint adheres to the use of dialect in Switzerland and Zurich bank directors speak it naturally among themselves.[22]

In effect, the *questione della lingua* has transcribed a circle and returned to the problems of the early eighteenth century. What is the proper language in which to teach ghetto children in a New York slum – black dialect or standard American English? Should Liverpool working-class children not first be taught in 'scouse'? Which benefits them more psychologically and socially?

None of these questions is easy and tempers rise in the discussion of them. What is common to all of them is the new assumption that dialect is itself as valuable as standard in expressions of culture. The language question has been democratised. In this process Antonio Gramsci played a part. He knew, as the only Italian-speaker in his Sardinian village, what an advantage this gave him, and when in 1911 he won a scholarship to study at the University of Turin (along with another young Sardinian called Palmiro Togliatti) he chose philology. His last work, the last of the so-called *Prison Notebooks*, is concerned with the question of grammar. To Gramsci it was clear that while there are many possible sorts of grammar, the choice among them is not neutral. The imposition of normative grammar is 'un atto politico'.[23] But why should political authorities choose one variant over another? In the Italian case the prestige given to the vernacular version of Italian – that is, medieval Tuscan, used by Dante, Petrarch and Boccaccio – established it as the norm of high speech. It was there for Manzoni to apply and to be spread by the *risorgimento*. In the case of Slovak, as Brock shows, the choice depended on the confessional and geographical divisions of the various valleys. In the case of modern Romantsch, the geographical dispersion of the speakers prevented the growth of any standard at all.

Gramsci was right in seeing the discussion about, and the imposition of, a standard language as the sign that other changes in class or political alignments were taking place. As he put it in the 'Notes to the Study of Grammar', 'Ogni volta che affiora, in un modo o nell'altro, la quistione della lingua, significa che si sta imponendo una serie di altri problem: la formazione e l'allargamento della classe dirigente, la necessità di stabilire repporti più intimi e sicuri tra i gruppi dirigenti e la massa popolare–nationale, cioè de riorganizzare l'egemonia culturale' (Every time that the language question appears, in one mode or another, it signifies that a series of other problems are beginning to impose themselves: the formation and enlargement of the ruling class, the need to stabilise the most intimate and secure links between that ruling group and the popular national masses, that is, to reorganise cultural hegemony).[24]

It is not necessary to accept Gramsci's Marxism to see that on an empirical level his observation is correct. When the French State set out to eradicate *patois*, when Professor Graur decided that Moldavian was a separate language, when Manzoni decided to write in Italian, these cultural expressions reflected more or less conscious political decisions and choices. To lecture in Italian in 1765 was not neutral; it was to assert the variety of the cultural world. To lecture in Latin was to affirm its unity.

Culture in the broad sense forms part of the authority which Gramsci understood by the phrase *egemonia culturale*. Correcting a child's grammar or accent enforces the majority or standard expression of culture on him or her. Just as the teaching of history in schools expresses the prevailing values of a society, so does the attitude to language.

The language question flickers in and out of the constant interplay between culture and power, but it is not, as too slavish a reading of Gramsci might suggest, language which merely reflects the changes in power or class relations.

The decisions taken by the poets and grammarians who made modern Slovak or modern Italian could hardly reflect power relations. The *Manzoniani* chose Tuscan because Dante, Petrarch and Boccaccio had written it, not because the Piedmontese court or the Italian bourgeoisie imposed its will. Ludovit Stur chose a central Slovak dialect because previous attempts using other variants had not worked. Choosing Tuscan or central Slovak affected power relations, not the other way round. Much of this is implicit, or at least ambiguous, in the whole idea of *egemonia*, for a vulgar Marxism would deny to culture anything more than a reflecting capacity. After all, Marx called these matters *Ueberbau*; economic relations were the real causal elements, the *Unterbau*. The evidence simply will not sustain such a view. Culture and language change reality, as much as reality changes culture and language. The circularity reflects the curious fact that history is made by objects who are also subjects.

Gramsci's question is not the only *questione della lingua*; there is also the problem of timing. A historian cannot escape the curious fact that for some thirty years in the middle of the eighteenth century questions about the origin, nature, superiority or inferiority, formal and informal uses, of languages occupied the minds of many of Europe's intellectuals. Is it just a coincidence that the issues of language and dialect, symbol and sign, speaker and speech, text and discourse, now dominate our thinking? Whether it be the language of class or gender, our age, like the 1760s or 1770s, has got linguistic preoccupations and anxieties.

Our age, and relatively recently at that, has rediscovered the reality behind the great assumptions of nineteenth-century nationalism. The equation *Volk = Sprache*, which Herder first established and which spread throughout eastern Europe, looks less obvious now. Neither term of the equation is unproblematic. The French are not quite the people who speak French, and the Italians until recently did not all speak Italian. Even today a substantial minority habitually speak something other than Italian in daily use, and Neapolitan has been declared Italy's second language. Language, the other term, has disintegrated under the analysis of dialectologists and sociolinguists. The borders between standard and vernacular, among vernaculars, within vernaculars, have become hazy. Like the eighteenth century we face the problems of definition and of the standing of claims that would have been self-evident even a generation ago. It is no longer clear which speech or which register is right in which situation.

Why should this new version of the *questione della lingua* have emerged now? Undoubtedly there have been very important changes in just the areas where Gramsci would urge us to look: relationships of production. Old industries decline and new ones emerge. The appearance of the computer, its transformation from its original form, the huge, electronic brain located behind closed doors and available to a few, into an item of mass consumption, and all the talk of information technology certainly push us to think about languages. 'Basic' and 'Fortran' are regularly so described, and we speak of machine language or machine codes. Academic linguistics and the computer industry overlap to the mutual profit of both. It may be that for the 1760s or 1770s an enterprising soul will indeed find that the nascent mechanisation of society pushed the language question into the minds of Herder and his contemporaries.

Another explanation for the return of the language question is, of course, the spread of Europe's version of nationalism to the entire world.

208   *The social history of language*

From India to Bolivia developing societies struggle with the relationship between high and low speech, between official standard and regional, local or tribal dialects. Mass migration from less to more developed economics has filled primary schools in Bedford and Düsseldorf with children who speak something other than the standard national language. The educational world has to cope with the advantages and disadvantages of 'mother tongue' teaching, as the jargon has it. Manzoni's problems are as well understood in East Africa as in western Europe. The 'mother tongues' differ.

Social and physical mobility, it might be argued, began to increase in the latter part of the eighteenth century, but it would be hard to demonstrate such a change. What is clear, and contemporaries saw it, was the growth of the increasingly unified central state. Germany was one nation in a literary sense by the 1770s; it took another century to make it one politically. The period which the French Revolution began and the Second World War ended can be seen as the arc of the rise and fall of the European nation-state. Since 1945 nationalism has been much more the property of minority communities – the Basques, the Frisians, the Welsh, the Scots, the Irish, the Bretons, the Jurassians, the Hungarians in Romania and so on – or of formerly dominant linguistic communities who have lost power against others, as in the Croat–Serb or the Walloon–Flemish rivalry. Alongside the ferocity of small nationalities has been the disintegration of the nation-state. Below a certain size the national economy runs into limits of markets and resources; regional supra-national bodies have emerged to meet that challenge. The European Economic Community erodes the sovereignty of its members and their sense of themselves. The loss of confidence in the national State and its naturalness has no doubt had an effect on the thinking of us all. The *questione della lingua* has re-emerged in unexpected forms and places. What would have seemed absurd in 1885 was not so in 1785 and is once again not so in 1985. In this sense, Gramsci was right. When the *questione della lingua* appears, it means that great changes are going on. The historian needs to think about them.

NOTES

[1] Tullio De Mauro, *Storia Linguistica dell'Italia Unita* (Bari, 1972), p. 43.
[2] Eugen Weber, *Peasants Into Frenchmen. The Modernization of Rural France 1870–1914* (London, 1979), p. 67.
[3] *Ibid.*, p. 92.
[4] R. I. McDavid, Jr, *Dialects in Culture: Essays in General Dialectology*, ed. W. A. Kretzschmar (Alabama, 1979), p. 13.
[5] Interview, in 'The Dark Wood of Dialect', by Jonathan Steinberg, produced by Stanley Williamson, BBC Radio 3 broadcast, 13 September 1978.
[6] Michael Bruchis, *One Step Back Two Steps Forward. On the Language Policy of the*

Communist Party of the Soviet Union in the National Republics, East European Monographs, Boulder, Colorado (New York, 1982), p. 149.

7 *Ibid.*, p. 151.
8 R. I. McDavid, Jr, *Dialects in Culture*, p. 13.
9 Eugen Weber, *Peasants into Frenchmen*, p. 73.
10 R. E. Keller, *The German Language* (London, 1974), pp. 485–6.
11 *Ibid.*, p. 486.
12 Melchiorre Cesarotti to Galeani Napione, *Letteratura Italiana. Storia e Testi*, Tomo IV 'Del Muratori al Cesarotti' (Milan, 1967), vol. 44, p. 17.
13 Antonio Genovesi (1713–69) to N. N., in vol. 4, 'il Settecento e L'Ottocento a cura di Giuseppe Petronio', *Antologia della Letteratura Italiana* (Milan, 1967), p. 1254.
14 A. Verri, *ibid.*, p. 1176.
15 J. W. von Goethe, *Dichtung und Wahrheit. Aus meinem Lebem*, II Teil (Munich, 1961), pp. 365ff.
16 Johann Gottfried Herder, 'Abhandlung über den Ursprung der Sprache', in Erich Hemtel, ed., *Sprachphilosophische Schriften* (Hamburg, 1960), pp. 30 and 51.
17 Tullio De Mauro, *Storia Linguistica*, pp. 43–4.
18 Rosario Romeo, *Il Risorgimento in Sicilia* (Bari, 1970), p. 274.
19 Nassau Senior, *Journals Kept in France and Italy from 1848 to 1852* (London, 1871), vol. 1, pp. 291–2.
20 *Ibid.*, p. 337.
21 Peter Brock, *The Slovak National Awakening* (Toronto, 1976), p. 47.
22 Jonathan Steinberg, *Why Switzerland?*, rev. ed. (Cambridge, 1980), pp. 100–8.
23 Antonio Gramsci, 'Note sullo studio della grammatica', *Quaderno* 29 (1935), 2341–51, in *Quaderni del Carcere a cura di Valentino Gerratana* (Turin, 1975), vol. 3, p. 2347.
24 *Ibid.*, p. 2346.

BIBLIOGRAPHICAL ESSAY

Since the social history of language, as the introduction suggested, is a recent development, readers can hardly expect an abundant bibliography. But there are books and articles which are well worth following up, some of them examples of a more traditional history of language, some dealing with sociolinguistics, and some sociohistorical studies in the strict sense.

1 History of language

a *English*

O. Jespersen's *Growth and Structure of the English Language* (Leipzig, 1905) remains a classic, like the many works of Eric Partridge, such as *Slang Today and Yesterday* (London, 1933). Barbara M. H. Strang, *A History of English* (1970), is a rather technical study, written backwards. On the Middle Ages, R. Berndt, 'The Linguistic Situation in England 1066–1204', repr. in *Approaches to English Historical Linguistics*, ed. R. Lass (New York, 1969); R. M. Wilson, 'French and English in England', *History* 28 (1943), 37–60; on the early modern period, C. Barber, *Early Modern English* (London, 1976); R. F. Jones, *The Triumph of the English Language* (Stanford, 1953), another classic; and V. Salmon, 'Elizabethan Colloquial English', *Leeds Studies in English* (1967). Oaths have attracted particular attention, from J. Sharman's delightful *Cursory History of Swearing* (1844), to F. A. Shirley's *Swearing and Perjury in Shakespeare's Plays* (London, 1979). On the propriety and efficacy of cursing, K. V. Thomas, *Religion and the Decline of Magic* (London, 1971), 502f; on the legal aspects, J. Sharpe, *Defamation and Sexual Slander in Early Modern England* (York, 1980).

b *Other European languages*

For a general survey of the Middle Ages, see P. Wolff, *Western Languages AD 100–1500* (London, 1971). On Latin, A. Maillet, *Esquisse d'une histoire de la langue latin* (Paris, 1928); F. Lot, 'A quelle époque a-t-on cessé de parler Latin?'; C. Backvis, *Quelques Remarques sur le bilinguisme latino-polonais dans la Pologne du 16e siècle* (Brussels, 1958); J. Bérenger, 'Latin et langues vernaculaires dans la Hongrie', *Revue historique* 242 (1969), 5–28.

Useful introductions to particular vernaculars include W. B. Lockwood, *An Informal History of the German Language* (1965), and P. Rickard, *A History of the French Language* (Cambridge, 1974). Classic in their own countries are F. Brunot's *Histoire de la langue française*, 14 vols. (Paris, 1905–); C. G. N. Vooys,

210

Geschiedenis van de Nederlandse Taal (Groningen, 1931); P. Skautrup, *Det Danske Sproga Historie* (Copenhagen, 1944–); B. Migliorini, *Storia della lingua italiana* (Florence, 1960); abridged edition, *The Italian Language* (London, 1966); R. Lapesa Melgar, *Historia de la lengua española* (Madrid, 1951); B. O'Cuiv, ed., *A View of the Irish Language* (Dublin, 1969).

2 Sociolinguistics

For a brief and lucid introduction, see P. Trudgill, *Sociolinguistics* (Harmondsworth, 1974). Although they necessarily omit the work of the last decade, three anthologies are invaluable: *Language and Social Context*, ed. P. Giglioli (Harmondsworth, 1972); *Sociolinguistics*, ed. J. B. Pride and J. Holmes (Harmondsworth, 1972); and *Explorations in the Ethnography of Speaking*, ed. R. Bauman and J. Sherzer (Cambridge, 1974). On the relations between language and class, B. Bernstein, *Class Codes and Control* (London, 1970), and his critics, such as H. Rosen, *Language and Class* (Bristol, 1972). On language and gender, R. Lakoff, *Language and Women's Place* (New York, 1975). On code-switching, C. A. Ferguson, 'Diglossia', repr. in Giglioli and J. Gumperz, *Discourse Strategies* (Cambridge, 1982). On insult, W. Labov, 'Rules for Ritual Insults', in *Studies in Social Interaction*, ed. D. Sudnow (New York, 1972). On language as performance, R. D. Abrahams, 'Black Talking on the Streets', repr. in Bauman and Sherzer; R. Bauman, 'Verbal Art as Performance', *American Anthropologist* 77 (1975), 290–306, and M. Bloch, ed., *Political Language and Oratory in Traditional Society* (London, 1975). On gossip, M. Glucksman, 'Gossip and Scandal', *Current Anthropology* 4 (1963), 307–15. On spells, S. J. Tambiah, 'The Magical Power of Words', *Man* 3 (1968), 175–208. Of general importance is D. Hymes, *Foundations in Sociolinguistics* (Philadelphia, 1974), from an 'ethnography of communication' perspective, as is R. Fowler, ed., *Language and Control* (London, 1979), from a Marxist point of view. It should be noted that most contributions are extremely recent. R. Robin, *Histoire et linguistique* (Paris, 1973), shows no awareness of sociolinguistics.

The question of whether literacy produces (or at least strongly encourages) a new mentality still divides anthropologists and other scholars. Those in favour include J. Goody, *The Domestication of the Savage Mind* (Cambridge, 1977), and W. J. Ong, *Orality and Literacy* (London, 1982). Expressions of scepticism include R. Finnegan, 'Literacy v. Non-Literacy: The Great Divide?', in R. Horton and R. Finnegan, eds., *Modes of Thought* (London, 1973), and B. Street, *Literacy in Theory and Practice* (Cambridge, 1984).

3 Social history of language

a *English*
D. Leith, *A Social History of English* (London, 1983), discusses questions of history and sociolinguistics but fails to bring the two closely together. G. Stedman Jones, *Languages of Class* (Cambridge, 1984), is a collection of essays in which 'Rethinking Chartism', in particular, tries to insert language into the social history of nineteenth-century England. K. C. Phillips, *Language and Class in*

212

212   *Bibliographical essay*

Victorian England (Oxford, 1984), combines richness of illustration with poverty of comment. R. Bauman, *Let Your Words Be Few* (Cambridge, 1984), discusses the symbolism of speaking – and silence – among the seventeenth-century Quakers. J. Barrell, *English Literature in History* (London, 1983), Chapter 2, offers a social interpretation of eighteenth-century discussions of grammar. O. Smith, *The Politics of Language 1791–1819* (Oxford, 1984), is concerned with the awareness of the problem among a small group which included Cobbett, Hone and Tooke.

b *French*

The relationship between language and politics in the French Revolution has attracted particular attention. M. De Certeau, J. Revel and D. Julia, *Une Politique de la langue* (Paris, 1975), discusses one aspect of this question; *cf.* P. Higonnet, 'The Politics of Linguistic Terrorism', *Social History* 5 (1980), 41–69; J. Y. Lartichaux, 'Linguistic Politics during the French Revolution', *Diogenes* 97 (1977), 65–84, and L. Hunt, *Politics Culture and Class* (Berkeley, 1984). For the nineteenth century, E. Weber, *Peasants into Frenchmen* (London, 1979), has an important discussion of *patois*, while T. Zeldin, *France 1848–1945*, 2 vols. (Oxford, 1977), 227f, has some interesting observations on rhetoric. Peter N. Moogk, 'Thieving Buggers and Stupid Sluts', *William & Mary Quarterly* 36 (1977), 524–47, discusses complaints about insults which came before the courts of New France, 1650–1760. Richard Cobb will discuss insults and politeness in a forthcoming volume, provisionally entitled *Chatting Up*. A pioneering study of rumour is G. Lefebvre's *La grande peur de 1789* (1932): English trans. *The Great Fear of 1789* (London, 1973).

c *Other languages*

O. Macdonagh, *States of Mind: A Study of Anglo–Irish Conflict 1780–1880* (London, 1983), includes a perceptive chapter on the politics of Gaelic. The appendix to G. Craig's *The Germans* (Stanford, 1982) deals with the relation between language and politics in the nineteenth and twentieth centuries. Recent work on rumour and gossip in German includes D. Sabean, *Power in the Blood* (Cambridge, 1984), and R. Scribner, 'Oral Culture and the Diffusion of Reformation Ideas' (forthcoming in his *Popular Culture and Popular Movements in Reformation Germany*). On Italy, P. Burke, 'Languages and Anti-Languages in Early Modern Italy', *History Workshop Journal* 11 (1981), 24–32, offers a survey and some references. On the period since 1860, T. De Mauro, *Storia linguistica dell'Italia unita* (Florence, 1965). G. Ruggiero, *Violence in Early Renaissance Venice* (New Brunswick, 1980), includes 'Crimes of Speech'. S. Raffaelli, *Le Parole Proibite* (Rome, 1983), deals with what could not be written in the nineteenth century (including expressions of foreign origin); L. Formingari, ed., *Teorie e pratiche linguistiche nell'Italia del '700* (Bologna, 1984), includes a number of interesting essays (such as P. Fiorelli's on *'la lingua giuridica'*). M. Barbagli, *Sotto lo stesso tetto* (Bologna, 1984), Part 2, uses the evidence of language to explore changing family relationships in Italy in the eighteenth and nineteenth centuries. Elsewhere research remains very thin on the ground, although W. Whiteley, *Swahili: The Rise of a National Language* (Cambridge, 1969), is a pioneering study which deserves to be more widely known.

There have been many studies of the history of literacy, although relatively few which are concerned, like the anthropologists cited above, with its consequences. Some of the most important contributions are collected in H. Graff, ed., *Literacy and Social Development in the West* (Cambridge, 1981).

INDEX